T0243398

CRYING IN THE RAIN

CRYING IN THE RAIN

The Perfect Harmony and Imperfect Lives of the Everly Brothers

Mark Ribowsky

Backbeat
Books

Essex, Connecticut

Backbeat Books

An imprint of Globe Pequot, the trade division of
The Rowman & Littlefield Publishing Group, Inc.
4501 Forbes Blvd., Ste. 200
Lanham, MD 20706
www.rowman.com

Distributed by NATIONAL BOOK NETWORK

British Library Cataloguing in Publication Information Available

Library of Congress Cataloging-in-Publication Data

Names: Ribowsky, Mark, author.
Title: Crying in the rain : the perfect harmony and imperfect lives of the
    Everly Brothers / Mark Ribowsky.
Description: Essex, Connecticut : Backbeat, 2024.
Identifiers: LCCN 2023035239 (print) | LCCN 2023035240 (ebook) | ISBN
    9781493077786 (cloth) | ISBN 9781493077793 (epub)
Subjects: LCSH: Everly Brothers. | Rock musicians—United
    States—Biography.
Classification: LCC ML421.E9 R53 2024 (print) | LCC ML421.E9 (ebook) |
    DDC 782.42166092/2 [B]—dc23/eng/20230807
LC record available at https://lccn.loc.gov/2023035239
LC ebook record available at https://lccn.loc.gov/2023035240

♾™ The paper used in this publication meets the minimum requirements of
American National Standard for Information Sciences—Permanence of Paper
for Printed Library Materials, ANSI/NISO Z39.48-1992.

For my son Jake, who, because of books like this, knows there was something before rap.

Contents

Introduction

High and Lonesome

[T]he importance of an individual's own sound [is] a notion that traces back to Mozart and before that to the ancient Greeks [and] the idea that timbre could overshadow melody and rhythm and become the dominant, identifying attribute of a piece of music was probably first shown by Ravel in "Boléro." What the Everlys . . . did with this idea for "Cathy's Clown" influenced music for the next several decades.

—Daniel J. Levitin, PhD, from the National
Recording Registry: The Everly Brothers
"Cathy's Clown," August 24, 2021

Phil's lorn howl ranged against Don's tender lead, their black jumbo guitars ringing synchronically and the evening, of course, [was] electric. An audience of every age, elders, excited children, one Japanese youth sits rapt like Keats before the Elgin Marbles.

—Penny Reel, New Musical Express review of the
Everly Brothers reunion concert, October 8, 1983

I had this haunted feeling all my life, of being [the] odd man out.

—Don Everly, 2014

1

This work tells an epic tale of the fussin' and fightin', steel-string acoustic guitar-strumming Everly Brothers and their vital place in nascent rock and roll, bridging it to the magnificent patois and pathos of American country music. Those times are of course now a long time gone—the three words they sang in their 1958 cover of the York Brothers' 1950 country tune "Long Time Gone" on the Everlys' second album, *Songs Our Daddy Taught Us*. In the song, Don and Phil Everly sang of being "cheated" and "left lonely," which they would all but repeat two years later in their top-ten hit "When Will I Be Loved?" in which they complained about being "put down," "pushed around," "cheated" and "mistreated." Oh, and there was also "Crying in the Rain."

That's a whole lot of grievance and self-pity, but Don and Phil Everly made dreamy, melodious carping a staple of country rock, their other-worldly harmonies and nifty structures creating an avalanche, pouring almost on top of one another the songs we all know by rote—"Bye Bye Love," "Wake Up Little Susie," "All I Have to Do Is Dream," "Bird Dog," "Problems," "(Till) I Kissed You," "Let It Be Me." "Cathy's Clown," "When Will I Be Loved," "Walk Right Back," "Crying in the Rain," and "That's Old Fashioned (That's the Way Love Should Be)." With dozens more that came down the mountain for fifty years, they recorded seventy-five singles, eleven of which went to number one, thirty-five going Top 100, twenty-six going Top 40, more than any other duo except Hall and Oates. The two beanpoles from Nashville probably saved Warner Bros. Records from early ruin after they signed a then-unheard-of ten-year, $1 million deal in 1960.

Unlike wilder rockers, they wore stiff suits and Brylcreemed, duck's-ass haircuts, never moving an inch out of their stage pose, their lower bodies inert, or as described by British rock writer Maureen Cleave, "rather fragile" with "an Asiatic mold of face . . . like Puck as sculpted by [Jacob] Epstein," their song arrangements "baroque." Some oddly disconcerted critics believed they lacked *manliness*—one insisting they had "an androgynous tone, strange and somewhat surreal." But that overlooked a James-Deanish diffidence, contrasting the untempered flames of Elvis, Jerry Lee, Little Richard, and Chuck Berry, all of whom can be credited with unleashing rock—though in Bob Dylan's estimation, the Everlys "started it all." They would change with the times but never seemed to lose teenage angst, the kind that created the coolest breakup song ever, "Cathy's Clown," vowing "I gotta stand tall / You know a man can't crawl" to the boom-ba-da-boom of a strip club beat.

They also, for a while, hid a secret—that they were coping with the pressures of fame in ways their fans could not have imagined, including, in Don's case, committing spousal abuse, abandoning his children, becoming alienated from his parents, being addicted to drugs and booze, trying to commit suicide, and undergoing electroshock therapy. Actually, both Everlys lived in perpetual agony, unable to stand each other, each harboring grievances, Don that he had to make room for Phil, Phil that Don was a petty tyrant. And it never really eased or ceased, even in the best of times. And after Phil died in 2014, Don's last years were still so disordered that he lived out his life with an often-arrested woman who, though it was little known, apparently tried to kill him and against whom he had to file two orders of protection. He also sued Phil *after* Phil died, his own mother sued *him*, and the brothers' estates were suing each other after both had died. Yes, this is no ordinary story.

The Everly Brothers were bred by an itinerant coal miner and country singer from western Kentucky named Ike Everly and his singing wife Margaret, groomed to sing and strum in unison, reflecting the folk, blues, and hillbilly music that dated back to the 1700s. In the Appalachians, they liked to say it was a high and lonesome sound. Many singers have sought it, but few have *sounded* as if they were whistling down the wind quite like the Everly Brothers, about whom Paul Simon said they were "the most beautiful sounding duo I ever heard, pristine and soulful." It wasn't just harmony. It was Blood Harmony.

Growing to manhood, they lived for a time in Chicago, where they became devotees of Bo Diddley, and would put his hambone beat into their songs. In the 1950s, when white stiffs stole songs by great Black artists by covering their songs in mayonnaise, Black artists were covering Everly Brothers songs. The equation was simple: Don sang a nasal baritone, Phil a nasally fifth of an octave higher, the mesh such that it was hard to tell who was singing which part. Don handled the demanding guitar riffs—the springy intro of "Wake Up Little Susie" would late in life win him the Riff Award from the Musicians Hall of Fame, and their black starburst Gibson J-180 "Flattop" models from yesteryear—the Don Everly model having been played at one time or another by a legion of top guitar men, including Paul McCartney, Jimmy Page, and Keith Richards—went on display at New York's Metropolitan Museum of Art. Because of those harmonies and steel strings, we got the Beach Boys, the Mamas and the Papas, Simon and Garfunkel, the Eagles—shit, the whole future of rock.

During the prime, their songs were mainly composed by the Nashville husband-and-wife team of Boudleaux and Felice Bryant and contoured in the studio by country guitar king Chet Atkins and the prime Nashville cats, ladling sweet innocence seasoned with some snarky brine. "Wake Up Little Susie" wasn't really about falling asleep at the drive-in but teen nookie. Keith Richards testifies that there was a "load of bluegrass in those boys," but they also spooned in Bo Diddley's beat. And did it so engagingly that they were on the biggest TV shows and as comforting as Johnny Mathis, Perry Como, and Nat King Cole. To a nation, soon the world, Don and Phil were like brothers, sons, imaginary lovers, cool cats.

Their body of work emerged and reemerged over and over, filling twenty-one albums of current and classic tunes, no album more criminally overlooked than *Roots*, a prime mover of late 1960s–early 1970s country rock. Two of their compilation LPs are king-sized, the 103-track *Heartaches and Harmonies* (1994) and the *198*-track CD/DVD *Chained to a Memory* (2003), both of which contain alternate takes, old homemade family tapes, and odds and ends only a mega-fan would appreciate. And there are mega-fans, here, there, and everywhere, just as there were idolaters in the music game who got the message from them, including the nascent Beatles, Rolling Stones, and Simon and Garfunkel. Their harmonies could be heard, second-hand, in the thousands of Everly cover songs. The 1999 Linda Ronstadt-Emmylou Harris *Western Wall* album was Ronstadt's longtime wish to "run off and be The Everly Sisters." She wasn't alone.

"Bye Bye Love" alone is one of the most covered tunes of all time, sung by Simon and Garfunkel on *Bridge over Troubled Water*, Bob Dylan on *Self Portrait* (on which he also covered their "Take a Message to Mary"), and Ray Charles. After Eric Clapton stole Patti Boyd from George Harrison, George's retort was the most bitter cover ever of "Bye Bye Love," which in Peter Jackson's *Get Back* John and Paul broke into as a relief from Beatle rigors. George and Paul Simon did the same while rehearsing for *Saturday Night Live.* A movie was made with it as the title. Like "Monster Mash," but for far better reasons, the damn song just refuses to die.

The Everlys' saving grace was their popularity in England, where Lennon and McCartney nearly called their early band The Foreverly Brothers, and may have appropriated the melody of "Cathy's Clown" for "Please Please Me." Years later Paul later dropped the words "Phil and Don" into his "Let 'Em In" and wrote a song for them, "On the Wings of a Nightingale," which he also played on. Dylan wrote a song for them, too, called "The Fugitive," and Buddy Holly wrote three—one being "Not Fade Away." But while the Everly Brothers were kept from recording them by their autocratic publishing company, only recording "Fade Away" as album filler in 1972, they only sang what they knew they could master. One can see their point. Even covers that outsold their originals—Ronstadt's "When Will I Be Loved," the Jerry Butler/Betty Everett "Let It Be Me" (itself a cover by the Everlys of Gilbert Bécaud), and the Carly Simon/James Taylor "Devoted to You"—lacked the same depth and sense of *being* and *believing* what they sang about.

This must be true, since by way of personal perspective, this writer was six, living in a nearly comatose suburb of New York City when "Bye Bye Love" entered the urban pop of Top 40 radio. The dial was vibrant then. Alan Freed had come to town and the idiom he named rock and roll dominated the medium on two legendary stations, WABC and WMCA, where the DJs played doo-wop shit that arose from the streets. Only snow in

August could have gotten Murray the K, Dan Ingram or Cousin Brucie to play anything "country"—even Marty Robbins and Johnny Cash were mostly strangers—every reason why it took this writer around forty years to be able to write a book about Hank Williams. Yet these Everly Brothers were a relentless entree. They sang in a nasal burr and played stringy guitars the way it just had to be wherever Tobacco Road was, but it aimed at the gut. It rocked not with rancor but a sweet melody, just like the doo-woppers did. No one knew it was doused with a condiment called Bo Diddley, but whoever these brothers were, they were good. Damn were they good.

There were, of course, a myriad of technical and supernatural reasons *why*, such as those given by the good doctor from the Recording Registry about "Cathy's Clown." Great songs, and how they were structured, helped. But the best instruments of classic Everly Brothers songs are those voices. The question is why. There are things like exact octaves, extended notes, slides, glissandos, portamentos—all of which to them was just singing the way their daddy taught them. But something made me think of the similarly tactile depth and sensitivity of Phil Spector's "Wall of Sound." When writing a book about Spector, his partner in the Teddy Bears, Marshall Leib, told me it was "more air than sound," transporting the mysteries of the sound. The Everly Brothers never raised their voices to shouting level, because that would have distorted the balance of air and sound creating harmonies that didn't seem possible in humans.

Many have tried to be just like them. Peter and Gordon were called "the Everly Brothers of the British Invasion," but as the *Washington Post*'s Geoffrey Himes noted in 1991, "that description is overly generous—and unfair to Phil and Don Everly." And if they couldn't be the Everly Brothers, they could drink from the same cup. Among the mass of other covers are Ray Charles's "Bye Bye Love," Robert Plant's "Gone, Gone, Gone," Nazareth's "Love Hurts," and REM's "All I Have to Do Is Dream," which was sampled by rappers O.G.C. in "Flappin'" and Jive Bunny and the Mastermixers' "Lovers Mix." There were three tribute albums in 2013 alone—the Billie Joe Armstrong/Norah Jones *Foreverly*, the Chapin Sisters' *A Date with the Everly Brothers*, and the Bonny "Prince" Billy/Dawn McCarthy *What the Brothers Sang*; another, in 2014, was *The Wieners Play the Everly Brothers.* God knows how many more there will be.

○ ○

The backstory is their leading role in the transformation of Nashville from a backwoods clearing to a power center where about *everyone* would record—Dylan his finest work in the 1960s. But when the pious Grand Ole Opry bugged them for not playing there enough, they told the Opry to fuck off. Moving from Nashville to L.A., they hit the heights, but the downside was losing a tug of war for control of their act with the powerful Nashville song publisher, not to mention their private lives going to hell, through their own devices. They also laid down some knowing, quite un-fiftyish intonations like "Let's Go Get Stoned," "Christmas Eve Can Kill You," "I'm Tired of Singing My Song in Las Vegas," "Ebony Eyes" (of a would-be bride girlfriend killed in a plane crash), and in "Devil's Child," being "scratched and bruised" and made into "a human sacrifice."

Some were hidden gems that went unreleased for decades—"Even If I Hold It in My Hand [Hard Luck Story]," a virtual suicide note, and "Lord of the Manor," about a fop banging the upstairs maid. And how crazy was it that Don would be able to tell audiences, "You won't hear our new song unless it's on FM underground." But then, their cover of Gene Vincent's "Be-Bop-a-Lula" was heard in the first great (and awful) underground film, Jack Smith's *Flaming Creatures,* and since then their songs have been used in romcoms and *A Nightmare on Elm Street.* The Everly Brothers mean whatever one wants them to mean.

That they could be so harmonious singing into a single microphone, and so disharmonious when not, is the Cain-and-Abel subtext, which led Phil to say in 1972 that it was "one of the great sibling rivalries of the Twentieth Century." Don was plainly the instigator, but both were speed addicts and Phil would smoke himself to death. Don was politically far left, Phil far right. To Phil the sixties "weren't my cup of tea." But Don bought it all, swallowing LSD, hanging with Jimi in London, lusting for Joni

Mitchell and God knows who else. Defining them was never easy. Don was called "ruthless, rude and self-centered" and "rootless, restless, mercurial," but also "warm, generous, very charming and excitable" with "lots of the qualities of a child."

Phil, his Rubenesque face differentiating him from the glare of Don's eyes, was less complicated, but one bystander called him "diffident and reclusive" and another that he "made me think of Holden Caulfield"—though Don's torturous brooding seemed far more Holdenish, his drunken firing of Phil in 1973 was like a scene out of *Catcher in the Rye*, coming *during* a concert and leading Phil to angrily smash his guitar to bits. For a decade, they were essentially divorced, recording solo, working with the likes of Paul Rothchild, Lindsey Buckingham, Albert Lee, Warren Zevon, Dave Edmunds, and Pete Wingfield, who explained the Everly Brothers' estrangement with titanic understatement— "The circumstances of their lives were so unusual."

After dashed hopes of a reunion, they did that in 1983 at London's Royal Albert Hall, but, always, they seemed to be living out "When Will I Be Loved?" or asking, as another song did, "So How Come (No One Loves Me)." Don, who understated that his personal life was "sort of strange," married four times, Phil three. Both were serial adulterers and cheaters—Ricky Nelson's number-one hit "Poor Little Fool" was written by one of Don's playthings about being made a fool by his lies. They seemed to be playing games with each other even in their private lives, Don even dating a woman ten years after Phil had split with her, who after Don had enough of her wrote a snarky letter to Margaret thanking her for "not having a third son."

Thankfully, the inane, psychologically disturbing feuds were put aside for their inductions into the Rock and Roll Hall of Fame, the Country Hall, the Songwriters Hall of Fame, and a Grammy Lifetime award. When Phil died in 2014 at seventy-four from lung cancer, Don said it was the "saddest day of my life," Last seen, he sang "Bye Bye Love" on Paul Simon's 2018 farewell tour stop in Nashville, three years before he died there at eighty-four, still in his psychotic last marriage. Of course, the song remains the same, taking two riders into that high and lonely wind, despite the squalls that always seemed to be blowing in the wind.

CHAPTER ONE

White Blues

If you happen to be in the State capital of Tennessee, you will literally never be able to forget you're in a place of fantasy the town wants you to call Music City. Actually, Nashville is part of a musical nexus; it and the Soul City, Memphis, are interconnected by I-40, and from Nashville one can take the last train north to Clarksville and the choo-choo south to Chattanooga. No other place, however, has its musical history so blatantly plastered all over its streets. Downtown, west of the Cumberland River, in what is officially called the Arts District, is Music Row (commemorated by Dolly Parton's 1973 "Down on Music Row") and the historic landmark, the Ryman Auditorium, a dumpy brown brick building that for three decades hosted Grand Ole Opry shows thrice weekly to sold-out audiences and on the radio across the nation.

A tour of Music Row can take you past the Johnny Cash Museum, Chet Atkins Place, and Chet's meticulously built RCA Studio B—its exterior marked by two oversized mock guitars, one with "Roy Orbison" painted on it and the other with an image of Elvis's face and the words "Heartbreak Hotel"—as well as Owen Bradley's Quonset Hut Studio A, the Columbia studio where Cash, Bob Dylan, Patsy Cline, and Elvis Costello laid down tracks. However, while the biggest of their hits were recorded at Studio B, "Everly Brothers" isn't on that outer wall at

Studio B, or any street signs or monuments memorializing them in Nashville such as the bronze one of Chet Atkins playing his guitar. One must find their way to streets in Iowa and Kentucky for that. Still, no one needs to be reminded of their place in the history of the "Nashville Sound," that mystical, part-mythical aggregation of country music's essential bits and pieces.

For around a hundred years, "country" grew to fruition as a synonym for political conservatism, thriving in a state where 21 percent of the Black population are disenfranchised, highest in the nation, and where the white-dominated state legislature expelled two young Black Democrats for wanting more done about gun safety after the Nashville church school killing of six people, three children. Yet the massive protests that helped return the pair to the legislature were just one sign that Nashville isn't your grandpappy's Nashville. Other signs are on those streets, reading "Rep. John Lewis Way," named for the Black congressman who spoke at Martin Luther King Jr.'s March on Washington in 1963—when Black artists were not welcome on the Opry stage—and on which the National Museum of African American Music is just down the block from Rosa L. Parks Boulevard, the intersection where the Country Music Hall of Fame and Museum sits, a three-story, glass-ceilinged wonderland where dozens of honorees have exhibits lined with photos, memorabilia, and push-buttons that play songs the faithful fans sing along with in various cacophonies. The Everly Brothers exhibit has a sign reading: "From Nashville to Rock & Roll Stardom."

It's as good a summation as there is about them, but it undersells them by thousands of words and hundreds of years.

○ ○

The story begins not in Nashville but Hessen, Germany. It was from there, in 1718, that Johan Simon Eberly immigrated to colonial America, settling with his family in Dauphin County, Pennsylvania, where he died in 1783, seven years after the Declaration of Independence was signed. Johan's son, Casper, who was also born in Hessen and later changed his surname to Everly, moved with his family to Magnolia County, West

Virginia, where dust-covered county records reveal that Casper was "paid by the state of Va. for working his horse in 1782." Casper died in West Virginia and was buried in the Fort Martin cemetery, as was *his* son, Simeon Oliver Everly, who fought in the Revolution and was called a "spy" in the state militia. He fathered eleven children, one of whom, Simeon Everly Jr., migrated to McLean County, Kentucky, in the early 1800s.

It's unclear whether any of the Everly men fought for Johnny Reb in the Civil War but Kentucky was where the Everly family tree was planted, and grew well into the twentieth century. Most Everly men were hardy, sturdy providers for their usually large families. The chain continued with Simeon Jr.'s son, Jesse Malone Everly, who earned his license as a country doctor, and then Jesse's son, Isaac Milford Everly, born in 1869 in Ebenezer in Muhlenberg County, the "dog's back" part of western Kentucky. Like most of the Everly patriarchs before him, he worked in the stifling mines and carried on singing Gaelic folk tunes, a common practice transferred from German life and passed down from Irish missionaries, songs that were the genesis of Gregorian chants. In modern times, during World War II, Nazi propaganda was broadcast on the radio in Gaelic to neutral Ireland, sometimes accompanied by the same folk music that the Everly families and scores of other German immigrants in America sang.

Indeed, an underexamined element of music history in the Appalachians is the widespread reach of Irish folk. As *Irish Music* magazine has noted of this fundament, "Folks grabbed acoustic guitars and Aran sweaters and banged away ditties such as 'Molly Malone,' 'The Wild Rover' or 'Whiskey in the Jar.' Bands playing Irish music sprang up all over the place." The idiom of Irish folk, like that of bluegrass and hillbilly music springing up at the same time, was rife with drinking songs, ballads, and laments done in a four-beats-to-the-bar format that would fuse into the standard blues and jazz structure, which would find its way northward up the Mississippi River as post-Reconstruction Black musicians joined the rush out of the Louisiana Delta.

Without really knowing it, people like Isaac Milford Everly were adapting Irish folk to the blues of the Deep South and

passing it down in their singing and strumming. The fifth of
Isaac's children, Isaac Milford "Ike" Everly Jr., born in 1908 in
Brownie, in Muhlenberg County, also worked in the mines, his
voice a figurative light in those dark corridors. Picking up the
backwoods thumb-picking style, he performed at amateur talent shows, sometimes standing on the back of his rickety pickup
truck. Ike was a handsome, smiling compromise cowpoke, not
a heavy devotee of hillbilly music but well aware of the musical
spectrum in Kentucky, with an eye on the growth of fake "high-
tone" country fare not far away in Nashville. He sang an engag-
ing mix of English-Irish-German folk and Kentucky country
blues, fitting the mix into an overall mold of hillbilly-acceptable
sound, not with professional-level skill but a boyish elan, getting
people to clap their hands, stomp their feet, and improvise dance
moves on unpaved dirt roads. They sang in unison about the
intrepid sea captains who ruled the waves of the North Atlantic,
the fairest of all being Grace O'Malley, who was as brave and
true as the queen. They also sang of the call of the hunt:

> When I was a bachelor airy and young
> I followed the bachelor's trade
> And all the harm that ever I done
> Was courting a pretty maid.

And finding the true one,

> Till at length we were married—myself and my darling
> All over the foggy dew.

It came with the territory of the Appalachians, even bound
to the mines. Ike's sister Lena Everly Guy married and moved
to Powderly, Kentucky, and when Lena died of tuberculosis in
1929 her young son James was adopted. Renamed James Best,
he would become a Hollywood actor whose enduring role
was as the bumbling sheriff Roscoe P. Coltrane on the *Dukes
of Hazzard*. Most of the Everlys, though, were focused on their
music. And a major influence on Ike, it turns out, was his sister,
called Aunt Hattie, who was also turned on to mountain music
by Ike Sr. Hattie liked to claim she created the "Drum Piece"

technique that made a guitar riff sound like a drum beat, with a down-up, up-down strumming—something necessary at the time, with drums considered vulgar in country music—and it would serve as a brushy percussive effect for Hank Williams and then Johnny Cash.

History disproves Aunt Hattie; the format was actually introduced by a thumb-picking Black man from western Kentucky, Arnold Shultz, who called the technique "Travis picking," after Merle Travis, whom he taught to play. Schultz, despite discrimination, played in white hillbilly bands, his technique to be adopted by other Nashville immortals like Mose Rager, Chet Atkins, and Doc Watson. It was Mose Rager in fact who turned up the stakes for Ike Jr., who met Mose when they were both teens. Hearing stories of Arnold Schultz's blues playing, they would find their way into the Black neighborhood where Schultz lived and hide under his porch so that they could hear him do his pickin', and Ike would unwind these techniques on stage, at times with Mose.

As his son Don would relate years later, "Mose and Dad used to play guitar around Muhlenberg County, picking and singing the blues at town halls and local dances. But that didn't pay the rent. So, like most Kentucky men and boys, they went down in the mines to make a living, loading coal on mules underground." But both kept tugging at the blues, singing songs about trouble taking place in the lowlands that night, and Ike did so with a big smile and a mane of jet-black hair. He was a real catch who could melt young girls' hearts. In 1935, when he was twenty-seven, he fell hard for a winsome Kentucky girl named Margaret Eva Embry, a pretty, willowy brunette with a mega-smile, whom he could instantly pick out of a crowd and who could hit high notes herself. She was from a family of "Honey Boo Boo"–type Kentucky natives, with nicknames to match—her father, Louatress, known as "Blue" and "Two Papa," her mother, Eva, as "Two Mama." Among her eight siblings were ones named Zirkle, Dimple, and Prock.

She was only fifteen, but when Ike met Margaret, he was sure he had met the love of his life and no one objected when they married only months later; they tied the knot at a church, the ceremony a hoedown, with both large families partying away. Soon, Ike added Margaret to his performances, the act billed as Ike and Margaret, her adorability gaining more and more gigs on the pickup truck. This was happening in the depths of the Depression, when lives teetered on the edge of hopelessness, and Ike took his work quite seriously. Working the Muhlenberg mines along with several of his brothers, they were said to have set the record for the most coal shoveled in a single day. Their escape was picking up guitars and singing the Celtic-based folk music the Everly family had adopted for two centuries.

The music that surrounded him was a full feast in a state where a real meal was always in doubt. Even in the best of times, Kentucky was one of the poorest states, and perhaps as a consequence, it has been said that more country music singers and musicians with a serious focus came from the eastern end of Kentucky than any other place east or west of the mighty "Mississipp." Its 144 miles of pockmarked roads called US 23 is familiarly known as the Country Music Highway. Radio host John Lair's 1939 country music "barn show" radio broadcast often referred to Renfro Valley as "Kentucky's Country Musical Capital." For many of its residents, that might have seemed small solace. For men like Ike Everly, it was the only way out of the darkness.

○ ○

Both Ike and his new wife were ambitious, and it was easy enough to find an audience, which, as one music historian asserted, consisted of "the common folk class of white people in the southeastern United States," who lacked the "requisite intellectual curiosity, or were not educated enough" for pop and jazz music offerings. Ike was well aware of those alien pop styles, seeking out blues artists who sifted through Kentucky performing for pockets of Black coal miners. But the Everlys knew the score, keeping their act simple but sneaking in variant styles.

Ike also knew that Margaret was not mere window dressing, and how important she was to the act. He had in mind to copy the path of singing families, the first being the Carter Family, the legendary brood of singing, guitar-playing sisters that had formed in the 1920s when the country idiom revolved around rugged men like Jimmie Rodgers, the woe-is-me "Singing Brakeman" who was country's first megastar. But the Carters also achieved national fame as the first country *group*, selling thousands of records, making songs like "Wabash Cannonball," "Can the Circle Be Unbroken," and "Wildwood Flower" into instant standards. (Hank Williams, too, would have a family act in the 1940s on Alabama radio with his wife, Audrey, and his young son, Hank Jr.) By the mid-1930s, the Carter family had their own radio shows in Texas, and lesser-known family groupings were able to land shows on radio stations around the South, the big station being Nashville's clear-channel WSM, the NBC network-affiliated carrier of the Grand Ole Opry show from 7 p.m. to midnight on Saturday nights.

Another was WWVA out of Wheeling, West Virginia, also a clear channel, saturating the airwaves especially at night with programs like *Jamboree U-S-A*, and WLW in Cincinnati, with its country show *Renfro Valley Barn Dance*—which actually paid homage to Kentucky, by referring to Renfro Valley, where the show would move in 1939. These stations made huge gains when they became affiliates of national networks, on NBC. CBS would get in the country game in 1943, picking up Louisville's WHAS, which ran the country favorite *Renfro Valley Gatherin'*. Family acts had won their spurs on these shows and stages. One, the husband-and-wife team Jack and Jill, an organist and piano player respectively, won an audience in the 1930s, played the Grand Ole Opry, and had their own radio show on Saturday nights.

Ike was convinced he could make giant strides in that same mold, but at his age there was only a short window of time left for it to happen. Not incidentally, he also wanted to start a family that might add flavors and voices to a family act. And midway through 1936, Margret was pregnant. She gave birth on February 1, 1937, at just seventeen, delivering their firstborn, Isaac Donald Everly, in Brownie, which would in time be made a part of Central City. Ike fixated on his son, teaching him how to thumb a guitar when he was still in the crib, and singing to him to sink the folk and country melodies into his head. Don, as he was called, mimicked words he had no understanding of, and seemed to have inherited a naturally resonant voice. Ike and Margaret would even take him along on gigs, with Don sitting in his stroller just off stage. Just a tot, he would soon understand how Ike sang and played a brand of country music that was neither fixed nor free of improvisation.

Ike was a stickler for detail, and superstitious; when Don began using his left hand to write, Ike wouldn't allow him to play the guitar left-handed, believing that playing it upside down, as lefties generally had to do back then, not only looked low-rent but might disturb the strict tuning he had achieved on it through endless tinkering and string tightening and loosening. What's more, just being left-handed was regarded by the righty majority as bad luck. As Don recalled, "My father said, 'You gotta learn it right-handed. They'll call you lefty otherwise. . . . It's a screwed-up world for left-handed people.' So I did. Everything else, I'm totally left-handed. Both Phil and I were." Years later, Don would say, "Country's not the right word for what [we] played. It was more uptown, more honky-tonk. I'll tell you the right word for it: blues. White blues." Their style would not change, but the path of the Everly family had a long, convoluted way to go.

CHAPTER TWO

Little Don and Baby Boy Phil

In 1938, Ike was still inhaling coal dust in the hellish mines, which he feared might savage his voice, given the prevalence of black lung disease among his coworkers. He was saving what he could, also taking some menial jobs to buff his savings, a necessity when, in 1939, Margaret was again pregnant. By then, having shoveled all that coal, record-breaking or not, when a great ball of fire ignited underground, missing him by inches, he took it as a sign from God that he needed to get out of the pit of hell and realize his dream of singing and thumbpicking for a living. And not in the choking terrain of Kentucky. Rather, he would try it in the big town, a *really* big town, where they played rhythm and blues and folk and country. And so, without waiting for Margaret to deliver, he quit the mines, packed up, and the Everly family was off to the wild snake pit of Chicago, with its elevated railways and speakeasies and famous names like Bugsy and Capone.

Ike moved the brood into an apartment in a tough Italian neighborhood, on Adams Street, then to 2201 Warren Boulevard. He found work as a manual laborer through Franklin Roosevelt's Works Progress Administration, but he continued injecting himself into the speakeasies at night. The blues melded with Irish folk, opera, and country, with the first nationally broadcast country radio program, *National Barn Dance*, debuting on WLS in 1924, predating the Grand Ole Opry's broadcasts by a year. The kaleidoscope of the clubs, the pulse, the fast life, was a kick to Ike, who played guitar as an in-house musician. He garnered steady work playing in the house band at the Kit Kat Lounge lakeside on North Halsted Street. Don would recall the joint mainly for the foul smell of booze, sweat, and blues hanging in the dank air. That aroma provided the background setting for the birth of his next son, Phil, born on January 19, 1939 (and, according to the birth certificate, given silver nitrate drops in his eyes to stave off conjunctivitis and future VD, a strange custom done away with in the 1980s).

They were the model of a working-class family as the Depression ended and World War II cast another pall in America—Ike was too old to be drafted, and had a family deferment—the parents and sons well-behaved, neat, church-going. Ike didn't make much money, but whatever he had went into buffing the family image. He left them no choice about being in the act, not letting lack of spending money get in the way. Ike could not afford to buy a second guitar, and so when they rehearsed songs that the family would sing on stage, he and the boys would all play the same guitar—at the same time. Ike would handle the strumming, Don and Phil the chords on the fretboard. It made a kind of layering effect that could make it sound like two guitars were playing, and even if it was something only done by established performers as a novelty or for *extremely* complicated classical arrangements, it accelerated their budding skills.

To Ike's delight, both boys also could sing. He would take Don, and later Phil when he was older, to the club scene along Michigan Avenue to soak up the blues feel. As Don recalled, "The first song I ever learned in my life was 'Paper Doll' by the Mills Brothers. Dad took me down to one of those recording booths they had for soldiers to record talk-letters back to their folks. And he made a record of 'Paper Doll,' with him playing his guitar." When Ike and Margaret would play in the sticks, the little guys dressed in pint-sized cowboy duds, for effect, though they were not the usual hillbilly act. Even then, their blend of voices was whipped cream smooth, meeting the ear with no distortion, which was remarkable given that the boys usually had to sing into an inferior microphone, which would magnify the louder vocals. But neither sang louder than the other, nor tried to outshine the other. Ike would have tanned their hides for that. And when these low-level gigs finally allowed Ike to buy two junior guitars, they were a three-guitar band, with Margaret lugging the big double bass guitar she'd had since they played the Kentucky hills. For Ike, that was real progress.

○ ○

Ike went further when he rigged up some cable and came up with a homemade amplifier, which he toted around with him from bar to bar. Don remembered one place where the owners put the amp in the doorway to Madison Street so that Ike's electric blues riffs would blast out onto the street, luring in more patrons. Amplifiers would soon enough be acceptable in country music, too, and Don and Phil would be well prepared when it was. Meanwhile, Ike made some strides in the Windy City, joining up for a time with a country group, the North Carolina Boys, and appearing on KXEL, Chicago's country station.

Things were happening in Chi-town. The young Red Foley, from Blue Lick, Kentucky, was chosen by WLS to sing with John Lair's Cumberland Ridge Runners, the house band on the station's *National Barn Dance* franchise. Foley also put some boogie-woogie blues into country but returned to Kentucky in 1937 to headline the *Renfro Valley Barn Dance*, then would go on to a long run known as "Mr. Country Music." (Not incidentally, he also would have a family act with his wife and their three daughters, who were called The Little Foleys.) But the small-time Everly family act was unable to get any real traction on big-city radio. WLS showed no interest in him and his family, and worse, there was no other option. Moreover, little country music was coming out of the city's recording studios once the Delta blues migration reached the area. Producer Lester Melrose, who produced blues records for RCA Victor/Bluebird, Columbia, and Okeh, led a lava flow of blues men into the studios, including Joe "King" Oliver, Big Bill Broonzy, Sonny Boy Williamson, Memphis Minnie, and Roosevelt Sykes. Soon, Muddy Waters arrived in Chicago in

1943, followed by Ellas McDaniel, a.k.a. Bo Diddley. That wave formed the soundtrack of Sweet Home Chicago.

In 1943, with America deep in wartime, he bundled the family up and drove to a more typical incubator of country folk music and American family life, the quiet Farm Belt town of Waterloo, Iowa, in the northeast part of the state, its population of 51,000 almost entirely white, a culture clash with Chicago. Not that Ike paid any attention to racial demographics. He believed there was work to be found on the radio. And when that didn't happen, they were on the move again, to Shenandoah, a small town to the southwest that bore the honor of being the "seed and nursery center of the world." It wasn't a hick town but one that had a thriving country station, KMA, on which an act called the Haden Family had a show. Their then-preteen son Charlie Haden would later bloom as a jazz musician after his throat was damaged by polio.

Founded in 1925, KMA melded farm news with hillbilly music, some of which would be recorded at its home base, the Mayfair Auditorium, where the station claimed over a million people had visited for shows that were broadcast at only 5,000 watts, too distant for many even within the Farm Belt, much less the Old South, to hear clearly on the radio. Yet the station's owner and on-air host, seed salesman Earl May, was so affixed in the culture that he was voted the "World's Most Popular Radio Announcer" in a 1952 *Radio Digest* poll. In fact, those shows, performed in the afternoon, based in a fictitious school and with May selling his seeds to audiences between songs, drew the highest ratings in the state.

Ike figured he needed to be on that wavelength and found a tidy home in a pleasant neighborhood at 800 West Sheridan Avenue. It wasn't long before he was taking the family out for gigs that began a small ripple for them. Soon they were making appearances on KMA. One of the earliest recordings of them came on Christmas morning, 1946, on a show hosted by "Uncle" Warren Neilsen, who introduced nine-year-old Don by saying, "You hear this young man on the air quite a bit. Good morning, Donnie." "Well, good morning." "Can you say Merry Christmas to all the folks out there?" "Merry Christmas." "Say it again real loud." "Merry Christmas!" Asked what he got for Christmas, Donnie answered, "A pocketknife [and] a football." With a studio band backing him, he then sang, "Santa Claus is Coming to Town" in a tender soprano, using the Southern pronunciation, "Santee Claus."

"That was really swell, Donnie Everly," Nielsen told him. "Thanks a whole lot."

He then brought on "Phillip," noting that the seven-year-old squirt had not slept all night: "You were rehearsing the song in your sleep, is that right?" In a seriously high voice, he squeaked, "That's what mother said," causing people in the studio to guffaw, knowing that Margaret liked to weave humorous fables around the boys. Baby Boy Phil's song was "Silent Night," full of tone variations and skillfully long-held notes. At the time, he was too young to master harmony, so he developed his pipes singing leads, gradually falling into the comfort zone of teaming with Don, who looked back at their development as the product of Ike alone.

"Dad did it," he said. "He sat us down every day, and we would rehearse and practice all day long. We also played a local barn dance on Saturday nights, and occasionally we'd get up on the back of a flatbed or pickup truck with speakers and go play for various little harvest-jubilee-type things. We never made a lot of money at it, but enough to get through, to get by."

All the while, the two little guys proved not only that they could sing—they could sing *together*, with a harmony that grew as they learned that it couldn't be forced but that each voice had to organically feed off the other. They were almost Stepford children—regulated, well-mannered, handsome, church-going, and when permitted their own time, showing quite dissimilar profiles. Don was thinner, darker-haired, more intellectually inclined and less comfortable before a crowd. He took to insular pursuits, such as artwork, reading, taking pictures, and even cooking. Phil, beefier, more comfortably smiling, more sandy-haired, and hammy. And neither had ever wanted to combine with the other. In Phil's toddler days, he would go into uncontrollable crying jags when Margaret all but ordered Ike to make the itinerant performing and radio gigs into a full-fledged family act. Ike had learned he could live easier if he just gave in to her demands, but neither of his boys ever really liked being paired up.

Indeed, Don was not happy to hold back his own development as a singer and guitarist waiting for Phil to become merely proficient. Phil disliked being the little shaver and had no desire to compete with Don by putting in the extensive work. He even put up with Don's little cracks about him messing up. Phil's discontent was evident, and if Margaret can be believed, many years later Phil rebelled by getting a can of black paint and covering the walls of his room with it, apparently to escape the daylight. Soon, though, Phil was content enough to be able to sing fairly well, if not with Don's power or finesse, and seemed to have what Don didn't—the approbation of Margaret. She never allowed Don to have a thought about rising in the business without his little brother, or Phil to believe he wouldn't.

She took this condition quite seriously, and Ike had no intention of crossing her, given her flaring temper. To keep her sons on the same beam, they were each year given only a single batch of Christmas presents and had to play with them together, not individually. They slept head to foot in one bed, even after reaching their teens. Their clothes were almost always identical and kept in a single closet. And Ike kept working the boys hard, almost maniacally. It paid off, too. Phil would never be much of a guitarist, so playing strictly rhythm was fine with him, as was singing harmony to Don's lead vocals. And here is where they really meshed. As Don would say of their symbiosis, "I sing the lead, and so I can drift off. Then we'll come back in together and the whole thing happens again. It amazes me sometimes." It also meant that whatever visions he had of becoming the next Hank Williams, they were as dead as Hank.

○ ○

As for his own dreams, Ike got only as far as his limited talent could take him. He got a break when KMA hired him for a half-hour show. He was paid fifty dollars a week, drew some loyal listeners, and spoke so much about his family that when the station offered him another twenty-five bucks if he made it a family show, he was flushed with this great leap upward for him and the brood. *The Everly Family* show debuted with Don and Phil winning attention as "Little Don and Baby Boy Phil." Gaining experience and stage instincts—standing in their assigned spots in front of Ike and Margaret, singing and playing guitar with Ike, and Margaret keeping the beat on her upright bass. Don and Phil would wear easy smiles, and display their wit and comfortability in the spotlight. An early takeout from Ike's show, from 1951, had him in character, going heavy on the drawl that was almost imperceptible off the air.

"Well, a great big howdy doo to all our friends and neighbors," he opened the show. "This is Dad Everly talkin' for the Everly family. And we're gonna play you some songs, neighbors, family style, also country style. And we got the whole gang, Mom, Don, Baby Boy Phil. Y'know, I kinda suggested we get the Everly boys teamed up on one here. Phil, what are you gonna sing?"

Phil, who at twelve chafed at still being called Baby Boy, said, "Well, dad, we'd like to do a number for the folks called 'Don't Let Our Love Die.'"

This song, recorded by the York Brothers in 1950—the B-side of "Long Time Gone"—was a remarkable choice for such young men, a pleading folk ballad begging a jilting lover "Someone stole your love and your heart / Is it really true you don't care for me?" Don would play lead with a fluttery, flamenco-like touch. They handled it so expertly that their youth seemed irrelevant. It was so remarkable that the Everly Brothers would revive it, with a fiddle solo put into the middle eight, forty years later on a BBC TV show celebrating Irish folk ballads, which included Irish-Scottish artists like Philip Chevron, Mary Black and David Spillane, Kentuckian Ricky Skaggs, and the Brit new wave rocker Elvis Costello; there was also a three-CD album made of the BBC show, *Bringing It All Back Home*, with a second Everly Brothers selection, "Rose Connolly," an old Appalachian lament sung by Charlie Monroe in 1947 and covered by the brothers as "Down in the Willow Garden" on their *Songs Our Daddy Taught Us* LP. (They also would use the 1951 studio recording of "Don't

Let Our Love Die" as the lead track of the massive, 103–song, 1994 Rhino Records release *Heartaches and Harmonies* and other old tapes on the even more hefty CD/DVD package from Bear Family Records, *Chained to a Memory*.)

The boys were naturals singing old-school country folk tunes—other examples being, besides "Long Time Gone," mountain anthems like "Barbara Allen," "Put My Little Shoes Away," "Who's Gonna Shoe Your Pretty Little Feet?" "Lightning Express," and another of those harbingers of the new lexicon to come along in the 1950s, "Rockin' Alone (In an Old Rockin' Chair)." Ike of course had the final say on their song selection, and had directed them to sing Gene Autry's teary-eyed "That Silver-Haired Daddy of Mine," paying homage to "a dear one who's weathered life's sorrows." These songs would cling to their minds all their livelong days, and be recorded by them as if by genuflection—the *Songs Our Daddy Taught Us* album including the Autry song. Gaining age and experience, they sang with a sort of restless desire that would keep getting stronger as they outgrew their precocity, sprouting from precocious ragamuffins into tall, resolute, string bean–thin teens with a Ricky Nelson look and a trail of concert performances around town.

As the main attraction of "The Everly Family" shows, they pushed Ike and Margaret into the background. Don even was given his own show on the station, "The Little Donnie Show," his theme song being one he wrote, "Free as a Little Bird as I Can Be." But Ike clearly gained work simply by having sired Little Donnie. He began to write songs of his own—the first was called "Have You Forgot Your Joe?"—and was given another radio show, on KFNF, 330 miles away, across the border in Oberlin, Kansas. Riding back and forth, he burned up a lot of miles and gas, but Ike was flying high knowing that he had a family gold mine. He was right, but he would from now on be reduced to table scraps from the sumptuous upward trail of his sons.

○ ○

They were much photographed as they navigated through their childhood, often wearing cowboy-style outfits. But by the early

1950s, with the rock fad growing, they wore jeans and casual shirts with the sleeves rolled up. And they had a rock compliant country sound. A photo of Don circa 1952 shows him seated and playing the guitar at a school dance with a local band named Clare Hornung Jr. and the Shenanigans, the name being a reflection of the teen culture. Still, beyond their progress through school, friends were sacrificed for the long hours spent mainly looking only at each other as they went through their paces on the guitar under Ike's gaze. Phil was able to requisition free time for himself by joining the Shenandoah High School's basketball and track teams. He would also test Ike by being late for their guitar lessons, and would relish being the "carefree" Everly Brother, who actually looked like he was *enjoying* himself, while Don always seemed in pain from some hidden grief—a permanent trait for as long as he lived.

Years later, Phil would muster a smile and say, "We aren't locked at the hip. We're different people, we like different things." Don would be more perfunctory: "When we get together, we sing. That's what we do. You know, we don't go on vacation together." Not that being brothers, and sons of a musician, didn't forge a bond between them. They were representing the *family*. They had their contentions, but their music was like a shared soul. And the education they gleaned from Ike was a ligament for both of his sons. As Don would say, "When dad taught me to play guitar, I discovered Hank Williams. All I wanted to do was write and sing songs, and be on the Grand Ole Opry like Hank Williams." That it worked out that way within only a few years was what separated them from their contemporaries by country miles. On the other hand, that it happened so soon may have been the problem. Because their juvenile differences would widen before they could be resolved, it would always be too late to turn back.

CHAPTER THREE

Nashville Cats

To be sure, their timing was dead-solid perfect. Country was their background but rock and roll their conveyance. Rock was in the early 1950s cracking out of the eggshell it had been in when some believed, and many hoped, that it was a passing fad. It could be backdated to the late 1940s, as America returned to peaceful contentment and cultural and limited racial expansion. One of the first rock records, Fat Domino's "The Fat Man," was recorded in New Orleans in 1949 with a fat, sassy backbeat, Fats boasting that "girls they love me 'cause I know my way around." It became the first R&B song to sell a million records, virtually telling the world to get ready, something new was happening here. Two years later, "Rocket 88," written and produced for sax man/singer Jackie Brenston and His Delta Cats by blues hepcat Ike Turner in Sam Phillips's Memphis Sun Records studio, flexed this swing beat (the chunky bass line created by a broken amplifier) metaphorically about a flashy car as an aphrodisiac—setting forth that cars and sex would be teeming topics of interest among maturing baby boomers.

In another old photo of the Everly boys, they seem genuinely pleased sitting in the front seat of a snazzy convertible, top down, Don at the wheel, Phil in the passenger seat wishing he could take the wheel. Rock had a way to go. American culture was adamantly mainstream. The big hits were by white

big-band singers like Johnny Ray, Kay Starr, Rosemary Clooney, Patti Page, and Eddie Fisher, with incursions made by a
few Black bebop veterans like the fabulous Mills Brothers. The
biggest-selling record of 1952 was bandleader Leroy Anderson's
"Blue Tango"; in 1953, Percy Faith's laid-back instrumental,
"Song from Moulin Rouge." No one really knew where to put
rock and roll; it had no idiomatic format until June 1951 when
Cleveland's hipster DJ Alan Freed attached the three words few
teens had ever heard to the race records he played on the air
instead of the usual bland white covers of them.

In truth, the phrase had been around for years; there was
even a novelty song called "Rock and Roll" in 1880, and in the
1930s it was slyly conscripted by jazz musicians as slang for sex.
Black artists like Sister Rosetta Tharpe, Roy Brown, and Ella
Fitzgerald stuck it in their songs. A real turning point was the
proto-rock "Sixty Minute Man" by Billy Ward and his Dominoes
in 1951, noting with a wink that "I rock 'em I roll 'em, all night
long." By the mid-1950s, it was firmly injected into the culture
when Bill Haley and His Comets, a white bop band that had
reached the top of the R&B chart with a cover of Big Joe Turner's
sexual feast "Shake, Rattle and Roll," recorded "Rock Around
the Clock" for the teen-angst movie *The Blackboard Jungle*, its
call to arms to dance the night and day away becoming the first
"rock" song to go to number one on the *Billboard* Top 100 chart.

The Everly Brothers were no strangers to the big beat,
Freed's other cryptograph for rock and roll. During the family's
Chicago stay, rhythm and blues entered their world. In fact, for
Don Everly, Bo Diddley's hambone beat, repetitive stop-time
pattern, and sense of drip-dropping cool would leave a lasting
impression, even as Ike was still hoping to cast them on the radio in the manner of the Delmore Brothers, the country family
act from Alabama who were a Grand Ole Opry favorite in the
1930s and 1940s singing high-revved gospel-flavored country—
though, as an early indicator that country could cross over to
other markets, they recorded in 1946 "Freight Train Boogie,"
which would be covered far and wide, including by the Everly
Brothers, who as aspiring songwriters were contouring country
with this as a model.

However, Ike decided nothing would happen for either him or his sons in Iowa. After his radio show was canceled in 1953, still no moss growing under his feet, he gave up on Iowa and went where other work was, in Evansville, Indiana, when the country station WIKY went on the air that year. And, as the wheel turned, being not far from the border to the Old South was soon the last steppingstone for the Everly family to retrace their steps back to where this travelog had begun, in the hills.

○ ○

Actually, Ike and Margaret had never put the South out of their minds or lives. Each summer, they would take their sons back "home," as Ike called it, to Knoxville, Tennessee, where both of their families had sunk roots. There the Everlys would stay until the cool winds of fall began to blow. When Ike moved the brood there in 1953, Don and Phil by now had grown and progressed as musicians to the point where they could play in public without the mantle of the family, as the primordial Everly Brothers. They were teens only in the technical sense, attending West High School, and Don would be able to garner his first recording opportunity, as the result of Ike all but forcing them on Chet Atkins.

The long, lean, taciturn guitar god, who ran the country music corridor in nearby Nashville, came to Knoxville for a show, playing the three-finger, thumb-strum technique that was the envy of all guitar pickers. Atkins had learned to play guitar in high school back in Georgia by tuning it in the boy's room, where, as he said, "the corner of my ears" could judge that the acoustics there were best. As a wunderkind, he moved up the country ladder by leaps and bounds, and in 1954 was in the process of building RCA Studio B, the first major studio in Nashville, implementing on sessions the "Nashville sound" he had helped unleash. Now thirty, he was RCA's top country producer while making his own records and those for non-RCA artists, so admired and near worshiped that Gretsch had named a guitar line for him.

As he had with many country music figures, Ike had met Atkins somewhere along the way and schmoozed with him. After the Knoxville show he elbowed his way backstage, with Don and Phil struggling to keep up with him, and introduced himself and the boys, then got to bragging about his precocious sons, who vamped a few nuggets right there on the spot for Chet, who said years later, "I can still see them lookin' up at me through the fence."

"They're writin' some good songs, too," Ike persisted, a quality he had honed.

Atkins, a nicer and more accommodating fellow than most, didn't brush them off. He told Ike to come up to Nashville with the boys and play some of their stuff for him in his own lair. Don recalled that as blissful, saying "Chet, bless his heart, gave us his home phone number, which was like the key to the city, a treasure." The brothers did as he suggested, and they and Ike rambled up to Nashville to sing and play for him. Chet again was impressed, mostly with a song called "Thou Shalt Not Steal," which was out of the trough of country betrayal, stealing a lover from a friend, the hook being, "In the Bible it says thou shall not steal / But I have found the love I want." Chet told Don to add a bridge between verses. "I was shocked he liked it," Don said. "So I took it home, made the changes, and a few days later I came back again to Nashville and played it for him. And he liked what I'd done with it."

There was more to it than that. In the record industry, there always is. Atkins had a ton of connections, and his main vine was Acuff-Rose Music, the giant Nashville publishing company that the noted country singer Roy Acuff had founded with a hard-eyed music agent named Fred Rose, its original intent being to shuttle Grand Ole Opry singers to record companies, as Rose did for his most legendary client, Hank Williams. Acuff-Rose, which after Fred's death was taken over by his son Wesley, demanded the publishing rights on all songs by their clients, who willingly traded them for a shot at fame. Atkins was the "inside man" in Nashville's power schema (as was Owen Bradley, who built Nashville's other major studio, Quonset Hut, for

Columbia Records), and could send demos from new singers to his bosses. He did that with Don's song, and before signing Don to an Acuff-Rose deal, he tested the waters by routing "Thou Shalt Not Steal" to various A-R acts. Don, who also mailed Chet demos from other songs, heard nothing until weeks later. Convinced it was all for naught, he got a letter from Chet, dated July 28, 1954. It read:

> Hello Don: It looks like we'll get a record on "THOU SHALT NOT STEAL." Kitty Wells likes it very much and says she will cut it in two or three weeks. I know you'll be glad to hear this news. So, if you sign the enclosed contracts, and return one to me, we'll be in business. As you are underage Don, I suppose you'd better have Ike sign too.

He added:

> I hope to get some records on the other songs, but it will take a little time to do that. . . . Also, we'll be trying to get you on record. Keep writing and let me hear from you.
>   The two new songs you sent are fine.

As Don recalled, "I was flabbergasted." Indeed, that planned meeting in Knoxville had joined him with country's femme fatale, Kitty Wells, whose classic tune for Decca, "It Wasn't God Who Made Honky Tonk Angels," had gotten her briefly banned by the Opry and some radio stations for its sassy, raunchy tale of being cheated on. "Thou Shalt Not Steal" was soon released, backed on the flip side by an old song written by Fred Rose, "I Hope My Divorce Is Never Granted," which in retrospect sums up Kitty's seventy-four-year marriage. This sort of top-level deal-making was alien territory for Don, who would now be owed his first writing royalties—six hundred bucks. He used the dough to buy much-needed new tires for the family car, and pink slacks and brown suede shoes for himself. He was comforted that he had Chet Atkins as a go-between, and convinced he could go it alone in the business, graduating from songwriter to singing star. But if he thought the game was going to be easy, he was about to learn how much he needed his baby brother to keep from falling flat on his ass.

○ ○

For one thing, Wesley Rose had decided not to offer Don a contract as an Acuff-Rose songwriter. For another, Ike and Margaret would not let his quick success go to his head, and forsake the family bond. The Everly Family now had a program on Knoxville's country station WIVK, doing the early morning *Cas Walker's Farm and Home Hour*, the host being the owner of a chain of local grocery stores. The show also had a TV version on WBIR. Walker, a corruption-fighting city councilman and future mayor of the city, had a large audience and took credit as a conduit for young and mainly unknown talent—with cause; in 1955, he would put on the air ten-year-old Dolly Parton, who three years later had a record deal and was on the stage at the Grand Ole Opry.

This seemed doable for the Everly boys, too, but it turned out that they were over the line for Walker. They were hardly rebels, and sang country blues that the audience reacted well to, yet Walker saw them as too rock-and-rollish. As Don recalled, "Our hair was a little long and we didn't sound as Southern as [Walker] wanted. He called us 'Yankees,' we didn't sound Southern enough. And we lost that job." Actually, the entire family did. This was a blow, and when Ike was unable to talk his way into another radio gig, he turned from music to becoming a barber in Knoxville, while Margaret took a job in a beauty parlor. It seemed the music pipedream was over. In 1955, Don was in his senior year at Lee High and Phil a sophomore at Peabody Demonstration High, a school meant for future teachers, where Ike and Margaret had transferred him in hopes he would buckle down and take life more seriously. And while Don seemed to be the only Everly still engaged in music, writing songs and going out with Phil for the same low-level, pickup-truck gigs that Ike had used to break in his own act, the real possibility was that the dreams of youth would lead both brothers into a place that made them shudder—the mines. And then, out of nowhere, another of the songs Don had given to Chet Atkins paid off.

This one was called "Here We Are Again." Chet had sent it to Mother Maybelle's youngest singing daughter, Anita Carter, who had gone solo, appearing several times on Kate Smith's TV show—the first female country singer to be on national TV—and recording with Atkins, Hank Snow, and her future brother-in-law, Johnny Cash. Although "Here We Are Again" was released by RCA, it didn't hit the chart, but did make a few more dollars for Don—and Chet—who could go rogue and register any songs that Acuff-Rose had passed on with one of his own publishing companies. For Don, it refocused his sights. As he recalled, "I was never really good at school, and here I had made a thousand-some dollars in royalties from my songs. So as soon as I graduated from high school, we packed the car up and high-tailed it for Nashville."

The "we" were Don, Phil, and Margaret, while Ike stayed in Knoxville doing his barbering. In Nashville, they rented an apartment while Don gave it his best shot at moving up. Again, the climb was limited to his writing. Working on another one of his endless contacts, Atkins had talked him up to another big shot, Grelun Landon, vice president of the New York–based songwriting and publishing company Hill & Range. Landon would within a year become head of RCA Records and sign Elvis Presley, who would come to record in Nashville, his first record "Heartbreak Hotel," with Chet Atkins on the session with Elvis's band. Landon had a lot of pull. Offered a contract, Don had no choice but to sign, but he did little writing. Instead, he tried to break into recording with Phil, who dropped out at Peabody, though he would get an equivalency diploma years later.

Chet again was his go-between. He prevailed upon no less than Columbia Records' Don Law, who headed the mighty label's country music division, to give the brothers an audition. Law, who had seen them in shows around town, invited them to record some songs at the Columbia studio built by Owen Bradley. This meant that the brothers were suddenly, and fleetingly, in the same galaxy as Tony Bennett, Doris Day, Rosemary Clooney, and Johnny Mathis, and country biggies like Bob Wills and His Texas Cowboys, Floyd Tillman, "Little" Jimmy Dickens, Lefty Frizzell, Ray Price, and a young Johnny Cash. But there would be less to the deal than met the eye. Their first real studio foray, on November 9, 1955, was booked for them to record four songs in a twenty-minute session Law squeezed in for them.

They came in accompanied by Carl Smith's band, though the backing was mainly a brush-stick drum line and a melodious pedal-steel guitar leaving room for the brothers' string guitar blend. Still, there were auguries in this session. Don and Phil had perfected playing in thumb-picking style but without a thumb pick, skimming the strings with a full hand sweep, thumbs playing the bass notes, the other four fingers stoking the high harmony. Impressed, Law acted quickly, signing them to a deal, with Ike needing to sign for the underage Phil. It was a conditional contract, just four cents per dollar on potential record sales, and the publishing on their songs owned by Blackwood Music, an arm of Columbia Records, which conflicted with Don's still-extant contract with Hill & Range. Don kept that part quiet, not knowing whether he could freelance with his songs if they were performed by his own act.

They were able to cram the four songs into twenty minutes, three written by Don and Phil—"Keep A' Lovin' Me," "If Her Love Isn't True," "That's the Life I Have to Live"—and "The Sun Keeps Shining," written by Don and Jerry Organ, a pseudonym for Troy Martin, an east-coast executive of Gene Autry's Golden West Melodies, a publishing firm that was under the CBS roof. Martin had also written swings for Lefty Frizzell and Ray Price. Don Law was the nominal producer, and the songs came out as conventional country fodder, with a fiddle and some quite poor acoustics. A single would be released with "Lovin'" on the A-side, the title being the "the secret to make our love last . . . if you just give me a chance." It was a little bit twangy, a little bit Hank Williams, the hook being "I've found a new love." The flip, "Sun," has them pining to find "a new love, a true love."

The disk was released in February 1956 as Columbia catalog number 21496. However, the brothers knew the songs were not ready for prime time. Phil would recall how he and Don walked out of the studio agreeing how horrible they'd been. Don Law agreed. The record, with no promotion behind it, never got any traction, was here and gone—which may have spared them any trouble from Hill & Range. And the two other songs recorded on that day were not to be dug out of the CBS vaults until 1981, when the German-based Bear Family label, which specialized in finding rare "first records," bought the copyrights on all four sides and released them on a twelve-inch EP. Even as rock gods, when CBS compiled its ambitious 2006 four-volume *Columbia Country Classics* series twenty-six-track "Nashville Sound," Volume 4, none of those four Everly Brothers songs were on it. Phil, looking back, recalled the songs as a dose of reality that their options were very limited. Having "died a death that was deserved," he said, they could almost smell the coal dust.

Failing so dismally with one of the biggest labels in the world, the only thing Don and Phil Everly could do was go back to their sidewalk act, hoping they would be noticed. Hanging out among a crowd of similarly unproven singers in the alley of the Ryman Auditorium, they also flubbed an audition by the Grand Ole Opry pooh-bahs, leaving Don with hard feelings about the Opry. As he explained years afterward,

> It was a monopoly. If you're not Grand Ole Opry music, you're not really country music. We were the outcasts. Our crowd had skin-tight pig pants and ducktail hair. I didn't want to wear cowboy suits and cowboy boots. I didn't feel like a cowboy. The Opry really wasn't our thing. You know, no drums were allowed in there on the stage. They decided drums weren't country music. It didn't fit. Well, neither did we. But we could do country music in a different way. Not the usual way, which was like a two-step dance beat, a Hank Williams beat. We put some rock, some blues rhythm, into it without sacrificing the country aspect. In Nashville, you had to make yourself fit.

However, being in the big shadow of the Opry was the only chance to get another shot at the carousel ring. And they were too good not to get on the Grand Ole Opry's summer road tours—the Opry's "minor league" circuit. During that summer of 1956, their appearances were often noted in the showbiz pages of the *Nashville Banner*. One blurb in the August 23 issue noted their concerts three days later across the Tennessee border at Deer Creek Ranch in North Vernon, Indiana, an "All-Star Show" featuring other lower-case names like Eddie Hill, George Morgan, Lee Emerson, Hal and Ginger, and Asher and Little Jimmie, though an ad publicized it as "one of the greatest shows ever to go out from the Grand Ole Opry. DON'T MISS IT."

These excursions, on which the brothers usually got an enthusiastic reception, seemed to reignite them at Columbia, at least according to an item in the *Banner* reporting that, according to Don Law, they would "wax more records for Columbia." However, it never happened. Moreover, it seemed the Everly family was in crisis. Margaret had by now gone back to Knoxville where Ike was getting restless again. Barbering had not worked out for him and the only work he could scour up was at a construction company back in Evansville, where he and Margaret packed up and went. And when that job ended, they landed back in Chicago, doing menial jobs. Their sons, meanwhile, were hoping against hope for the break in Nashville they seemed to have gotten, and blown. As Phil remembered, "We were out of money. All [we] had was a stick of butter and a box of cornmeal. And Donald made egg muffins from that cornmeal and we put the butter on it. I've never had anything that good, because we hadn't eaten for a day or so."

If not for Chet Atkins, that would have been the last roundup for the Everly Brothers. But he continued to think there was something special in them, and kept touting them. He now sent another demo they had written and recorded, "The Life I Have to Live," to Justin Tubb, the "Texas Troubadour" Ernest Tubb's son, who'd had a few top-ten country hits but was better known as a songwriter, one being Hawkshaw Hawkins's "Lonesome 7-7203." Tubb liked "Life" enough to put it on the B-side of his hit song "I'm a Big Boy Now" early in 1957. That was worth several hundred dollars in royalties and an invitation to go out on the road in a show headlined by the banjo-playing, singer-comedian Grandpa Jones.

Along the way, Don had become the object of affection for Ernie Tubb's daughter Elaine, whose crush on him had helped her convince her brother to record "The Life," and as Don recalled, she soon became his ad-hoc "girlfriend-manager." She was, he said, "a year or so older—but a little more worldly. I was a very naive young boy. Mom and dad had never left us alone before. We'd traveled together, done everything together. Elaine got us on the Ernest Tubb Midnight Jamboree, and we got up and sang with her and by ourselves."

It was then that a fortuitous moment occurred—winning the attention of another big-time Nashville player, Wesley Rose, a Falstaffian figure, the chubby, balding, mustachioed son of the storied Fred Rose who was now president of Acuff-Rose. And though the firm had gone only so far with the Everlys months before, Wesley had seen enough of them to proffer a contract to Don and Phil. The sticking point was Don's contract to Hill & Range, and while he had gotten away with recording his songs for Columbia, signing a deal strictly as a songwriter would step directly into Hill & Range's purview, though that relationship had all but withered away. This time, however, Don didn't blindly go ahead. Wesley had big visions, and getting the Everly Brothers another record deal through Acuff-Rose's enormous reach was his intention. Not willing to put that at risk if Hill & Range made a stink about losing the publishing on Everly Brothers songs that didn't fail, Don went to see Grelun Landon, who was initially truculent.

"Nobody gets out of those contracts," he said. "You signed for five hundred dollars [per song] for the rest of your life."

But Don was a persuasive young man, remembering years later that after some sincere pleading, Landon "got us released, bless his heart."

Free now to sign with Acuff-Rose, Rose turned right away to landing a record deal for the Everlys. Fatefully, Don said, "Wesley had Cadence Records coming in. He said if Cadence wouldn't do it, he'd put us on Hickory [the small Acuff-Rose house label]."

Things seemed to be falling into place, but Don would recall that he heard the same refrain from more than a few Nashville singers trying to move on up—"Watch Wesley," whose labors on behalf of his stable's writer-singers were primarily for the benefit of the company. Don had no reason to believe Rose wouldn't do well for the Everly Brothers, and saw no need to question the contract he and Phil signed, which was common for the times, securing for Acuff-Rose by far the lion's share of those publishing royalties. It also seemed fine by him that Wesley would be their manager, as unethical as that was, since managers theoretically existed to drive a hard bargain with a record label and song publishers. In this case, Wesley bargained with no one. His word was law. And in the broad sense, it worked out pretty damn well for Acuff-Rose-affiliated performers, such as when he drove a deal for the Everlys with the quite prominent label he had his sights on from the beginning.

○ ○

Cadence Records was right in Rose's crosshairs. Founded in 1952 by New York bandleader Archie Bleyer, a tall, bespectacled trumpeter who had been the musical director on Arthur Godfrey's radio and TV shows, the label was small but on the grow. For two years, it had been a mere sidelight for Bleyer, but then Archie was blindsided by the sanguine but hideously imperious Godfrey suddenly firing him and the show's matinee idol singer Julius La Rosa, who recorded for Cadence, for "lacking humility"—a euphemism for the betrayal Godfrey felt when Bleyer recorded a spoken-word album by a competitor, Don McNeill, host of the long-running radio show *Breakfast Club*. Worse, Bleyer violated a Godfrey blue law when he began dating Janet Ertel, one of the Chordettes, the candy-cane group who had a massive hit with "Lollipop" and sang on the Godfrey show, and she was deemed off limits to the show's men. And so in 1953, Godfrey had dismissed both Bleyer and La Rosa, the latter on the air, right after he had sung the last notes of a song, his misdemeanor being that he had hired an agent, offending Godfrey's prickly sense of insecurity, explaining that La Rosa had the temerity to "become his own star."

Bleyer, who soon after the firing married his Chordette, turned to upgrading his label, producing big hits for it across the music spectrum, and incorporating country into his big-band-style offerings. He traveled often to Nashville for country songs and meetings with Wesley Rose, and when he came through in 1957 on one such pilgrimage, Wesley talked up the Everly Brothers. Although Bleyer had previously passed on an Everlys song during their panhandling days, he was convinced by Hal Smith, the manager of another young Nashville singer-songwriter, Dave Rich, who was tight with Don and Phil and asked Smith to help get them signed. Bleyer had not heard the act recently but agreed to an audition. Don and Phil would later laugh about how they rushed to get to see him before he left to go back to New York. Speeding through the streets of Nashville to the Sam Davis Hotel where Bleyer was staying, they damn near crashed Phil's battered Ford and parked it in a no-parking zone. They ran up the stairs and banged at his door, and when he opened it, Phil recalled, inside the room was "his mistress."

Sitting in his underwear, and clearly impatient, Bleyer heard them sing and, perhaps eager to get back to work, told them he'd sign them when he returned to Nashville on February 1, three weeks later. And he meant it. Indeed, he even had a song for them to record, a rock-friendly country tune, "Bye Bye Love," furnished to him by Rose, cowritten by Rose-Acuff writers Boudleaux and Felice Bryant. He had tried to place it with one of his label's acts, over twenty in all, but couldn't find anyone who wanted to record it. Lore even has it that Elvis turned it down. Another, Porter Wagoner, had accepted it, but when he demanded a chord change Boudleaux Bryant refused, and Porter pulled out. Wesley assured Bleyer that the Everly Brothers would not turn it down, not if he had anything to do with it. And though the Everly Brothers knew nothing about the song, or how he and Phil would sing it, once again Chet Atkins entered their world. Walking down the alley outside the Ryman, he ran into them hanging out there.

"Don said, 'We just signed a deal with Archie Bleyer,'" Atkins recalled. "I knew how happy he was because he said, 'Won't you join me? Let's play some Bo Diddley.' And I said, yeah, man, just call me. We'll do it."

Chet kept his word. He came to the first of the Everly Brothers sessions at his newly opened Studio B, hired by Archie to play his wizardly Gretsch; and the rehearsal takes made him blink. Years later, after they had proven it scores of times, Atkins would summarize why. "They filled a void," he said. "They had a different arrangement: The Nashville Sound combined with Bo Diddley beats."

And those harmonies. Good lord, those harmonies.

Until they died, Don and Phil would be explaining how they managed the delicate mechanics of that harmony to a world that couldn't possibly imagine how. "I have to pay attention every second with my harmonies," Phil would say. "It's like playing tennis with someone who is really great. You can't let your mind wander for even a microsecond, or you'll be left behind." Nor did he elevate his supple high octaves into dramatic arpeggios, as it would have interfered with the exact balance between them. Watching Don's fingers as he played the guitar, and singing along with every little diversion in Don's vocals as if by premonition, Phil was wraithlike. "When Phil and I sing," Don once said, "I swear that there are times that what comes out is not either of us but the voice of a third person." That was how spooky the Everly Brothers were—in effect, the Everly Trio.

Far in the future, Art Garfunkel was nearly haunted by it. "I sing to James Taylor [songs] before every show I do," he once said. "Then I go from James' bass-baritone to tenor singing with the Everly Brothers—first Don, later Phil." Even for him, just getting close was perfect enough. But in 1957, the Everly Brothers were already fully there. The top musicians in Nashville had yet to hear them in a studio setting, but that mythical but all-too-real "third" Everly Brother would enter with them when they recorded "Bye Bye Love." And never leave.

CHAPTER FOUR

Big Juju

"Bye Bye Love" was a strange brew, a woe-is-me tale about losing a girl who had run off with "someone new," yet it was unclear whether the agonist was holding her responsible, or himself. Losing love, sweet caresses, and counting the stars above was painful, but there was no intention of getting her back. With this, the Bryants massaged the country template of wallowing in lost love, but the reason it had been rejected by so many singers was likely the apprehension within the 1950s culture about casting a woman, especially a teen girl, by inference as a cheater. But while Archie Bleyer was a classic prude, and no fan of rock and roll, he was in business to make money, and knew a good song when he heard it. With "Bye Bye Love," he was willing to go for the country and rock market in one shot.

Among the limited roster of acts on the Cadence label at the time, the top drawer was occupied by Andy Williams, who that year hit number one pop with a cover of country singer Charlie Gracie's "Butterfly," the Chordettes, and Bleyer's fellow victim of Arthur Godfrey, Julius La Rosa. Some others on the label were sax man Sal Butera and the Yiddish, jazz-singing Barry Sisters. By signing the Everly Brothers, Bleyer believed he could conquer rock with songs that had a little bite but bathed in soft country overtones. As it was, he was horrified by another act in his employ, North Carolina guitarist Link Wray and His Wray

Men, who had logged a rock and roll hit for him in a seething instrumental with a fuzzy feedback guitar, "Rumble," which was parlance for gang warfare. Catching rock's rebellious fever, it would rise to number sixteen pop and number eleven R&B, but Archie still dismissed Wray from the roster instead of having to suffer through a "Rumble–Part 2."

Bleyer wasn't even sure about "Bye Bye Love" until he sent a demo of the record to his teen stepdaughter, Jackie Ertel, who lived with her biological father in Sheboygan, Wisconsin. She said she loved it and so did her friends, and so Archie committed to it. As for the Everlys, any side issue about women and girls' infidelity was silly, since country songs often dealt with messy, multi-blamable love triangles. With the issue settled, Wesley Rose arranged a session to record it and three other songs on March 1, 1957, at Chet Atkins's RCA studio, which was inside a drab one-story building at Seventeenth Avenue South and Hawkins Street, which would later be renamed Music Square West, and then Roy Acuff Place. The studio, built to his specifications, was 40.5 × 26.5 feet, a chamber that would turn out to be far less perfect than Atkins's guitar skills. Technical experts would come to see the room as acoustically inferior due to the thinness of the walls that prevented the booming effect of the lower frequencies, which explains why the Everly Brothers recordings were fairly thin at the bottom, but this flaw made the high guitars so crackling sharp.

The best feature of the studio was its echo chamber in a small step-up room above the thirteen-foot ceiling, controlled by a mixing board that was ahead of its time, able to produce futuristic effects like reverb and delay. When a new engineer, Bill Porter, arrived in 1959, he made some refinements, such as lining the hardwood floor with checkerboard tiles, having the walls curved, and hanging triangular-cut ceiling panels at different lengths—known famously as the "Porter Pyramids"—making the room look like an obstacle course. And though it seems hard to fathom now, he also drew X's on the floor at points where sonic resonance was least problematic. The most potent X spot— the "Sweet Spot"—was just inside the door, where the Everly Brothers, Elvis, Roy Orbison, and basically all of Nashville sang their greatest songs.

All of it is still there, as well as an old Steinway piano against one wall, a vibraphone nearby, a beat-up drum kit against another, amps arrayed on the floor, music stands with almost obliterated "RCA" circles on them, and creaky seats lined up on one side. And one can almost hear the Everly Brothers and Atkins working their magic here. Unlike today, when every sound is fed into auto-tune, auto-intelligence computers that automatically measure them down to the lowest megahertz, anyone back then with an idea about how to create the right sound could make something special happen—such as Orbison stacking coats, tablecloths, sheets, anything he could find, on a coat rack right behind him to dampen the acoustics and heighten the grimness of his woebegone songs. There were only four tracks at most then, and most songs were recorded with the vocals and instruments done at once, not in separate tracks, which is why they sounded so intimate and spontaneous, with little mistakes left in as part of the live feel, and requiring only a few takes per song.

This was quite beneficial to Archie Bleyer, who would produce the first Everly Brothers sessions, which of course included Chet, who would often freelance on sessions there for other labels than RCA. When the Everly Brothers entered for the first time, Atkins was joined by some other "Nashville A-Team" stalwarts, elite pros who were regulars in the house band at the Grand Ole Opry—guitarist Ray Edenton, bassist Floyd "Lightnin'" Chance, who like Atkins had played on Hank Williams sessions and as his backup at the Grand Ole Opry, and drummer Buddy Harman. Chet would play lead guitar on his electric Gretsch tweaking a high-treble sound on top of Don and Phil's steel-string strumming. This tight coterie rehearsed "Bye Bye Love" with Don and Phil, as well as the Bryants, who made lyrical changes they saw fit.

After some fitful starts, it was agreed that the boys would forgo starting with the verse and go right into the hook—"Bye bye love, bye bye happiness." As an intro, Don rehashed a guitar riff he had used in an early demo he'd made with Phil for Acuff-Rose of "Give Me a Future," a feisty love song that would itself be reprised by the brothers down the road. The intro was Don scratching out, Bo Diddley style, the chugging *ba-da-da-da, chicka-chicka-chicka* riff. In geek terms, Don and Edenton strummed in open-tuning and Phil in regular tuning, Don hitting chords high on the neck. And Atkins hit saucy notes on his electric guitar, a tasty seasoning. Phil called it "a rhythm and blues intro" and that "Archie really liked it. He said, 'Gee, that's swell.' That's how Archie talked. And Don and I said, 'Yeah, it is swell'—because we knew we were gonna get sixty-four dollars for the session, as working musicians. That was a big deal for us."

And, as it turned out, for pop music. As Don said, "All the guitar players in Nashville were trying to figure out how to do it." Their harmonies of course were smooth as apple butter, Don on the lows, Phil on top with a never too forced yowl. It all fell into line, every note and accent on target. When Don took the lead on the verses, wrenching out the agony of him being "through with romance" because his "baby" was through with him, he stretched out the line that he was "so bluuuuue," and both he and Phil killed on the hook. It was a two-minute-twenty-second backwoods sonata, easily understood teen fodder with some splendid subtleties and country backbone and affectations such as singing that hook as "I'm a-gonna cryy-y, so bye-bye my love good-byy-y."

In retrospect, the song is a hell of a blues number, as was the song chosen as "Bye Bye Love's" B-side, "I Wonder If I Care as Much," a yearning country ballad with a horseblock percussive effect and a whining pedal steel line, a wonderful prop for the brothers' country-nasal and openly sentimental vocals. As a debut single, it was one hell of a wallop.

○ ○

Bleyer had on the same day also produced a session for Gordon Terry, a Nashville singer-fiddler, and apparently one of the horde of singers who had passed on "Bye Bye Love." A story the next day in the *Banner*'s "Country Music for Everybody" column by Ben E. Gross touted Bleyer's foray in Nashville and wrote that "reports from New York indicate" that Bleyer "was highly pleased with the first record session held for his firm in the country music field." Archie had the record pressed in RCA's New York studio, and out on the market, with the Cadence catalog number 1315 only a week after being recorded. The Everly Brothers had by then headed out on a tent-show tour of Mississippi and Louisiana on a bill headlined by Bill Monroe, the mandolin king of Kentucky bluegrass, riding from stop to stop with thirteen other people in Monroe's two Cadillac limousines.

Singing Southern-fried covers of blues rock such as the rockabilly "Be-Bop-A-Lula" and Ray Charles's "Leave My Woman Alone," the troupe rolled through the Deep South. Don recalled the trek fondly, saying that "Jimmy C. Newman and Rufus Thibodeaux took me to my first shrimp boil" and "I got my first beer down there." Seeing the Gulf of Mexico for the first time, he got up early one day and walked down to the water to dip his toes. The brothers split ninety dollars a week, which Phil said saved them from "having to go get a job with jackhammers." Nonetheless, they had no expectation that their record would make any inroads. Indeed, the first time they heard anything about the song was when one member of the troupe told them he'd heard that "Bye Bye Love" was on the radio—not their record but one that had been quickly covered by Webb Pierce. In a panic, Don called Bleyer long distance and told him about it. Archie chortled, "Webb who?" Whether or not he knew of Pierce, who'd had thirteen consecutive top-ten country hits, Archie assured Don that it didn't matter, that the Everlys' original was "hittin' pop," scrambling up the pop chart.

And he was right. Pierce's version, which he sang in a country trill, didn't do much business. But on the way back home to Nashville, Don and Phil heard their record hittin' pop all over the dial. As Phil would say years later, "It was like, big juju."

○ ○

For Don, there were other things happening that would impact his life. He had taken a liking to one of Elaine Tubb's girlfriends, a dark-eyed brunette secretary named Mary Sue Ingraham. Born in Nashville seven months after Don, they were still under twenty-one when she became pregnant. Needing to marry before she would give birth, they couldn't elope in Tennessee, where marriage was prohibited under the age of twenty-one, so they took it on the run and got hitched in a Baptist church in Ringgold, Georgia, on March 25, 1957, a month after Don's twenty-first birthday, and then moved into a comfortable home on Forest Acres Drive in Nashville's Madison suburb.

As if marriage was a statement of independence, especially from Margaret, who reacted bitterly to Don eloping because he had had knocked up a girl Ike and Margaret didn't even know. And Don himself kept the marriage quiet. Even a year later, when asked about romance in his life by an interviewer for one of the typically juvenile fanzines aimed at lonely-hearted teen girls, *Sixteen*, he pretended to be on the lookout for a wife, who he said had to be "sincere" and have a mind of her own. (In the same article, Phil's only requirement was to find a blonde as a wife—which he never did—and that she need not be all that smart.) But it didn't take long before the marriage was out in the open, and on the surface Mr. and Mrs. Don Everly were an All-American couple, who were seen in magazine and newspaper photos doing things like riding horses and cavorting while on vacations. But, while waiting for the birth of their child, Don began to feel straitjacketed, and Mary Sue was as hard-headed as he was. They would stick it out, but "Bye Bye Love" seemed to be their ultimate flip-off to each other as the record began its ascent and made the pop and country charts in early May.

Up in New York, meanwhile, when the early sales figures came in, Bleyer ran ads with attitude shots of Don and Phil, hair tousled, handsome faces grinning gleefully, *Billboard* putting it on the "Coming Up Strong" pop list right behind Johnny Mathis's "It's Not for Me to Say." The song was the biggest-selling country song in Memphis ahead of Jerry Lee Lewis's "Whole Lotta Shakin' Goin' On," and the third-biggest in Nashville. This was what crossover was all about, and for an obscure country act to hit the pop and blues charts simultaneously made the Grand Ole Opry take notice. Having labored out in the sticks on Opry-sponsored shows, getting an invitation to play on the big stage at the Ryman was a mind-blower. The Opry, after all, was the summit for country-burnished performers, putting them into the thick of the Opry's Saturday night live fishbowl, with thousands of radios across the map tuned to the happenings on that stage.

It had been this way since 1925, when the Opry began and men started putting on cowboy clothing fashioned on old pictures of Bat Masterson and Wyatt Earp—snappy suits with pearl snap fasteners and vaquero designs to go with Stetson ten-gallon cowboy hats and black cowboy boots, their wives in blue gingham and chambray skirts and Buffalo Bill-type fringe blazers. Hundreds of white country fans snapped up tickets to the shows, with two other, non-radio performances during the week, whooping it up as rhinestone cowboys decked out in charro suits, vests, neck bandanas, and shirts with glittering patterns did their thing on the stage. This kind of folderol became a huge business in the 1940s, when Nudie Cohn, a Hollywood designer whose "Opryware" symbolized the country industry, was the Ralph Lauren of a farcical leisure culture that latched onto conditioned Southern racism and denialism, sold to music fans at a price—though the Everly Brothers never thought it necessary or helpful to don those corny duds, sticking with the coolly fashionable "square" motif of sock-hop jackets and ties.

By 1957, the Opry was godlike, an ersatz god of profit and exclusionary common law—one of which was that Black performers need not apply for admission to the first church of country music, and that country singers could not bring to that stage drums, horns, or anything else that might make country reek of sinful rock and roll hoochie-koo. This was so even while country music splayed tales of drinking moonshine into a stupor, though when the sainted Hank Williams got on the stage drunk, the Opry mucks fired him (not that it kept them from putting him in their Hall of Fame). It was into this mire of self-appointed righteousness that the Everly Brothers stepped on May 11, as part of the second show of the evening of what was billed as "Prince Albert's Grand Ole Opry," for the tobacco company that sponsored the show with endless commercials.

Carrying their guitars and dressed in gray pinstriped jackets, black slacks, light gray (not blue) suede shoes—with not a cowboy hat or boot on them—when host Grant Turner, a WSM DJ, bid the audience to "make 'em feel good," they smiled nervously, perching in front of a group of musicians that included Chet Atkins, Lightnin' Chance on his big standup bass—and Buddy Harman on drums, a seeming violation of Opry rules that only an act with a smash record could have maneuvered past, though Harman had to make do using only a snare and a cymbal, and use brushes instead of sticks. Even that, Don recalled, was historic, boasting that "Phil and I were the very first to have drums on that stage. And we were very proud that we had gotten on it."

Situated a few feet in front of the famous stage wall sign "Martha White's Grand Ole Opry, Goodness Gracious, It's Good"—the slogan for the Martha White flour company—they took their places at a microphone stand festooned with a banner reading "Grand Ole Opry" in red letters. With no fanfare, they broke into a spirited and typically flawless rendition of "Bye Bye Love," Atkins adding some nifty glissandos. When the song was done, Turner brought onto the stage Archie Bleyer, whose New Yawk accent must have amused the crowd as he said, "We're all happy to present the Everly Brothers with a gold record, each of them, for passing the one million mark [in sales]. Boys, congratulations to both of you."

Taking the boxed gold records in hand—those sales having been racked up while it was still rising on the charts—Don said, "Thank you, Mr. Bleyer. We'd like to say this is gonna be a moment that Phil and I will always remember, even when we get kinda old and gray." He thanked "everyone responsible for this" and he and Phil then performed a weepy rendering of "I Wonder If I Care as Much." Then they took half-bows and exited, greeted warmly by the crowd, some of whom likely had heard them on the radio as Little Donnie and Baby Boy Phil.

The town seemed riveted by it, at least to judge by a review by a hyperventilating Gross in the *Banner* hailing the brief performance as "the greatest sensation in Grand Ole Opry circles here within almost a year. [There were] screams from the high schoolers, roars from the men and high soprano cries from the women. Many were in tears, including Roy and this writer."

He went on that "two great stars had been born," and wove it as "an almost unprecedented event" and "Nothing like [it has] happened since Johnny Cash came into the picture almost a year ago. [They] should be great for 50 years if they keep their humility, their poise, their love for people, their sincerity. And they will be because they've been brought up right," though Ike and Margaret were not in attendance, still mired in Chicago.

The stodgy Opry board snubbed their own rules on members being recognized as official Opry members only if they had played the Ryman at least a dozen times. Perhaps the Opry was seeking to control the brothers on their upward thrust as clear-cut country performers, not rockers, at a time when the Opry's eminent role was being challenged by the rock crowd. Another example was that the Opry's general director, W. D. Kilpatrick, waived the company's prohibition on any Opry functionary, from executives to the house musicians, from working with non-Opry-affiliated acts. As a result, studio sessions in the town had risen by 30 percent in six months. As the Opry viewed the new realities through their rosy lens, this was allowable, since the Everly Brothers would surely keep Nashville safe from the heathens outside the gates.

○ ○

By early July, "Bye Bye Love" would zoom to number two on the pop chart, between Elvis's "Teddy Bear" and Pat Boone's "Love Letters in the Sand"; to number one on the country chart ahead of Marty Robbins's "White Sport Coat" and Jim Reeves's "Four Walls"; and to number five on the R&B chart. Even in August, it was still sitting at number three pop. And Bleyer had the brothers knee-deep in touring around the country. Although they identified more with rock's gritty idealism, rebellion and style, they were by design square-looking fellows. This was to their benefit, as the new idiom had quieted down a bit. Elvis for example had detoured from the "Jethro" nature of early 1950s country to a neatly pleated, matinee-idol image at RCA, backed by the smooth Jordanaires, a far cry from the Ed Sullivan gig in 1956 when he was shot only from the waist up, virtually amputating his swiveling legs and hips. Naturally, Sullivan needn't have worried about Don and Phil, who barely shook any part of their anatomy when they performed on the Sullivan show for the first time on June 30, 1957.

However, Sullivan didn't give them their first national TV exposure. Eight days before, Bleyer had arranged with Julius La Rosa to have the Everly Brothers on the summer replacement show La Rosa had been hosting since 1955, which ran three nights a week on NBC. Like Bleyer, he was no fan of rock and roll. As with most of the middle-aged TV and radio hosts, he was prone to making cracks about the "kids" and their silly fixation, which he did when the brothers came on.

"Eighteen, twenty, "LaRosa began his introduction of them. "I think Pat Boone is old enough to be their grandfather," sparking some mild laughter from the studio audience. "They have a wonderful record, 'Bye Bye Love.' Sing it."

Don and Phil, on their first trip to New York City, came onto a stage where a week after Count Basie was the musical guest. Don went into the opening guitar riff, and he and Phil sang a higher-pitched version of the song in front of a backdrop of fake trees and shrubbery, to a few yelps and squeals from the teen girls in the audience. And that was it. But they had done what they were there for, to sell more copies of "Bye Bye Love" for Archie Bleyer. After spending another week in the big town, lodging on Bleyer's tab at a swanky hotel, they made their way to the Ed Sullivan Theater for the Sunday night show. Wearing light-colored suits, they launched into "Bye Bye Love" and took their half-bows to healthy applause, Phil smirking, Don barely blinking. It was a short but important stride in rock and roll's encroachment on mainstream American culture in 1957, but the real market was out there in the underbelly of the culture, in music halls where teens came en masse to see new idols, and on the side and back roads where rock caravans on old buses came to spread the gospel in tent-show-like venues before moving on again. And Bleyer had made sure they would be a near-fixed presence on these meanderings.

That summer, they were on Alan Freed's Summer Festival, one of his periodic shows in Brooklyn's cavernous Paramount

Theater, where the eminent DJ, who had moved his show to New York, drew the top shelf of rock to perform for peanuts while Freed skimmed the box-office revenues. The summer installment ran from July 3 to July 10, headed by the Everlys and Chuck Berry and reiterating older acts like Clyde McPhatter, Frankie Lymon and the Teenagers, the Moonglows, Big Joe Turner, Johnny and Joe, and the Dubs. Freed's house band for the shows had some monster talent itself, with jazz sax greats Sam "The Man" Taylor and Big Al Sears, and drummer Panama Francis. Freed's creed, as he wrote in the program, was that rock and roll "is bigger than all of us now," and the full houses were encouraged to go wild, leading Don to recall the experience as "hysterical," and Phil to say, "We loved it, but it also scared us. It made us wonder what kind of craziness we'd gotten ourselves into." But the perks were cool. Freed put the big acts up at the ritzy Park Sheraton Hotel, where Jackie Gleason had an entire floor for his office and lodging. "New York was great," Phil acknowledged. "I remember walking through Times Square with Chuck Berry, and him buying us our first cheesecake at Lindy's.

Their image was already entrenched. On July 28, a wire story about them, titled "Teenage Parade Continues Now It's the Everly Brothers," made room for them among an odd crowd: "After Presley, Boone, [Tommy] Sands, [Frankie] Layne and all the others, the newest [sensation] are a couple of brothers from Madison, Tenn. They have good looks of the peculiar smoldering type so sought after these days, they pluck guitars in unison, they sing a blend of rock-and-roll and country-and-western that's called rock-a-billy. . . . They have one car—a conservative sedan—between them, don't like fancy clothes, are sober and respectable citizens, admire Elizabeth Taylor mightily, and otherwise are perfectly normal young men." That was exactly what Archie Bleyer wanted to read. And the brothers knew it was going to be their flavor, no matter how long they would be around, and as less than normal as they would be.

CHAPTER FIVE

Perfectly Normal Young Men

Ed Sullivan was so smitten with the Everly Brothers that only a few weeks after their debut on his stage, they were booked again, on August 4, even with no new single to sell. Instead, they regurgitated "Bye Bye Love" and in another segment, chose a cover of bluesman Titus Turner's "Hey Doll Baby," which they had recorded with a harder rhythmic core, but the record would sit on the shelf until Bleyer could decide if it was in their mien. When he did release a second single, it was another Boudleaux and Felice Bryant song, "Wake Up Little Susie," a wink-and-nod to teenage maneuvers in the dark, couched by artfully inoffensive lyrics and the brothers' irresistibility.

The session for it, on August 16 at RCA Studio B, pretty much followed along the same glide path as "Bye Bye Love," Don's boppy intro shuffle was almost the same but with a tad more layering and impatience—a three-second killer riff. The chords were also almost identical, in double-time downstrokes for the chorus, the lyric a sheepish lament about the two teens famously falling asleep in the darkness of the movie, or drive-in, theater. They hit some splendid low-string shuffles and made hard dramatic stops at the end of lyrical passages, driving home that something more interesting was happening that made the night as memorable as paradise by the dashboard light.

The Everlys verbally amended the title phrase to "Wake up a-little Susie" and didn't even try to disguise the Bryants' clever musings, like "our goose is cooked, our reputation is shot," and "What're we gonna tell our friends when they say 'ooh la la'?" When they would sing the song on TV, Phil would do the "ooh la la" with a sly eye roll, while Don displayed a pinch-faced grin. It was full of sheepishness but also braggadocio. Combined with their latent itchiness, it came out just right, the embellishment being Chet Atkins's rock-style accents in the recesses and Lightnin' Floyd Chance's skipping bass line. It rolled out as a jumpy country blues burr, guilty pleasure in every word, but unlike the quickie session for "Bye Bye Love," the brothers, Atkins, and Boudleaux were at first unhappy with the product. As Bryant remembered, "We had problems with getting it right. They worked a whole three-hour session on that one song and had to give up, they just couldn't get it right. We all trooped back to the studio the next day and got it down first take. That's the way it happens sometimes."

The record, the B-side of which was a slow-dance around imminent love written by Don and Phil called "Maybe Tomorrow," leaped from the radio and refused to let go. And mainstream TV was again right there to help the Everly Brothers get traction. On August 21, they were on the summer replacement for the CBS sitcom *December Bride* hosted by big-band singer Vic Damone. And then, in a what's-wrong-with-this-picture side light, they somehow were booked on *The Arthur Murray Dance Party*, a longtime favorite of sclerotic Americans who tuned in to watch the bow-tied, sixty-two-year-old Murray and his wife, Kathryn, who owned the famous chain of dance studios, waltz with the guests, who were required to take a few dance steps with the show's dance instructors. Don and Phil, clad in tuxes adhering to the show's dress code, sang "Bye Bye Love" then tiptoed across the floor with young instructors.

These efforts paid off, even withstanding a now-comical stage when "Wake Up Little Susie" was banned by some stations in Boston and New York, which baffled the brothers and Bleyer, given that rock had weathered actual sexual come-ons such as "Sixty Minute Man," "Backdoor Man," and "Shake

Rattle and Roll." Even Dean Martin's innocuous "Mambo Italiano" was banned by some stations. As Don recalled, "It didn't dawn on me that someone would get the wrong impression about [the song] and figured we were corrupting the youth." (It also wasn't so much on logic—why wouldn't the two "sleeping" kids have been chased out after the movie ended?) And in the end, their innocence shamed the prudish stations, which backed off when the song became a must-get, must-hear for their target audiences, carrying the record to number one on the Best Sellers in Stores chart the week of October 14—pimped by yet another Sullivan gig when they did a flawless live version. A week later, it sat atop the Hot 100, displacing Jimmie Rodgers's "Honeycomb."

Of underlying significance is that "Susie," "Honeycomb," and Elvis's double-sided "Jailhouse Rock"/"Treat Me Nice" were vying for these coveted slots. It meant that three country rock acts were supreme on the pop, country and R&B lists—setting the still-existing achievement of being the only song ever to be number one on all three charts at once, though it must be said that in the prism of the times no white artists of the 1950s were *actual* R&B performers on the level of any Black performer; the buy-in was that a white act could sell records in the Black market. Over in Memphis, the country blues rocker Carl Perkins was making these idiomatic connections more overtly, his 1957 stomp "Boppin' the Blues" ending with the hook "Rock, bop, rhythm and blues." And there were quite viable reasons why the Black market embraced the white interlopers enough to put their songs on the R&B charts, to the benefit of both, and why almost all of them were country performers, as this was a ligature formed by a hundred or so years of similar economic history in the South. As country music historian Bill C. Malone writes, "virtually all [country singers] from Presley to Buddy Holly to the Everly Brothers came from Southern working-class homes" and "celebrated sensuousness and physical abandon," displaying "urges that lay at the core of Southern masculine culture, the contest between piety and hedonism."

The Everly Brothers, he added, "exuded boyish charm and innocence [and] brought out the mother instinct in many women," including Black women. Yet, on a broader level, "Susie" was also cleaning up outside the United States, hitting number one in Canada, number two in England, number three in Australia. The undeniable lesson was that the Everly Brothers were amenable to a wide expanse of culture and geography that overwhelmed parochial deceits. Don and Phil would have the last laugh often, such as when years later they would play in Boston and tell the audience, "Here's a song that was banned in this city in 1957," evoking great laughter. But even back in 1957, to size them up as rock and roll rebels slipping poison pills into white cultural sanctions was a nonstarter. They had .defined themselves as being something for everyone, the safest ground that any performer could ever tread on.

○ ○

As it happened, 1957 saw the rise of other viable newcomers with a deep store of universal acceptance. Buddy Holly had brought rattling rock to the South. Born a year before Don, the wiry Texan with the thick horn-rim glasses and hiccupping style of singing was on a surge. Produced in the near anonymity of Clovis, New Mexico, by studio owner Norman Petty, Holly and his band the Crickets had hit number one on the pop chart and number two on the country chart in the spring. And it was with a keen sense of symmetry that the Everlys and Holly joined in rock caravans. The first such teaming came with an eleven-week, seventy-eight-city tour called the "Biggest Show of Stars of 1957 Fall Edition," the roster assembled by promoter Irvin Feld was a banderole celebrating the 1950s—the Everlys, Holly, Fats Domino, Chuck Berry, Frankie Lymon, Lavern Baker, Clyde McPhatter, Paul Anka, the Spaniels, the Drifters, Johnnie and Joe, the Bobbettes, Buddy Knox, the Diamonds, and the Paul Williams Orchestra.

However, as this list proves, booking the Everly Brothers and Buddy was something of a bold move—in a reverse-racism context—as they and Paul Anka were the only non-Black acts on the A-list in the troupe, and the latter would be barred in the Deep South from staying in the same hotels as the white acts, instead forced to find accommodations in Black rooming houses or in the bus, always remaining wary of what might happen. Indeed, some white acts had declined the tour, but Don and Phil and Buddy, wouldn't hear of it, though if they hadn't already known the extent of racism in the music subworld, they would continually see it on this tour. Feld, in fact, had to move a show from D.C., where he lived, to Annapolis when the all-white D.C. city commissioners banned Fats Domino because his raucous presence might lead to a riot among Black fans, requiring every policeman in the city. Worse, the tour meant riding in a creaky, cramped bus, hired by Feld, that lugged the troupe across twenty-eight states and five Canadian provinces. Paul Anka and Frankie Lymon slept in the luggage racks, and soul diva LaVern Baker in the aisle with suitcases as a pillow. The foot-slog began on September 6 at the Syria Mosque in Pittsburgh. Astonishingly, the troupe wouldn't have a day off until October 21—the *only* day off until the tour concluded on November 21 at The Mosque in Richmond, Virginia, where the second show of the excursion was held. Feld's placards for the tour looked like a beehive, the stars' names etched across every inch. Out of respect, Fats usually got top billing, but the Everly Brothers and Buddy and the Crickets were billed high when, during the tour, Buddy's newly released "Everyday"/"Peggy Sue" and "Wake Up Little Susie" both went nuclear.

For the Everlys, this subtext seemed to outreach the tour. Indeed, when it pulled into Hershey, Pennsylvania, on September 13, they spent the afternoon appearing on an after-school TV dance party called *American Bandstand*, hosted by a youngish Philly DJ named Dick Clark. It had only been on the air nationally since August 5—when the first show featured none other than the Chordettes, including Archie Bleyer's wife, Janet Ertel. Archie had that kind of reach, and the Everlys rode it hard, making the new scene by schmoozing with the "world's oldest teenager" and lip-syncing "Bye Bye Love" and "Susie." For the next eleven consecutive episodes of *Bandstand*, "Bye Bye Love' was on Clark's "Top 10" board, with the requisite comments by the kids that it had a "good beat" and was "easy to dance to." And though the song was by now becoming dated, it no doubt moved some more vinyl to school kids, as "Susie" kept screaming up, to number one on the pop chart two weeks in a row—beating out Elvis's "Jailhouse Rock"—and on the country and R&B lists in early November, achieving that still-unmatched feat. It was also number one in Canada, number two in Britain, and the nineteenth-highest-selling record of 1957—eight slots behind "Bye Bye Love." (The highest was "All Shook Up.")

As well, Buddy's "Peggy Sue" rose weeks later to number three on the pop and country charts. And one other chart was fascinating: "Best Selling Artists on Singles," which calculated from August 5 through October the biggest-selling records based on store sales. Elvis was on top. Number two was the Everly Brothers. But the significance was that Elvis had eighteen releases on the market in that time frame, from "Heartbreak Hotel" to "That's When Your Heartaches Begin." In all that time, the Everlys had released just four songs, the A-sides "Bye Bye Love" and "Wake Up Little Susie." They also finished second to Elvis on the Best-Selling R&B Artists in Stores. Again, to be clear—in no way other than this were either Elvis or the Everly Brothers in the same R&B league as Little Richard, Nat King Cole, the Coasters, Larry Williams, and Clyde McPhatter. Yet, by these metrics, they were believably more popular in that fold than, say, the vanilla Pat Boone, who had released fifteen singles, and overall, The Everly Brothers were not far from even the King himself.

○ ○

As for Buddy and the Crickets, they too were red hot. Holly, who had failed to get any traction when he came from Lubbock, Texas, to Nashville early in his career and was produced by Owen Bradley, could read the future of rock. Putting the latest version of the Crickets together, he hired Niki Sullivan, making for the first electric double-guitar alignment in rock, along with drummer Jerry Allison and bassist Joe B. Mauldin. And Buddy also was taken with Don and Phil, whom he saw as opposites, Don more serious and urbane, Phil the lighthearted and a sometimes-goofy court jester. Don not only tutored Buddy on the guitar but advised him that the rumpled jeans and T-shirts that Buddy and the Crickets wore on stage needed to be trashed, just as the Everlys had once they moved on up.

When the tour set down in New York, recalled Don, "We took him and the Crickets down to our clothes stores in New York, too: Phil's Men's Shop, Lefcourt's for shoes. We had just learned to dress a little sharper ourselves, and they noticed it, so we took them to all the places. If you look at pictures from back then, you'll see all of us in the same jackets—Ivy League, like. Same photographer, too: Bruno of Hollywood." Buddy and his band even wore tuxedos when they went on the *Ed Sullivan Show* a second time. However, it was what the two acts did when they got out of their Oxfords that made the endless tour even more memorable. Holly, a notorious skirt-chaser with an endless sex drive—Little Richard once said that Buddy was the wildest man he ever saw, even compared to Richard himself—opened the brothers' eyes to what was possible on the road, and the brothers enjoyed the creature comforts of the rock lifestyle.

Phil, looking back, said, "Buddy Holly put me to bed with a girl. And he laughed. But I can remember him another night playing me all of his songs and asking me why [it was so hard] to get a hit record, he was so low." Buddy at times climbed into the same beds Don and Phil were occupying with a woman of the night, and helped himself. Fascinated by him, if a little grossed out, they took to wearing the dark sunglasses just like Buddy wore off the stage, all three of them chain-smoking cigarettes and stepping cool. Yet, as Phil's memories of him made clear, Buddy was a manic-depressive and impulsive, who a year later proposed to a secretary at his record label, Mary Elena Santiago, on their first date and married her two months later. But as wild as he was, he was a real friend to the Everlys. Their music was totally compatible, stemming from the same compulsions about rejection being too temporary and near-deathly, And in time, some less-than-erudite fans would even conflate them. When George W. Bush was running for president in 2000, asked what his favorite song was, he said, "'Wake Up Little Susie' by Buddy Holly." After Buddy was gone, the Everlys would sing "That'll Be the Day" as a tribute on many of their gigs, Don practically tearing up his when singing *"someday well I'll be through."*

They were indeed like bookends to Buddy, and even had ideas for each other's songs. Buddy gave them one he'd written called "Love's Made a Fool of You," and the Everlys gave him a Boudleaux Bryant song, "Raining in My Heart," though this interplay posed a problem, since the brothers' contract with Acuff-Rose precluded recording almost any song by writers outside the company. Clearly, Buddy's effect on Don was palpable. A late bloomer to casual sex, seeing Buddy collect and copulate with little effort, Don's road trips became a license to violate his marriage vows. Through the summer and early fall of 1957, he had not seen or spoken by phone with Mary Sue as she neared giving birth. Then, after a quick respite at home, he and Phil joined up with the "Biggest Show of Stars of '57" tour, as it wound through a labyrinth of cities in Ohio, Pennsylvania, then the Forum in Montreal and down through New York State, then down through Dixie.

In Birmingham, Alabama, New Orleans, and Tulsa, they, Buddy, and Paul Anka were taken off shows for the foulest of reasons—Jim Crow laws prohibited white and Black performers from appearing on the same stage, and most shows in general forced Black attendees to sit upstairs or in back rows. During one freezeout, Buddy and the Crickets went to Tinker Air Force Base and recorded four songs in the Officer's Club lounge, including "Maybe Baby," his second-biggest hit. When the tour made it to the West Coast in mid-October for a stop at the Shrine Auditorium in L.A., the other end of conditioned racism prevailed; several Black acts were dropped and white performers Eddie Cochran, Buddy Knox and Jimmy Bowen added. Such was the reality of life that rock fans hid from behind their music.

○ ○

In late October, when "Wake Up Little Susie" was breaking wide open on the charts, Bleyer called Don and Phil and instructed them to head back to Nashville for the next Cadence session to be held on November 3. Upon his return to Mary Sue,

Don seemed to be more distant and short-tempered with her. She was having a difficult pregnancy that could not have been helped by the distance of her husband even when he was home. When she went into labor on October 10, the child, a daughter they also named Mary, was born critically ill. Tragically, she died shortly after. The trauma seemed to age Don overnight, as the little girl was buried in Rose Hill Cemetery in Central City, Kentucky, where Ike Everly had years before purchased a twenty-by-twenty plot of land to be the burial ground for the family. Tears were shed that day, yet like the marriage itself, this terrible event was kept hushed, with the local newspapers agreeing not to run any stories about it, in order to give them their cone of peace. A few days later, Don's mourning seemed to turn to music as a salve. He and Phil rehearsed songs that they would be recording on November 3.

Bleyer would surely have rescheduled the session to give Don more time to heal, and neither would Phil have objected. But Don was living more on Everly Brothers time than that of his own family, and he kept the date intact, as he would in rejoining the All-Star tour right after. Nothing, it was clear, could deter the path he now saw as his life.

○ ○

At that session, Bleyer wanted to shift them from countryish, teen-tempting rock. He had them cover Ray Charles's 1955 song "This Little Girl of Mine," which was based on a gospel tune from the 1920s and went on the B-side of Ray's number one R&B hit "A Fool for You," and number nine R&B hit on its own. Fans of Bo Diddley that they were, this was something the boys wanted to do, and not only did they excel at the R&B meters but Chet Atkins almost blew a fuse on his Gretsch. Don and Phil needed to not stretch or embarrass themselves in the Pat Boone mold by singing lines that for Ray were a goof—"She knows how to love me right down to her teeth / If she does any wrong, you know she keeps it from me" and trill-out chants like "Oh wella, oh wella" and "oh yeah, oh yeah."

Nor did they have any hesitation plugging the song even before they recorded it with their fourth slot on Ed Sullivan's show months before on August 4, sans guitars and clapping in time while doing some Elvis-like hip-swiveling in between gyrating dancing girls. They looked like they never had more fun, with Phil unable to keep from cracking up after the final note. The irony was that Ray Charles did the song as a bold attempt at crossover to the white market—as he did again, in 1962, when he covered of all things "Bye Bye Love" in brassy big-band style on his *Modern Sounds in Country Music*—while the Everly Brothers and Ricky Nelson were extending their appeal to the Black market. Crossover worked both ways.

As the auspicious year of 1957 came to an end, Archie slapped "This Little Girl" onto a hastily created Everly Brothers debut album to further profit from their two major hits—a common practice, as albums were strictly window dressing for already-established songs, to which were added B-sides and other filler, which on the album would also include unreleased songs like "Little Girl," Don and Phil's "Should We Tell Him," Don's "I Wonder If I Care as Much" and another frenetic Ray Charles cover, "Leave My Woman Alone." There were three more blues-rock covers: Little Richard's "Keep a Knockin'" and "Rip It Up" and the song they'd had so much fun with on Sullivan, "Hey Doll Baby"; Boudleaux and Felice Bryant's "Brand New Heartache"; and a cover of Gene Vincent's primordial rockabilly-punk anthem "Be-Bop-a-Lula," upticking Vincent's slow, seductive moaning for "my baby doll" into a romp innervated by Atkins's bouncy licks that sounded quite like "Bye Bye Love."

Whatever it was intended to be, what mattered was the name "Everly Brothers" on the album cover. But a close listen to the tracks is a revelation, broadening the width and breadth of what was routinely defined as either a country or a teen-idol rock act. Those *Billboard* R&B charts that put them right there at the top proved that they knew as well as any white act how to bridge the distance between idioms. Remarkable is how naturally compatible they were with the Ray Charles and Little Richard stuff. On "Keep a Knockin'," they needed no histrionics or Richard-style shrieks to walk the bridge. Not daring to try and "sound black," their harmony patterns were transferred to a quicker gait, their semiotics just country enough to retain their identity but stoking a soulful strut such as on the outro of Richard's final repetitions, bending the "Keep a knockin'" riff to lower the pitch to a deep growl for ". . . *but you can't come in.*"

"Rip It Up" went the same route, the brothers un-self-consciously repeating Richard's pledge to "rip it up" and "shake it up," their one concession (per Bleyer) being to alter Richard's then-semi-risqué slang "and ball tonight" to the safer "*Have* a ball tonight." Bleyer would release the album titled *The Everly Brothers* in December, the cover a wide angle shot of the Everlys riding on one motorcycle, their Gibsons draped down their backs, smiling back at the camera, while on a cycle next to them Chet Atkins rode down the road, his Gretsch over his back. Bleyer—who had released a Chordettes album with the same exact cover design, the girls looking backward from a convertible—made sure he wasn't left out; he wrote a short text next to the brothers' image about how the "Frails sent mail by the bale"—in English, fan mail—to the boys after the first two smashes, and above the text, "They're off and running, says Archie." He also wrote the bio on the back cover.

At the time of its release, the already lofty duo was back in New York for another important TV gig, NBC's top-rated *Perry Como's Kraft Music Hall* on December 7, the first of four appearances on it within three years, sharing some valuable space with Ethel Merman, Red Buttons, and the *Look* All-American Football Team. From there, they slipped back down to Philadelphia for another *American Bandstand* drop-in, then were the headliners of the Alan Freed string of holiday shows at the Paramount, which again co-featured Buddy and the Crickets. It was another wild interlude, five grueling shows a day for twelve days starting on Christmas Day, with the teen girls screaming from opening to closing song. Staying on Sullivan's dime at the Park Sheraton Hotel, they partied like nobody's business. Phil related later that "Eddie Cochran was in town and we were all up in his room there. Buddy was having a drink, and he asked me to make sure he got [through the] night, and I did. . . . I don't mean to make it sound like we were a bunch of drunks. But once in a while you'd go out and tie one on, you know, always knowing what you were doing, though. In the Fifties, we were all pretty sane, compared to the Sixties."

Don and Phil would go back on tour as the LP climbed up the album chart to number sixteen, high enough for the single of "This Girl of Mine" and "Should We Tell Him" to be undersold on the charts, though each side would hit number twenty-six on the pop chart, "Girl" reaching number four on the country chart and "Should" number ten. But they were only placeholders until Archie would summon them again to Studio B, the result of which proved they were here to stay, even if they would take themselves from the fire into the frying pan.

CHAPTER SIX

"His Britches Fell Off"

A s 1958 rang in, rock was in a three-way tug-of-war between the white pop crowd, the country crowd, and the blues crowd, and the Everly Brothers were part riders in all three. That meant hit songs and lots of money, the profitability of the Nashville Sound having attracted Northern interlopers into the new paradigm. These included Jack Scott, born Giovanni Domenico Scafone Jr. in Windsor, Ontario, whose hiccupy country-pop tune "Goodbye Baby" was a practical redo of "Bye Bye Love," and Guy Mitchell, born Albert George Cernik to Croatian immigrants in Detroit, whose bouncy, whistling "Singing the Blues," went to number one on the pop and R&B charts and sold heavily in the South. Not incidentally, the song was written by Nashville singer-composer Melvin Endsley, who introduced it at the Grand Ole Opry and saw it go to number one on the country list when later recorded by Marty Robbins.

These were the headwinds of the new music, and the Everly Brothers were pointing the way, aided by Cadence PR people and the General Artists Corporation (GAC), one of Madison Avenue's biggest personal servicers agencies, who repped both the Everlys and Buddy Holly and the Crickets, gaining for them up to $4,000 per show. In lieu of the glitterati of serious music journalism, which would not emerge for another decade, record reviews were the province of pidgin English blurbs in *Billboard* and *Cash Box* along with teens offering the standard "has a good beat, can dance to it" on *Bandstand*. The adolescent-aimed fanzines were a dervish of fresh-faced, mainly white hunk idols placed in pinup poses on the covers like a continuous mayonnaise spill. The Everlys of course were a regular item in the pages of *Sixteen*, *Modern Teen*, and the somewhat less pandering *Photoplay* and *Song Hits*. In a *Sixteen* profile of them, in which they were called "Woosome" and "Those Dreamy Everly Brothers," Don—who was put in the same macho man category as Gary Cooper (and Phil with Alan Ladd)—did some slip-slidin' away from telling of his marriage, with no fear anyone would call him on it.

Yet even within these puffball pieces, they could sometimes reveal their dislikes, especially Don, who apparently had quite a few. For example, he questioned whether Harry Belafonte's calypso rhythms would have lasting value—though he saved his misgivings about Elvis for later platforms, when he would say Presley "didn't have the kind of voice I liked, nor a sound I liked. I was listening to Ray Charles, Brownie McGhee and Sonny Terry, and Bo Diddley." Mostly, he and Phil played it silly, joshing each other, such as Don pricking Phil when he claimed to be five-foot-ten and 150 pounds: "Hooey! You never were 150, soaking wet and carrying rocks in your hands. You're 5 feet 8 inches and weigh maybe 130." Don figured himself to be five-nine, 140. Phil retorted that his big brother was five-seven, 135.

Not that they couldn't unwittingly provide some bare clues about some static between them. One fanzine reported that Phil was "an impulsive buyer who once wanted to buy an island in Canada, but Don dissuaded him" and that he "usually beats Don at cards because [he says] 'Don is careless.'" But, as *Sixteen* observed, all anyone needed to know was that "They're two well-behaved lads, pleasant and soft-spoken, delightful to talk to." The truth was that it took very little for Phil to feel upstaged. His round, smiling face was trained to be just that in public, when he seemed everyone's best buddy. But it pricked at him to see, even in the mindless fanzines, a shot like "Don broods more and thinks more deeply about the future than Phil." In his own deep thoughts, though, he knew it was true.

For Don, there was certainly more pressure to deal with. While he and Mary Sue pressed on with their failing marriage, any subject matter other than the Everly Brothers' next gig or session was irrelevant to him. Still just twenty, he was the All-American dude no one knew was brooding about anything serious, or that he was getting off by being a cad to women. Somewhere on the rock circuit, he met a dark-eyed eighteen-year-old from Newport Beach, California, Sharon Seeley, a budding songwriter who would strike oil with "Poor Little Fool," which made her the youngest female to write a number-one hit, in 1958, when Ricky Nelson recorded it. Only among the music in-crowd was it known that she had written the song from a feminine point of view about an adulterous affair she had with Don, whom the lyrics burned for promising her that "we'd never part" and "hold me close and kiss me but [his] heart was full of lies." And, to be sure, she would be far from the only girl he sweet-talked and then played for a fool.

Playing these games with women's hearts seemed to elevate him as a man who needed to win, no matter the cost to others. It may have stoked his obsession to outdo other high-flying macho men like Buddy Holly, Sonny James, and Marty Robbins. This was the fuel that made the act run so powerfully in his voice as Bleyer continued to book them everywhere he could. On December 2, they were beckoned by Dick Clark to be the only musical guests on a primetime special presentation of *American Bandstand* and just after the new year for the fifth time on the *Ed Sullivan Show*. Wedged between Johnny Ray, dancer Rod Alexander, tumblers the Armandis, and the Vienna on Parade Orchestra, they did a spirited run-through of "Wake Up Little Susie," though the producers thought, incorrectly, it would be better embellished by not-so-swinging horns from the show's band. Three days later, they were back out on the bus with Irvin Feld's next blitzkrieg tour, "America's Greatest Teenage Recording Stars," again with Buddy and the Crickets, Eddie Cochran, Paul Anka—and more modest ones like the Rays, the Shepherd

Sisters, the Mello-Kings, the Tune Weavers, Danny and the Juniors, and the Hollywood Flames.

The tour got underway at the Charlotte Coliseum before rolling through the South and Midwest, with a detour to Toronto's Maple Leaf Gardens. When that was done, they barely took a breath and went out on the "Big Gold Records Stars" caravan along with Buddy and the Crickets, Bill Haley and His Comets, Jerry Lee Lewis, and the Royalteens, which opened on February 20 at the Kellogg Auditorium in Orlando, Florida, and ran for the rest of the month. Basically, everywhere one looked, there were the Everly Brothers. After only a year up and running, with only two major hits, only Elvis was bigger. Getting there took a toll on them, but there could be no time for kicking back. There would be more pressure on them every day, and dangerous ways to deal with it.

○ ○

On March 6, 1958, three weeks before they were booked to return to the Grand Ole Opry, Bleyer set up the crucial session to cut a follow-up to "Wake Up Little Susie," It turned out to be a song Archie took from the Boudleaux and Felice Bryant folder, a cottony soft, yearning ballad. As Phil recalled, "I remember hearing 'All I Have to Do Is Dream' on an acetate with Boudleaux's version on it, and I said they could have put Boudleaux's out and it would have been a hit. It's just a great, great song. The man borders on genius." Though it was a risk to do a ballad, the now formative synergy of writers, singers, and Chet Atkins would perfect what was, like all of the Everly Brothers' big early songs, a weave of very simple chords and transitions. Atkins's deft touch this time was to create the sound of a sigh, even a falling tear, by applying a tremolo effect, which was normally played by violins, organs, and harps in orchestral passages, which Chet—years before the invention of the "whammy bar" and pedals for such effects—did by rigging up a rudimentary bridge between the amp and his Gretsch to accommodate higher modulation, which would be a part of his famous 6120 Hollowbody model guitar, as a Bigsby vibrato tailpiece.

His first teardrop licks came right at the start, which trembled into the brothers' opening incantation of "Dree-ee-ee-ee-eem, dream dream dream . . . ," kicking into Buddy Harman's two-one-two-one backbeat with Lightnin' Chance's taut bass line. The tremolo jangling kept defining the mood as Don and Phil grieved about feeling blue in the night "when I need you to hold me tight." Don's handling of Felice's bridge was perfect, with the phrase "Only trouble is, gee whiz," which broke it down to a teenage level of pining—and one that Felice related was a bit of luck. "I can't explain why I put that in there," she once said. "It was just a lucky rhyme fall." Such luck could make a song, or a career, as could the right take. After trying it at different speeds, Bleyer took the slowest, least rockish version, which deepened their voice a tad and slowed the tremolo as well into a tearier sound. And the right take happened to have a sour note, too. As Phil would remember, "I sang a bit of wrong harmony. I always tell Donald that's what made it a hit! Because it doesn't have to be perfect. Sometimes the best versions are those with mistakes, It just has to sound right to be right. We learned that as kids."

The B-side was a song that had been written for them by Roy Orbison, "Claudette," after the sixteen-year-old girlfriend he married in 1957. "The idea," said Phil, "was always to put the best up-tempo song and the best ballad back-to-back. And when we were in Chicago [playing the Civic Opera House], Roy was there, and we asked him if he'd got a song for us. He gave us 'Claudette.'" Roy had tailored it to the brothers' pitch and tempo, the intro a similar acoustic guitar riff to "Bye Bye Love" and the up-tempo shift upon meeting the "greatest little girl I've met," was primordially Everly Brothers-like. Little wonder that Bleyer inserted his name on the 45's label for the first time, a notation under the brothers' names reading "Orchestra Conducted by Archie Bleyer."

Released in mid-March, the single was on the move when the Everly Brothers made their Grand Ole Opry redux on March 28. The show that night was hosted by "Gentleman" Jim Reeves, whose job seemed to be dutifully stuffing the words "King Albert," the pipe tobacco that was the Opry's main sponsor, into almost each of his sentences. Affable as usual, Reeves came on

and shouted out several Opry regulars, first being Chet Atkins—
"the king of the guitar!" said Reeves—then WSM DJ Grant
Turner, country comic Rod Brasfield, fiddlers "Stringbean" and
Tommy Jackson, June Carter, the Opry Square Dancers, and
the Opry Gang, before interjecting, "and our special guests, the
Everly Brothers!" He spoke with Brasfield for a few seconds but
cut it short to cue the Everlys, the opening act.

"Rod," he said, "I wonder about you. I really do. Well now,
I know all of you are anxious to hear from our guests. So here
they are, Don and Phil, the Everly Brothers!"

On a stage that was always congested with humans in designer cowboy wear, Don and Phil strode onto ground they had
already conquered, this time not in drab sport coats but gleaming white Nudie jackets with jet-black string ties black slacks
and shiny black loafers. Atkins, Chance, and Harman again
gathered behind them as Reeves met the boys on stage, saying,
"Don, Phil, it's good to have you back here in Nashville, especially after all the big doin's up in New York."

"It's good to be back, Jim," said Don.

"I'll say!" Phil tacked on.

"Well, say fellas, you know, we all know you record for
Cadence, and we know you have a brand-new record. So let's
premiere it here on the Grand Ole Opry tonight. The Everly
Brothers and their brand-new record, 'Claudette!'"

It was somewhat odd that the Opry billed as the "new record" the B-side of the record, but it was more country, and it
sparked whoops and squeals in the hall. They were then rushed
off stage as Brasfield darted out to begin a commercial for Prince
Albert—"the best smokin' tobacco a man can load his pipe
with." A few minutes later, after Chet Atkins performed "Please
Don't Talk about Me When I'm Gone" on his guitar, Reeves sang
"I'll Fly Away" then did a strained comedy bit with June Carter
on another King Albert spot that continued into an introduction
of the Everly Brothers' second number.

"Where is he, where's he at?" she began. "That little Everly
Brother that I like so well, that little Phil Everly; that's the one
I like. I was out with him today, he's got one of them little hot
rods that he rides around in, y'know? And we had a terrible

catastrophe happened. We got in it out there in Madison and we was comin' into the Grand Ole Opry, and he got in and he forgot to fasten his safety belt, and we rode on in here and he got out and he unfastened his safety belt and his britches fell off."

After some mild laughter at the botched joke, Reeves welcomed back Don and Phil to sing "the other side of their new recording, 'All I Have to Do Is Dream!'" They ran through it and then were all but shooed off as Reeves brought on "the banjo-pickin' boy himself, Stringbean!" And that was it. No more bows or encores. The Opry ran on a tight schedule, with the performances secondary to the business of selling tobacco and keeping the radio audience from getting fidgety. Yet the gig no doubt helped "All I Have to Do Is Dream" flourish, as would another Irvin Feld tour, the "Show of Stars for '58," also featuring top acts such as Sam Cooke, Paul Anka, Clyde McPhatter, Frankie Avalon, Lavern Baker, Jackie Wilson, the Monotones, the Playmates, and Huey "Piano" Smith and the Clowns.

This trek ran from April 5 in Norfolk then through Pennsylvania and New York and all the way through the May 29 closer in Charlotte. And that month, "All I Have to Do Is Dream" made it to number one on the pop chart, beating out the David Seville novelty hit "Witch Doctor," The Platters' "Twilight Time," and Elvis's "Wear My Ring around Your Neck." A week later, it moved into the top five on the country and R&B charts. A week later, in early June, beating out Don Gibson's "Oh, Lonesome Me" on the country list, it again was tops in all three categories, the same clean sweep that "Little Susie" had been the first to accomplish. It stayed at number one pop for three weeks, and on *Billboard*'s year-end best-sellers chart was second to the Italian crooner Domenico Modugno's "Volare," ahead of Elvis's "Don't." It would be endlessly covered, for example by Orbison in 1962, *Dr. Kildaire* actor Richard Chamberlain in 1963, Bobbie Gentry and Glen Campbell in 1969, and Andy Gibb and *Dallas* actress Victoria Principal in 1981.

However, this monster of a song was ignored when the first Grammy awards were given in May 1959 and rock and roll was shafted for mainstream comfort food—"Volare" beating out mainstream standbys like Perry Como, Peggy Lee, and Frank

Sinatra for Best Record. But for Roy Orbison, ending up on the backside of an Everly Brothers hit (one that he would record himself in 1989), didn't hurt him a bit; when "Claudette" broke off on its own run, going to number thirty pop and number fifteen country, not only did he receive writing royalties but it eased the way for him to repeat Elvis's musical conversion from struggling bluesman in Memphis to sunglass-shielded Nashville country rocker signed in perpetuity to Acuff-Rose (though Elvis's publishing was owned by Hill & Range). His ascension bore testament to how the Everly Brothers, without knowing it, had helped transfer power and influence to Music City, where, ironically, they only rarely spent their time now, and would less in the future. "All I Have to Do Is Dream" was a cause célèbre in another way, lingering far into the future. It would become the crux of a sound that not only defined Nashville in the rock orbit but bred what rock nerds would codify as jangle pop, that is, weepy songs with a dreamy beat, some examples being the Byrds' "Mr. Tambourine Man" and Simon and Garfunkel's "I Am a Rock."

Given all this, the irony was tangible that the Opry was becoming fixated on them despite Jim Reeves's factual statement that the Everly Brothers' "big doin's" in New York reflected their own lessening tie-in to Nashville except for their recording sessions. To court them into blind loyalty for the Opry, the panjandrums had approved the playing of their songs on an "Everly Brothers show" before the Saturday broadcasts on WSM, a perk given the biggest country stars in the radio block from six o'clock to eight-thirty. In June of 1958, the brothers' six-forty-five segment followed Roy Acuff, Johnny Cash, and Ernie Tubb, and was followed by Hank Snow, Acuff, Cash, Flatt and Scruggs, and Don Gibson. And after the Opry, the shows were recycled, with the Everlys on at eleven-fifteen.

But, as Reeves noted, they were spending more time in the land of the Yankees than in the Old Confederacy, the latest return trip being for the June 14 *Bob Crosby Show*, Bing's younger and less famous brother's summer replacement show for Perry Como Saturday nights on CBS. Not that the turf was always friendly to the two hicks; Don would recall that "when we walked down the streets of New York City with a guitar case, people would yell at you back in those days and look to see if you had shoes on." Yet they become comfy in those uptown hotel suites and at Archie Bleyer's swank East Side apartment, a retreat a visitor could equate with "Hernando's Hideaway," the show tune from *Pajama Game* that Archie had recorded with his orchestra in 1954. They would sit in Archie's plush living room deciding on future songs, and not incidentally, Phil really dug Archie's stepdaughter Jackie Ertel when she would come in from Sheboygan.

Back in Madison, where Don and Mary Sue had their home, the brothers had brought Ike and Margaret back home from Chicago, buying a house for them across the street on three woodsy acres at 888 Forest Acres Drive, in which they would live for the rest of their lives, and where Phil would live with them until 1959. As difficult as it was for Ike to accept now being in *their* shadow, he and Margaret wanted to get back in the music game. They began to appear, billed as "the parents of Don and Phil Everly," at events around Nashville, and do interviews about their sons. As a sop to his meal tickets, Archie Bleyer had even recorded a few songs by Ike, though the tapes were never to be released. Ike and Margaret had no compunction doing low-level functions, serving as masters of ceremony at talent shows at the National Guard armory in Paducah, Kentucky. Ike knew his time for stardom was gone, but seeing his name on a billboard got the old boy's veins popping. With Don and Phil kicking in a portion of their income to him and Margaret, never again would he need to cut hair or shovel coal for a living.

For his sons, the world was about to get much bigger than the region that spawned them, their appeal so broad worldwide that a road trip would sometimes mean across several oceans. Their guest shots on the Sullivan show had been carried in many countries, including Canada, England, and Australia, where they now regularly made the charts. And those recorded appearances were something like tutorials within the culture of would-be musicians who had caught the rock and roll fever and boogie-woogie blues. A week after the Opry gig, they also were the headline act on Dick Clark's primetime ABC version of *Bandstand*, produced in a Times Square studio and colloquially called the "Beech Nut" show, for the show's bubble gum sponsor, with Clark shamelessly requiring the kids in the audience to wear buttons saying "Beechie" and to chew gum. Even lip-syncing "All I Have to Do Is Dream" and "Wake Up Little Susie" no doubt demanded the focus of budding rockers, from the guitar strumming technique to every slight contortion of their mouths.

Such tutorials seemed particularly important for British leather bands trying to play American blues and rock. Few established Brit acts carried as much weight in the 1950s, and worse, the BBC's radio programs had an unwritten ban on rock and roll songs until the mid-1960s. The alternatives were the pirate radio ships out in the Channel, and juke boxes in beatnik bars inland, where, as playwrights Andrew Lloyd Webber and Tim Rice, the team behind the rock operas *Phantom of the Opera* and *Cats*, recalled, it was a near out-of-body experience hearing the licks of "Bye Bye Love" as teenagers. The Brits had their own fanzines, too, and as early as Christmastime 1959 the Everlys would be on the cover of *New Musical Express*, with their note, "Thanks—and season's greetings to our friends in Britain. We look forward to seeing you soon—Don and Phil."

One other pertinent pair of Brit amateurs, schoolmates named Lennon and McCartney, were also listening to and studying Everly Brothers songs found in the Liverpool record shops, and came perilously close to adopting the name the Foreverly Brothers for their band. Even later, when the Beatles themselves would be the beacon of the next teen generation of rockers, the Everlys were still standard bearers on both sides of the sea. Young Americans had risen on the gospel-like connection between the Everly Brothers and guitar rock. Ads in the puerile teen mags vowed: "Let the Everly Brothers Teach You Guitar," with an offer to mail a couple bucks to a post office box in Queens Village, New York, rented by a company affiliated with Cadence Records. They would "send you their 'Lightning' way to play Guitar . . . the Everly Way!' Start playing Western, Cowboy, Rock and Roll, Hillbilly, and Gospel songs quickly, easily, right away!" for "only $1.98." For future Queen guitarist Brian May, playing something dubbed the Everly Way "thrilled me to the core [and] it will be in my head till I die. I learned to play rhythm guitar and how two-part harmonies work, how different emotions are evoked using different sequences of intervals, finding the moments that chill your spine. You'll find echoes of it in a lot of our old Queen songs."

Yet, even as they were helping to build this city on rock and roll, Don and Phil Everly felt like suckers. As Don would later say, "we used to go into television studios and the directors and technicians used to be positively offensive about pop music. They'd make it clear we were there on sufferance, and they'd get rid of us as soon as they could. You know—they were often unpleasant. Elvis above all, had to take an awful lot of rudeness and he—like the rest of us—had to be unfailingly courteous to these people." And so they were. In the 1950s, rockers with an attitude were troublemakers, personas non grata. The only recourse was to put some attitude in their songs, even the ones that begged for love and respect. If it helped get them through a rough session, hey, it helped pay the freight.

CHAPTER SEVEN

Bird Dogs

The Everly Brothers were like sons to Archie Bleyer, yet one of their gripes was that he still wasn't paying them more than token advances on royalties and kept their per-record royalty as low as he could without seeming like a piker, maybe a penny or two more than the industry standard four cents per record sale. To be certain, they were making good bread, their 50-percent cut on publishing royalties from Acuff-Rose like dollars from heaven—enough to buy themselves new wheels. They needed to do nothing to have their faces on TV shows that other rock artists couldn't beg their way onto. Black artists couldn't dream-dream-dream of it—and even when they could get on TV, they suffered the indignities of conditioned racism.

America's Original Sin was not going to go away just because Black artists were crucial to the rock and roll wave. Jim Crow was all in for encouraging lynchings and for Dixie governors to stand in school doorways attempting to blunt the Supreme Court's outlawing of school desegregation or in lunch counter doorways wielding axes. Rock's own doors were blocked by the entertainment media's upper-level cowards. In 1957, Alan Freed was given a national TV show on ABC as competition for Dick Clark. Freed himself walked a thin line of illegality by taking payola—pay for play—from record companies to find places for their songs on the air, as Clark was accused of doing on

Bandstand. On Freed's TV dance party, when his guest Frankie Lymon danced with a white girl, thirteen stations in the South canceled the show. That was just the start of trouble awaiting Freed, who would rip off rockers from fully deserving pay at those back-breaking Paramount shows.

As it was, few would be taking up the case for artists of all colors who earned a pittance from royalties and appearance fees far beneath their market value. The Everly Brothers and Buddy Holly were among the exceptions, yet on TV gigs they received no more than union scale, generally a couple hundred bucks. But they still were in a fast lane, and could be in the literal sense, spending thousands on custom cars. Phil would tell a perhaps apocryphal story about buying one of his many wheels, saying a salesman had shooed him off the lot thinking he was a kid with no way to pay for it. Whipping out a wad of big bills, he told him, "This could have been yours," then walked to a lot across the street and bought a car there.

Phil had the bread, all right, and the moxie—in 1959 he was arrested for a drag race in which he almost drove his sports car off the road, incurring a fine and a police record—but he was still barely twenty, bunking in his parents' house that he owned a part of. That was how fast they had ripened, though the fickle nature of the business necessitated that they keep striking while the iron was hot, to live on the road and always be ready to record. In July, with "All I Have to Do Is Dream" in heavy rotation, they were given a song called "Bird Dog," written by Boudleaux Bryant originally as a goof playing off Elvis's "Hound Dog," using the bird dog as a metaphor of a girlfriend being stalked by another guy, "Johnny," with the warning "Hey, bird dog get away from my quail / Hey, bird dog you're on the wrong trail." Cleverly silly as it was, it began by ragging the guy as a "joker," with Don interjecting, "He's a bird" and "He's a dog"—which, phonetically, came out *dawg*. For the brothers, though, it seemed like filler. Don recalled later that "I thought the song was one of those corny things" and Phil that it was "a strange song."

Both were right, but so was Archie Bleyer, who smelled a hit and had the final say. He even tried to force on them a sillier idea for it. As Phil remembered, referring to the TV puppeteer Paul

Winchell, "There used to be a ventriloquist on television with [puppet] Jerry Mahoney, who had a dog called Farfel. Archie wanted to get Farfel to do the 'he's a bird,' 'he's a dog,' but we just weren't going for it. We said, 'Uh-uh!'" The session at Studio B was threadbare, backed by Chet Atkins and Lightnin' Chance, the Everlys' guitars supplying the melody for the droll song that became a thumping call and response, the stinging strums on the intro repeated between verses. Their harmonies were superior, of course, and Chet's rock accents superb, turning the song into a hell of a put-down line for scores of jealous teen boys. (Not incidentally, Wesley Rose would produce a cover of it in 1966 with the pop band the Newbeats.)

Before it went out, however, an issue arose when a second song recorded at the session, Boudleaux and Felice's airy ballad "Devoted to You," seemed better-suited to the Everly Brothers, a heart-melting "jangle pop" ballad and ideal wedding song, with Chet's chiming licks applying tremolo sprinkled into pledges that "I'll never hurt you," never be untrue, and that "I'd be un-happy if you were blue." The chord changes were slick and emo-tionally charged, and it gave Archie shpilkes having to decide which one would be the A-side. He took the best route he could, releasing the record as a two-sided single. Getting airplay first, "Bird Dog" in October hit number two pop (kept from the top by Tommy Edwards's "It's All in the Game"), number one country for six weeks, and number two R&B. And "Devoted," given its own release, hit number ten pop, number seven country, and number one in Canada—thus making it their third two-sided hit, Though they had a way to go—Elvis had thirty-nine two-sided hits and Fats Domino and the Beatles twenty-four each. But this was another marker of success, en route to racking up thirteen, keeping them in the fast lane.

○ ○

That fall, the lane led them to another *Perry Como's Kraft Music Hall* on September 27, guesting with actors Ann Sheridan and Ray Walston, and composer Arthur Schwartz—a square peg/round hole that could make it seem as if they alone were representing the rock and roll side of pop music. On October 22 there was ABC's *Patti Page Olds Show,* hosted by the "Tennessee Waltz" pop-country singer who was the most successful female act of the 1950s. Then it was back to Dick Clark's "Beech-Nut" show on November 1, co-headlining with Bobby Darin. Ducking in and out of Irvin Feld's "Show of Stars for '58" tour, they leaped into higher-paying standalone concerts. They were all but a turn-key operation. Archie was constantly amazed by how long their records remained high on the charts—even with "Bird Dog" and "Devoted to You" on the rise, one could check some chart or another and still see "Bye Bye Love" or "Wake Up Little Susie," since the album was also long on the charts.

They were singing by rote their year-old "classics" on the top-watched shows, And now Bleyer began considering the foreign markets as additional gold mines. The Everlys were already winners on that asset sheet, Cadence's international distributors, London Records, pumping up royalties in Europe and Australia, where there was a phenomenal outgrowth of American rock music, in no small part owing to the Everly Brothers. Wesley Rose, with Bleyer and GAC, were contracting with promoters on both continents for major tours, which had been ongoing, the earliest such transoceanic tour by an American rocker being by Little Richard, who was mobbed by fans in England and Australia—though during his Aussie tour in 1957, he had a breakdown that led him to quit the business, the first of his periodic religious retreats. American acts could clear as much as $10,000 a show abroad, where native rockers were mainly paupers who had taken to trying to sound like American rockers.

In England, where rock and roll was banned on the BBC, the biggest acts were skiffle and beat singers such as Tommy Steele (aka "The British Elvis," who covered "Singing the Blues"), Wee Willie Harris, Emile Ford and the Checkmates, the very young Cliff Richard, and Tony Sheridan, who would be best known as the guy who hired John Lennon and Paul McCartney as backup in Hamburg in 1961, after John, Paul, and then George Harrison had themselves begun their rock journey playing and singing Everly Brothers and Buddy Holly songs. In Australia, there was but one rocker who could even marginally qualify as a star,

Johnny O'Keefe. But there were promoters who could fill up venues with names like Little Richard, the most aggressive being Lee Gordon, who packed the rafters in Sydney and Melbourne even though in 1957 there were only three Americans on the bill, Little Richard, Eddie Cochran, and Gene Vincent. The native fodder included O'Keefe and singer Alis Lesley, who was billed as "the female Elvis Presley." The Everly Brothers would be sure to sell out houses, and Gordon staked them to top dollar. England would also be nailed down, though their first entree there before setting off for Australia would be a brief promotional stopover along with Bleyer, who foresaw them returning in 1959. What he didn't know was that, by then, his future with them was growing shorter by the minute.

○ ○

As the clock slid away from 1958, Bleyer issued "Brand New Heartache" from the now-graying *Everly Brothers* album, a laid-back, more sorrowful expression of foreboding than "Bye Bye Love." On the B-side was the album's Ray Charles cover "Leave My Woman Alone," a jumpy snort of country blues. Not given the promotional juice of the Everly Brothers originals, they failed to chart. In October, though, they recorded a new Boudleaux-Felice composition, "Problems," yet one more flesh wound of teen angst about uncertain love that had even their teacher worried about them, the session bathing it with the brothers' insanely perfect vocal blend, a fully blown rock tempo and almost ear-grabbing rhythm surges. Rare for the Everlys, it ended with a vocal fadeout of their melodic moans of "problems, problems, problems all day long . . . ," as if the hopelessness had no solution.

Perhaps only the Everly Brothers and Roy Orbison could turn such bleakness into a bubbly spritz of country pop, though the title would in time be a metonym for them, given its woebegone lines like "Worries, worries pile up on my head / Woe is me, I should have stayed in bed." Paired with the Bryants' "Love of My Life" on the B-side, a simple, acoustic, Frankie Avalon-ish melody, the single sprinted with the usual gusto.

Within a month, it reached number two on the pop chart, kept from the top by the Teddy Bears' near narcoleptic love pleading "To Know Him Is to Love Him," Phil Spector's first record. It also hit number seventeen on the country list, number six in England. And it became an ideal launch pad for more album fodder—which turned out to be a sort of double album around Christmas time, with two LPs released almost simultaneously— *The Best of the Everly Brothers*, another twelve-track collection of A and B sides of their first six singles, including "Problems," and what they insisted be a backward glance in tribute to Ike Everly—*Songs Our Daddy Taught Us*.

The latter, contemporizing the country stuff they had sung as Little Don and Baby Boy Phil on Ike's radio shows, was notably less high-strung, with only Lightning Chance and his double bass and no hint of any electric embellishment as they harmonized and strummed on a journey through traditional gut-bucket bluegrass and folk. Some were peaceful country ruminations—Bob Miller's "Rockin' Alone in My Old Rockin' Chair," the Charlie Monroe "Down in the Willow Garden" (renamed from "Rose Connolly") that they would revive on the BBC's 1991 country folk CD *Bringing It All Back Home*, Frankie Bailes's "Oh So Many Years," the Gene Autry "That Silver Haired Daddy of Mine," Bradley Kincaid's sad ballad "Lightning Express" about a boy who boards a train to see his dying mother, and Henry Prichard's "Kentucky."

Fans who had seen them in concert were already familiar with "Kentucky," which they would introduce as elegizing "our home state." It actually was a forerunner of the style that had come to define them, with its simple but deft guitar riff by Don and their glissando syllables, here in their pronunciation of "Kennn-tucky-yyy . . . you are the dearest land outside of heaven to me-ee" Other songs were about the desperation of all-too-mortal men, such as Merle Travis's "Roving Gambler," Karl Davis and Harty Taylor's "I'm Here to Get My Baby Out of Jail"—the plight of a woman begging the warden to trade her diamond ring for her man's release. There were also three traditional tunes of unknown provenance, "Barbara Allen," "Who's Gonna Shoe Your Pretty Little Feet," and "Put My

Little Shoes Away," which were all credited as "arranged by Ike Everly." And of course there was "Long Time Gone," its writing credit attributed not to Leslie York but, incorrectly, the cowboy singer/actor Tex Ritter and songwriter Frank Hartford, who had written a different "Long Time Gone" that was recorded by Ritter in 1946.

The song had Don and Phil doing their best Lefty Frizzell lonely-days-and-lonely-nights guise, vowing, "There'll be a day you'll want me only / But when I leave, I'll be a long time gone." Listen to it now and, unlike Ronnie Van Zant's future declaration as a free bird, the brothers sang of needing an excuse *not* to fly away. With the album's mélange of uneasy highs and inevitable lows, Ike's boys expertly framed Dixie pride, shame, contentment, and amorality, all things that would arise within themselves in time. All of it was gorgeous, and in the broader sense, this wasn't an Everly Brothers album; it was about the depth and breadth that was American country music. The cover was a pensive shot of them gazing away from the camera as though peering back through time, which is what every one of their songs can now be said to exemplify.

Yet, the departure from rock and crossover teen-friendly superficialities made it an unfortunate exception and was fairly lost in the clutter of rock's late 1950s buffet, as was the best-of album, which was more surprising. But *Songs Our Daddy Taught Us* would have a respectable afterlife, in numerous rereleases by various labels and remade in 2013 by the Billie Joe Armstrong and Norah Jones *Foreverly* tribute LP. Future critics did a make-good for the real-time neglect. A 2015 retro-review by the All-Music site's Richie Unterberger called it "quite a surprise from a top rock & roll act, and considerably ahead of its time." Nathan Brackett in the 2004 *New Rolling Stone Album Guide* dealt it four of five stars, venturing that not even Elvis "had the nerve to do an album as rootsy." Amen, brother.

○ ○

As high a gear as they were in, when 1959 arrived, it brought a devastating jolt. On February 3, forever metaphorized, quite wrongly, as "the day the music died," Don and Phil, like the rest of the country, woke to inconceivable news: Buddy Holly, who was on the cursed Winter Dance Party tour of the frozen Midwest, promoted by GAC, had hopped on a tin-can of a plane after a gig in Crystal Lake, Iowa, and crashed in a field, killing Buddy, Ritchie Valens, and "The Big Bopper" J. P. Richardson. Had this been a year before, the Everly Brothers may well have been on that tour into the tundra. Buddy could have avoided it, too, having grown beyond constant rinky-dink touring.

While not as omnipresent on TV as the Everlys, Holly had excised the Crickets from his act when he moved to New York, got married, and began recording blues and jazz-backed songs and even collaborated with the eighteen-piece New York Symphony Orchestra. Yet, just weeks after "It Doesn't Matter Anymore" was released, he had decided to jump in on the winter tour because he believed Norman Petty had skimmed much of the money due Buddy, whose new wife was pregnant, and money was a concern. Though the Everlys hadn't seen him in months, the bond between them was so tight that they spoke often with him by phone and Buddy encouraged the Crickets to back the brothers up when needed.

Out in Iowa, Buddy had paid to hire the infamous single-engine Beechcraft Bonanza plane that allowed him to bypass the bus with no working heat that most of the troupe had to ride between gigs, one of whom, drummer Carl Bunch, had already been left behind in a hospital, treated for frostbitten feet. After the Crystal Lake concert, two of Buddy's bandmates, including future country "outlaw" Waylon Jennings and Tommy Allsup, gave up their seats to a flu-ridden Richardson and Valens, who won a coin flip with Allsup. The end of the story was the crushing news, upon which Buddy's new wife collapsed in grief and suffered a miscarriage. As the music world awakened to the radio reports, both Everlys nearly collapsed themselves. At the time, Buddy and Phil had intended to start a new label for Buddy's recordings. At his last session, he recorded a song for that purpose written by the great sax man King Curtis called "Reminiscing."

The crash also killed that objective. ("Reminiscing" would be released, postmortem, in 1963 on Coral.) Buddy's family asked the brothers to attend the funeral in Lubbock on February 7; only Phil would go, while Don was so torn up that, as he recalled, "I wouldn't go. It freaked me right out when Buddy died. I just took to my bed, out of it mentally. I couldn't even fly in a plane for a while." Phil talked himself into attending. "I flew down to Lubbock for the funeral, went down and sat with his parents and Maria Elena," he said, and although the family requested he be one, "I wasn't a pallbearer. I didn't want to see him put down in the earth." Instead, as if zombified, he sat almost immobile, staring into space, tears running down his face, during the service and burial.

He returned to Nashville as uninterested as Don to deal with recording and touring. And for Archie Bleyer, there was major worry that his meal ticket's mental condition might ruin his plans—the Australia tour was only three months away, with a seemingly endless plane flight needed to get them there. He hoped pressing business like that would snap them out of their funk. It seemed hopeful as well that Don was awaiting the birth of his second child. On April 16, Mary Sue gave birth to another daughter, Venetia Ember, named for a B-actress from Britain, Venetia Stevenson, whom Don had met in New York when the brothers were there for an Ed Sullivan gig in 1957. And there may have been more to it than Don simply liking the name.

The actress, the daughter of the British playwright, director and actor Robert Stevenson and British actress Anna Lee, who in her younger days was called "The British Bombshell," was herself quite a bombshell. Tall, blonde, sophisticated and kittenish, to this day, she is still seen on the label of Sweetheart Stout beer cans and bottles. Having acted in movies and TV on the cowboy series *Sugarfoot*, she was a prize catch for young hunky actors and also was a "beard" for young, secretly gay stars Tab Hunter and Anthony Perkins. When Don met her, she was in the process of divorcing Russ Tamblyn, and they may well have engaged in some bawdy byplay in New York. If so, naming his daughter after her could have been a little inside joke between them, and on Mary Sue. If so, it was, well, psycho, and as future events would prove, they had hardly ended their connubial conjunctions.

After the birth, Don spent little time with mother or child. Mary Sue was accustomed to him being home only temporarily, and just days later Don and Phil were gone again, to New York to do the *Dinah Shore Chevy Show* on April 26, singing "Bird Dog" and the still-unreleased "Take a Message to Mary," written by the Bryants, a weeper about a guy in prison whose heart is achin' for the girl he left out there, identified by repeating cries of "Maarry," with the end line an ecclesiastical "Oh Lord, this cell is cold"—which was likely how the "Mary" back in Nashville felt about life with Don Everly.

"Message to Mary" was recorded during a time when the brothers' upward progression could be measured by the larger core of musicians at Studio B. Looking to add punch, Archie Bleyer added to the usual core of Atkins, Chance, and Harman the great pianist Floyd Cramer (whose "slip note" technique would stamp his own 1961 hit instrumental "Last Date"), pedal steel guitarist Jerry Byrd, jazz guitarists Hank Garland and Barry Galbraith, as well as the Crickets' refugees Jerry Allison and guitarist Sonny Curtis. And the soon-released single would have a more lasting effect than its limited stay on the charts, due to the deepening of the Everlys' vocals. The L.A. session guitarist Waddy Wachtel, who a decade later would back the Everly Brothers on the road, calls "Mary" "the closest that anyone has ever come to singing in perfect harmony. I do believe every word and syllable are as close to perfect as is humanly—or in their case, inhumanly possible—because I feel humans could never sing this well."

The same case could be made for "Problems" and two other songs Cadence released early in 1959—the banging Little Richard cover "Rip It Up" from the debut album, and "Take a Message to Mary's" flip side, the Bryants' "Poor Jenny," a rollicking tale with a cowboy flavor. For "Jenny" Harman created a percussion effect by tapping a screwdriver against a Coke bottle—as the brothers sang a tale about a girl who got caught in a rumble, was mistaken for a gang member, and thrown in jail, with her dad wanting to "ride me out of town on a rail" for not rescuing her. Radical as it was for the fine, upstanding Everly Brothers, it didn't raise eyebrows, but it did sales across the board, help-ing "Mary" reach number sixteen on the pop chart before going off on its own run to number twenty-two pop. Bleyer promoted these songs heavily in Australia, where each made the hit chart, "Mary" going all the way to number two, only a step behind "Bird Dog" and "Poor Jenny" to number twenty-two.

It was a proficient means of promoting the tour Down Under, which Don looked forward to as an escape from his personal Nashville blues and lingering mourning for Buddy Holly. The tour got underway in late May, when Don and Phil packed up and boarded the interminable flight to Oz. It had also been ar-ranged that when the plane touched down first in London for refueling, they would crack into the British rock market, ap-pearing for a quick interview on the aptly named TV show *Cool for Cats*, a fifteen-minute, teen-based *Bandstand* clone produced by the ITV network. Then it was off to Australia, as headlin-ers of what was called "The Big Show," to begin on May 28 in Melbourne, promoted by Lee Gordon, a guy with a murky past. An American-born native of Detroit, some assumed he was con-nected to the Mob. But Gordon moved in high circles, gaining financing from Australian businessmen, and his shows had been running since 1954.

Australia had never been an entertainment stop and had once banned African American performers under the White Australian Policy; one Black jazz band led by Sonny Clay had even been deported way back in 1928, the effect of which was to ban American jazz idols like Louis Armstrong from playing Australia until 1954 when Gordon managed to secure Frank Sinatra, Ella Fitzgerald, Armstrong, and other jazz greats— though Sinatra canceled another tour when Gordon refused his demand for a DC7 and Frank's manager punched the promoter in the face. Johnny Ray was the star of the first "rock" tour, sparking mob scenes by fans far more loyal than Ray's vanishing American following. A Bill Haley–headlined tour in 1957 drew over three hundred thousand people, and Johnny Cash had been in a few months before the Everly Brothers. The brothers' trip was a nightmare, their single-engine plane needing to refuel numerous times, and this only a few months after Buddy Holly went down in a such a plane. As Phil recalled, "The first time we flew to Australia was by prop, and it took thirty-two hours. You shaved twice; it was ridiculous."

However, Phil must have had some hallucinations on the way, since he would later weave a story for a *Rolling Stone* article about one of the passengers putting the extended time to good use. "Eddie Cochran got laid on [the] flight," he said. "Only person I ever knew that knocked a stewardess off. Got her in the back of the plane. The flight was so damn long, they got well acquainted."

Good as it sounded, though, this could not have happened, at least not on that flight, since Cochran was not on the tour, his Australian gig having come two years earlier on that fabulous gig with Little Richard and Gene Vincent. For their part, Phil and Don sweated out the thirty-two hours. When the plane landed, they were amazed that there were several hundred teenagers waiting on the tarmac at the Melbourne airport, with a large contingent of young girls breaking free to mob them when they descended the ramp from the plane, tugging at their shirts and even their shoelaces, giving a whole new meaning to "Who's Gonna Shoe Your Pretty Little Feet?"

Gordon had booked a lineup headed by three American acts, the only authentic rock and roll one being the Everlys. The others were Tab Hunter—whose only credits as a singer were a lifeless cover of Sonny James's "Young Love," which in the nature of the confused times went to number one in 1957, a lesser hit with "Ninety-Nine Ways," and the movie adaptation of the musical *Damn Yankees*—and the swarthy actor Sal Mineo, who besides supporting roles in the James Dean flicks *Rebel without a Cause* and *Giant* had a couple of mild teen pop hits. All the Americans were given obligatorily staged mob scenes at the airport and hotels, despite Hunter and Mineo being secretly gay.

These charades were fun, and the tour, with Aussie acts like Johnny O'Keefe, Col Joye and the Joy Boys, Johnny Rebb and the Rebels, the Delltones, and the Dee Jays, drew well in Melbourne, on two dates in Sydney, two more in Brisbane. Don and Phil, who were stunned at how well the audience knew and sang along with their songs, would pocket a cool ten grand for the trip, making the long trip back home easier to take. They would return to Australia in 1960 (and far in the future, again in 1989), but by then would be on a different locus, having made a critical decision about their future that put them on a road they alone controlled.

CHAPTER EIGHT

New Frontier

There were, indeed, big things brewing when the Everly Brothers returned home. The extended time spent killing the hours on the trip had them mulling over taking a stand on recording songs that they wanted to, including those from outside the Acuff-Rose domain, and also fattening up the royalty rate. It was a risk for artists to challenge their record labels then, especially artists who were already making more money than they dreamed possible and who seemed solidly planted on an assembly line of hits. Don and Phil couldn't really bitch about the money, though the lack of comforting advances by Archie Bleyer was a thorn. They would close in on $1 million in the bank by the end of the decade, and spent like thieves on cars, clothes, and, for Don, expensive artwork he didn't mount on his walls in Nashville, as if saving them for future homes elsewhere, possibly with another wife.

As it was, they had dropped quiet hints to Wesley Rose that they wanted more creative control of their records, relying less on the Bryants for songs they wanted to write, and on Bleyer for what songs would be recorded, the latter a key issue now that their contract with Cadence was due to expire at the end of January 1960. When they returned home, they took their case again to Rose, who was hiding a little secret from them. Already duplicitously managing the Everlys while trying to maximize

Acuff-Rose's bottom line without increasing their publishing royalties, he also had veto power over any song that he alone deemed unworthy (read: not owned by Acuff-Rose). He had approved an occasional cover such as the ones of Little Richard and Gene Vincent songs, but these were not the songs that were meant to make the big bucks. Only one of the brothers' hits up to then had been written by them. Still, Rose talked Archie Bleyer into bending a bit on their sales royalty rate, bumping it up to six cents a record, and to accept more songs written or chosen by Don. As a sop, both sides of the next single, "(Till) I Kissed You" and "Oh What a Feeling," had an Everly credit.

Mollified for now, Don and Phil recorded the songs in early July at Studio B with Bleyer producing and backed by the crew of Chet Atkins, Floyd Chance, Sonny Curtis, Floyd Cramer, and on drums this time, ex-Cricket Jerry Allison. That the Everlys had begun to take on more spit polish and less country gravel was obvious in the opening notes of "(Till) I Kissed You"—a song that Don explained years later was based on an adulterous fling in Australia. "I wrote it about a girl I met on that trip," he said. "Her name was Lillian, and she was very, very inspirational. I was married, but . . . you know."

It wasn't a guitar-centric intro but rather a jazzy jam of Chet's funky licks, Cramer's springy keyboard, and Chance and Allison's rhythmic bottom. The butter-melting verses were separated by Allison's *bad-dum ba-doom fills,* and the tempo was slowed for Don's soft vocal solos on two bridges that went: "You don't realize what you do to me / And I didn't realize what a kiss could be." The song was infectious from first to final note, bearing an unmistakable resemblance to a typical Buddy Holly song—no accident, since Don wrote the song only weeks after Buddy's death and had called in Jerry to further strike the feel. The harmonic resonance of the fadeout repetitions of "I kissed ya, uh-huh / I kissed ya, oh yeah" alone made it worth a listen—except perhaps for Mary Sue Everly, who might have wondered just who he kissed. On the flip side was "Oh What a Feeling," a romantic ballad on which Phil's treble gushed so high it might have scraped some of the paint off Studio B's pyramided ceiling.

To support the single, the Everlys once more showed up on the Perry Como *Kraft Music Hall* on September 30, as "('Til) I Kissed You" ramped into the top ten, to peak at number four pop, number eight on the country chart and number twenty-two on the R&B chart, narrowly missing another Gold record. However, the good vibes with Bleyer inevitably began to erode when he refused to go with a song they had liked, "Lonely Town," written by Dave Rich, the singer-songwriter they believed they were indebted to for helping them get an audition with Bleyer, and about whom Don would later say, "If not for this man, Phil and I would be coal miners today." But Archie gave the song instead to Andy Williams, who had a hit with it. They also tried to turn Bleyer on to another Rich song, "I Think I'm Gonna Die," conflating the lines of "Bye Bye Love"—"I think I'm gonna cry" and "I feel like I could die." But Bleyer and Rose rejected it, too, as old news.

Wesley did bend some more, allowing them clearance on the non-Acuff-Rose "Let It Be Me," written and recorded by French composer Gilbert Bécaud in 1955 with original lyrics by Pierre Delanoe as "Je t'appartiens." It had been covered with English lyrics in 1957 by leggy American singer Jill Corey but was only a middling hit. Archie, who had a yen to record it himself, suggested that the Everlys do so. He didn't need to persuade Don, who had heard the song as an instrumental on a Chet Atkins album and recalled it as "one of the great songs of my lifetime. I said to Chet, 'I love that melody. Is there a lyric?' He said, 'Yes, and it's a great one.' I went to Archie and told him I wanted to do it with strings." Bleyer of course loved that idea, and told the brothers to record it in New York, in a studio that Archie had used to record his own string-heavy instrumentals.

Don and Phil made the trip with Rose, who would produce the song at a December 15 session with Archie's own favorite musicians—jazz guitarists Howard Collins (who would play on Bob Dylan's *Freewheelin'*), Barry Galbraith (who had worked with Billie Holiday and Sarah Vaughan), and Mundell Lowe (Benny Goodman and Jimmy and Tommy Dorsey), bassist Lloyd Trotman (Duke Ellington, Ray Charles), and Hank Rowland (Cootie Williams). Only Jerry Allison came in from Dixie.

Given this splendid cast, Don and Phil saw the song as a symbolic breakout beyond the Nashville skyline. Wesley was satisfied that the B-side was an Acuff-Rose product, Don's "Since You Broke My Heart," but one of the Everlys' qualms was that Rose, like Archie, had been a nominal producer, with Don barely paying attention to him in the studio, working mainly with Chet on the arrangements and chords. Years later, he would insist the typical studio process went like this: "[Phil and I] would find the song, do the arrangement, go in, tell the musicians what we wanted, tell the engineer. We'd produce it in the studio. There was nothing for Wesley to do but time it."

That might have been a tad harsh, but as Don believed, "His part and Archie's part has been overplayed. Basically, they did not care about the music in the way that Phil and I did. I loved it. They looked at it as money. Their idea of what was going to hit was sometimes absurd." Don's memory of the New York session became almost a personal slap at Rose, who clearly was out of his element. "Wesley," he said, "just sat there pouting through the whole session like a kid." Which, if so, didn't prevent "Let It Be Me" from becoming a tour de force for the Everly Brothers. Immersed in layers of delicately tailored sound taken higher by the lush strings, their impeccable harmony was spooned with convincing sentimentality, not mawkishness— "Each time we meet love I find complete love" sung by Don as if shooting from a hydrant. Indeed, the Everly Brothers seemed to grow to full manhood just within the two minutes and thirty-three seconds of the recording.

Archie was so delighted he went back to listing himself on the record's inner label as the conductor of the orchestra. The single dropped just after the new decade arrived and ran up the charts, en route to hitting number four on the pop chart, number eight on the country, twenty-two on the R&B, and just missed going to number one in England, Canada, and Australia. And Bleyer, who was optimistic that its success would be an inducement for the brothers to re-sign with Cadence, also sent into production another compilation album, only a year removed from the last. This one, *The Fabulous Style of The Everly*

Brothers, naturally featured "Let It Be Me" along with "(Till) I Kissed You," "When Will I Be Loved," "Poor Jenny," "Take a Message to Mary," the covers of "Rip It Up" and "Be Bop-a-Lula," and several B-sides. Once a gamble, the Everly Brothers were now a fracking franchise.

○ ○

Still, there was no agreement to renew their Cadence contract, and when it ran out Bleyer simply went on with the recording schedule as if he owned them in perpetuity. But Don and Phil had put Wesley Rose on assignment to explore signing them to other labels, at the very least as a test of their lofty status. And the song they laid down as possibly their farewell to Cadence, "When Will I Be Loved," happened to be the one that reeked with feelings of being cheated and mistreated, though these feelings were hardly about Archie Bleyer alone. It also was their hat tip to Muddy Waters and Bo Diddley, the churning *ba-da-da-da-da, bomp bomp* beat of Muddy's "Mannish Boy," cowritten with Bo, as bluesy as they would ever get.

Intriguingly, "When Will I Be Loved" was written not by Don but Phil, proof that his writing could stand with his brother's, telling of hearts that could be broken all too easily, and their whining that "It happens every time" one hell of a whine. But by the time the record was pressed in May with the B-side being the cover of "Be-Bop-a-Lula, it was Archie Bleyer's heart that was broken. Right after recording "When Will I Be Loved," Don and Phil finally committed to walking on Cadence. For weeks, Wesley had been dotting the i's and crossing the t's with both Warner Bros. Records and RCA, In the end, though, Warner Bros., a new kid on the block in the music business, won out by digging deeper into the company's coffers. And so, as the presidential race began with John F. Kennedy vowing a New Frontier, the Everly Brothers had found their own new frontier, which would challenge them to be their own men in a highly fractious environment. No longer were they small-world, but would that be good or bad?

92 / Crying in the Rain

○ ○

What made the difference for Warner Bros. was their willingness to sign off on a pay scale that was much higher than even Elvis had gotten from RCA in 1954 (to be accurate, the leftovers Elvis was given when Sam Phillips, in financial straits, sold his Sun Records contract to RCA for $40,000, tipping Elvis only $5,000; with his manager and Svengali "Colonel" Tom Parker then making $40,000 for himself licensing Elvis's movie merchandising rights.) Remarkably, the Warner payoff turned out to be $1 million over ten years—the industry's first million-dollar contract. (Not that it seems so much by today's warped, nine-figure standards, and even back in 1982, RCA gave Kenny Rogers a $20 million contract.) It happened when the financial guardians of the label suffered through two years of mediocrity that began in 1958 as a means for Warner Brothers Pictures to control music soundtracks that had previously been farmed out to other labels, as well as to cash in on rock and roll's profit pie. For the latter purpose, the studio signed Tab Hunter, who was contracted to the studio and wanted a singing career. However, Hunter sank like a stone, and nearly all of the label's talent was aimed at a mainstream market, including songs by the stone-faced *Dragnet* "Sergeant Friday" Jack Webb and the dour William Holden.

The only major hit for Warner Bros. Records was *77 Sunset Strip*'s Edd "Kookie" Byrnes's painfully idiotic "Kookie, Kookie (Lend Me Your Comb)," a duet with *Hawaiian Eye*'s "Cricket" Connie Stevens, which went to number four on the pop chart despite such imbecilic lines as "I've got smog in my noggin' ever since you made the scene." While Bob Newhart's comedy albums did alright, one of the studio's many DOA albums was *But You've Never Heard Gershwin with Bongos*. Worse, the first rock-and-roll-oriented signing was Bill Haley and His Comets, whose "Shake, Rattle and Roll" days were long over and never to dust the charts again. In their first two years, the label lost $3 million and were in dutch for two-thirds of the advances they laid out.

This hardly presaged a long future, and heads were on the line when the label's president Jim Conklin took one last stab at making it work, one that most industry people thought was insane. Herman Starr, the gruff president of Warner Brothers Pictures, signed off on it, but with one condition, telling Conklin, "If the Everlys are so hot, go get the signing money from your distributors." Conklin did. He wheedled the record distributors with vows to repay them with interest, raising the money that guaranteed the brothers their ten-year, $100,000 advance against their 7 percent royalty rate, with $525,000 coming up front and the balance coming over the next nine years.

Wesley, who had seen it all—and in 1961 would be BMI's top publishing earner, owning the rights to eight of the top seventy-nine songs, three of them by the Everlys—was astonished that it got that far, the hundred grand being his highball starting point. Of course, it was impossible for the Everlys to refuse, not with the assurances Rose had gotten from the company that no Warner executive would interfere with the brothers' artistic choices, something that Wesley still reserved for himself, a blister sure to erupt. That was when Archie Bleyer got word that the concessions he made were not enough. He nearly choked hearing about the price that lured them away from the "family." Even with "When Will I Be Loved" in the can, Don and Phil wasted no time getting into the Warner family, though it was a daunting prospect.

"When we first went to Warners," Don recalled, "they had no record label at all. They used us to sort of subsidize the other albums they put out. They had no offices then, just a room over the street from Warner Bros. Pictures."

They did keep Nashville in their lives and creative process. With the temptation to move to the West Coast, they would soon do just that. But they would drive a hard bargain to keep coming back to record in Studio B with Chet Atkins and company. Their initial Warner product would be recorded there on March 18, 1960, as usual under the watch of Wesley Rose. And the song they banked on would be their finest piece of work, and the most contentious piece of property they would ever fight over.

○ ○

"Cathy's Clown" was based on Don's recollection of a story Ike used to tell about a girl back in his school days who dumped him, prompting his friends to slag him with taunts like "Mary had a little Ike." The name of the femme fatale in the song derived from an old girlfriend of Don's in his school days named Catherine, whose full name he said was the very alliterative Catherine Castle Craven Coe. He wrote the melody and most of the chorus, then—in what would be the thorny backstory for decades—called Phil to his home and he finished it, adding to the verses. Eons later, Don would obsessively try to obviate this scenario, maintaining that he had added Phil as cowriter because Wesley Rose believed they would sell more records if the public believed they wrote it together, and because they "wanted to keep [Phil] happy."

The consequences of this mini-drama would only grow into a scab that never healed. But in real time, the song was patently in Don's hands. He dressed up the arrangement of their first Warner Bros. Records entry, cribbing from the 1931 Ferde Grofe five-movement classical tone poem *Grand Canyon Suite*, which had been recorded by many other orchestra leaders (and again, by Andre Kostelanetz, in 1961 as *The Lure of the Grand Canyon* with a spoken narrative by Johnny Cash). Don's fascination with the grand orchestral suite included using distinct melodies and themes from the Grofe movements, which had been named "Sunrise," "Painted Desert," "On the Trail," "Sunset," and "Cloudburst"—which to Don sounded like the phases of his own life. For example, for the "Desert" theme he conveyed the strutting atmospherics of cowboy movies, which he apprised as "the sound of mules going down the path, down the canyon, that sort of gave me the inspiration."

In recording it, Don had to do without Chet Atkins, who was busy elsewhere. Thus, Don and Phil's chill acoustic picking was a rhythmic driver that Studio B engineer Bill Porter made thick with some tape looping, doubling Buddy Harman's bump-and-grind cadence, which he took from his days playing boom-lacka-

lacka drumbeats at a Nashville strip club. As Harman would explain the florid synergistic effect, with some matter-of-fact, for him, tech talk:

> If you listen closely, the drums sound like two drummers playing. I had gotten a tape loop from RCA New York that ran 60 ips, and there were four different playback heads which you could switch in and out and then move them around the tape path. So I heard this rhythm pattern and I thought, "God, this would be great for this song.". . . I hooked it up, fed it back into the console and got the balance, and then I switched it off on the verse and on during the bridge. I just did it manually with a switch [and] it's right in tempo and right in sync [giving it] the effect of two totally different drum sounds.

There were no choruses, only verses—the opening lines being an adamant directive to the girl: "Don't want your love anymore" or any kisses either, that's for sure. There were subtleties like the word "love" undulating for six beats and on the third beat Don deepening his vocal as Phil raised his, both keeping the note true all the way through. There was a four-note guitar arpeggio, then a four-note descension. And there was a simple, tart message within the sharper harmonies and Don's gruffer lead on the solos—that the Everly Brothers were now mature men, or as Don sang, "I gotta stand tall / You know a man can't crawl."

It was as if they were saying, "You've heard us—but you really haven't heard us." And Warner Bros. decided to make that point by having them record an album of original material right off the bat. The label mandarins named the LP *It's Everly Time*, making it seem like the Everlys' three-year joy ride at Cadence was merely a warm-up for what they would be accomplishing now, as men in the real world. Wesley Rose produced it and, like "Cathy's Clown," the work would be released in both mono and stereo, catering to a small but growing audiophile market, whereas Cadence only sent out records in mono until the early 1960s, when it had to remaster the Everlys catalog to keep up with the times. The album track list would not include "Cathy's Clown," which would be released around the same time in the early spring. And this made sense, as the album was more down-home in the manner of *Songs Our Daddy Taught Us* with a country blues-rock kick. In fact, the overall theme of *It's Everly Time* was the title of a Boudleaux and Felice Bryant song called "Nashville Blues," which actually would have made for a far better title of the album, drawing much from the Nashville rockabilly blues underbelly.

The dozen tracks would take five days and include the returned Atkins, Harman, Cramer, and the estimable Hank Garland, who had played electric guitar with Little Jimmy Dickens, Marty Robbins, and Patsy Cline but also big-band leader George Shearing and even jazz saxophone king Charlie Parker, and he also designed Gibson's Birdland model guitar. Garland, Atkins, and Cramer also played with sax man Boots Randolph and Black violinist Buddy Banks in an integrated band that played after hours at the Carousel Club. For the Everlys they were a godsend on an album that would have no song familiar to their fans. Only one came from the brothers' songwriting stack, Don's leadoff cut "So Sad (To Watch Good Love Go Bad)," a mournful ballad with some of the most perfect and saddest vocals they ever laid down, the self-jabbing bravado of "Cathy's Clown" turned into self-grieving moroseness about losing the "good times together," so much so that "It makes me cry to see love die."

"Nashville Blues" would leap from turntables with funky licks by Atkins and Cramer that sounded like something from out of a Printer's Alley bar—the Music Row watering hole referenced in the song. Three other Bryant songs on tap were "Oh True Love," "Some Sweet Day," and "Sleepless Nights," a trail of tears of lost love and endless nights that "will break my heart in two" that has been covered at least eleven times. One more tune, from Boudleaux Bryant, "Just in Case," used army induction as a grim metaphor of love about to end. All this love-hurts-but-we-still-need-it testifying was balanced by some mainstream pop, with covers of the nostalgic "Memories Are Made of This" and Bob Montgomery's "That's What You Do to

Me," letting them scat around with patois like "Bom do-dee bom do-dee bom bom bom ba do-dee. That's what you doin' to me." There was also a breezy remake of Ray Charles's "What Kind of Girl Are You" and the Fats Domino "I Want You to Know." And there was a cover of Dave Rich's "Carol Jane," paying back their old Nashville ally.

The cohesive but wide-reaching album was a superb delineation of who they were—a wise AllMusic retro-review pegs it as "one of the very greatest pre-Beatles, non-compilation rock albums, balancing all sides of the Everlys' repertoire." And as the album and "Cathy's Clown," were released, *Billboard* revealed the big news in the industry, the Everly Brothers' jump to Warner Bros. Records with a notice that actually understated the money figures: "Warner Bros. Records, six months ago a label that had a tough time getting its records played, has suddenly sprung to life. . . . WB accomplished its face-lifting by trimming off a lot of fat, putting in a whopping bid ($800,000) to pick up the Everly Brothers contract and working hard on the new releases."

Hard, indeed. The sessions for *It's Everly Time* ran so long that they produced enough material for yet another album, which would be called *A Date with the Everly Brothers*, to be released in October. It would run the same route, with the bonus that it would include "Cathy's Clown." Other tracks included the "Lucille" cover and one new song written by both Everlys, "That's Just Too Much," reiterating old ground for them by blaming a woman for losing "that tender touch" and the lips that "once thrilled me"—another possible jab at Mary Sue. They covered Jimmy Reed's 1960 crossover hit "Baby What You Want Me to Do," in Reed's swampy, swaying style, and four more songs by the Bryants—"So How Come (No One Loves Me)," heralding that they were "the loneliest creatures in the world" and "ugly ducklings," There were also "Donna, Donna," a "Bye Bye Love" echo about being "snowed under" by a fickle gal who "led me on and lured me on" and then "turned me down flat"; "A Change of Heart"; "Always It's You"; "Stick With Me Baby," written by Nashville singer-songwriter Mel Tillis; and Boudleaux Bryant's "Love Hurts," which noted that "love is like a stove, burns you when it's hot"—a subtlety that would be lost in the amped-up decades later when covered by the hair band Nazareth.

Wesley Rose, who was putting in overtime along with the Everly Brothers, producing this massive quantity of music, had time to be interviewed for a March 28 *Billboard* cover story about the foreign market boom, which now had grown for the Everlys with stops in Paris, England and Australia in April. Rose also got the chance to be smug about landing the brothers their million-dollar deal, an event that shook the industry to its core, either in excitement by artists or despair by the corporate overlords. Among the latter was Archie Bleyer, who must have felt torn that his stepdaughter Jackie was becoming more involved with Phil. Even so, Archie, who had taken a fatherly approach with the Everlys rather than treating them as mere clients, still corresponded cordially with them at times on the phone, and though he would lose a meal ticket he would gain a son-in-law. He would also be sending them royalty checks for years for songs he would keep recycling on compilation albums.

The problem for Archie was that he could only stretch the Everly Brothers' product so far. The only other rock and roll type he had on hand now was pop singer Johnny Tillotson, whose "Poetry in Motion," recorded in Nashville, went to number two pop in November 1960, behind only Ray Charles's "George on My Mind." And Bleyer would suffer another body blow in 1962 when Andy Williams left to sign with Columbia, where he'd remain for the next half-century Knowing he still needed the Everlys, Archie had ratcheted up the release of "When Will I Be Loved" and *The Fabulous Style of the Everly Brothers*, and profited handsomely when both sides of the "All I Have to Do Is Dream" / "Claudette" single went to number one in England and Australia, where "Bird Dog" had gone number one and "Message to Mary" number two. In both England and Australia, as well, "(Till) I Kissed You" went to number two, and, with no break in the seam, "Cathy's Clown" was climbing briskly up the charts.

To milk these new gateways, the Everly Brothers headed to England in late March. The tour there was promoted by Charles Lockier and Arthur Howes of the British agency Churchill &

Son, with talent agent Leslie Grade, the brother of producer/ impresario Lew Grade, both of whom founded the Grade Organisation in 1943 and basically owned the English entertainment industry. Don and Phil came in with Crickets Jerry Allison, Joe B. Mauldin and Sonny Curtis, all of whom outshone the supporting English acts, The Five Dallas Boys, Cherry Wainer and Don Storer, Lance Fortune, Danny Hunter, Flee-Rekkers, and the Freddy Lloyd Five with Tony Marsh. There would be twenty-two hectic gigs there, the first on April 3 at London's New Victoria Cinema, then a hopscotch path through England and Scotland. Along the way, they made their first two appearances on British TV, on the BBC's *Startime* on April 6 and April 14. Three days later, after their April 17 show at De Montfort in Leicester, they found themselves enmeshed in another of rock's new sub-context of inherent tragedy.

The day before, Eddie Cochran, who had been touring England for four months and partying with the Everlys when their paths crossed, played the final gig of his tour at the Bristol Hippodrome, paired with Gene Vincent. Following the show, Eddie, Gene, and Eddie's fiancée—who, small world, was Sharon Seeley, Don's former adulterous flame who wrote a huge hit about him playing her for a fool, and had also written hits for Ritchie Valens—were riding with a tour manager in a hired car headed for London's Heathrow Airport. Speeding on Bath Road, the driver lost control and crashed headlong into a lamppost on Rowden Hill. Cochran, in the backseat, tried to shield Seeley but the impact tore a door off and ejected him from the car. He suffered a massive head injury when he hit the ground. All the riders except the driver were badly injured and taken to St. Martin Hospital in Bath, where Cochran died the next afternoon, Easter Sunday. When Don and Phil heard about it on the news, they were as dazed as they were when Buddy Holly died.

Gene had fractured his collarbone and his legs were damaged, the tour manager fractured his skull, and Sharon badly injured her back and legs. After the Everlys and Jerry Allison rushed back to London to get to the hospital, Eddie had died, and Sharon was still sedated. When she awoke, she saw Phil and Jerry at her bedside, but Don avoided seeing her and rekindling old awkward memories. He was shaken up and would have terrible lingering insecurities about the perils of constant travel on these madcap road trips, a malaise that, as with Buddy's death, would take the Everly Brothers off the road for what would be a year and a half when they would land back home. But they had dates left in Bristol, Leeds, Manchester, Cardiff, Birmingham—and on April 24, at the Empire Theater, Liverpool's biggest music hall.

It's unknown whether Liverpudlians Lennon and McCartney were there. They had played the club with the Quarrymen and again with Johnny and the Moondogs, and the Beatles would appear there in 1962 and 1965. However, it is known that George Harrison was in the house that night. A few months later, in October, he would sing during one of the Beatles' first live performances on the BBC "So How Come (No One Loves Me)," proof that the Beatles' working knowledge of the Everly Brothers extended all the way to the innards of their albums. George did Phil's high part and John did Don's lower one. But it seems that the Fab Four would not personally meet the brothers until a later trip to England, apparently their only encounter. When the tour finally ended, every show had drawn an overflow crowd. There were the same constructed mob scenes at hotels and outside the halls. And until Eddie Cochran died, they were on a high, not only because some of the Brit acts and rock hangers-on passed them weed, but because a whole new window of opportunity had opened wide. It was still early on the British rock clock, and the Everlys were far more popular than any UK act. And given the VIP treatment they were given, they would have certainly agreed with fellow Nashville singer Roger Miller's description of the island country a few years later, that England swings like a pendulum do.

Making the scene at the rock clubs in their new Fleet Street suits, the Brits' odd fascination with the Everlys found context. Philip Norman, the music writer of the *Sunday Times*, would note that "Their slightly feminine Southern charm [had] a strong effect on the Yorkshire manner, which as a rule is dour and defiantly familiar." Whatever that was supposed to mean, it seemed the Everlys had dazzled the usually restrained Brits. As a result,

"Cathy's Clown" went crazy on the chart in the UK, hitting number one and staying for seven weeks, a future Beatles-like feat, and then went to number three Down Under when they capped the tour in Australia. That tour, a five-day affair again promoted by Lee Gordon, commenced on May 10, the backup acts being Americans Bobby Rydell, Motown's Marv Johnson, the Champs, rockabilly singer Billy "Crash" Craddock, and "the Australian Elvis" Lonnie Lee.

But despite another series of sellouts, unlike their budding second life in England, this would be their last journey to Australia until their 1989 reunion tour—not only for them but most worldwide stars, as Gordon met an unkind end, his drug habit and impending bankruptcy undoing him. Facing drug and back tax charges, he soon fled Australia and in November 1963 was found dead in a London hotel, a rock casualty few noticed but which took the fuel out of the Australian touring scene. Still, for the Everly Brothers, the roaring crowds in England were a real high, and another crowning point of the new frontier they had stepped into. Yet even as million-dollar supernovas, the rigors of it all were already compromising their relationship and their lives.

CHAPTER NINE

Doctor Feelgood

The brothers' change of direction in midstream had become a running story in the trade papers that was hard to decipher. For example, the May 30, 1960, issue of *Billboard* had this seeming non sequitur: "Although no longer affiliated with Cadence, they are in the Billboard Spotlight with a single just released by Cadence, 'When Will I Be Loved.'" On the page reviewing new albums, the mag had Warner's *It's Everly Time* ("a lot of good new stuff here") right on top of Archie Bleyer's first rerelease album *The Fabulous Style of the Everly Brothers* ("A fine collection [that] should generate plenty of action from the fans"). Essentially, the Everlys were competing against themselves, but profiting from whichever records were bought. In concerts, they would be singing songs on two labels at the same time.

To their fans, this meant not a whit, and many didn't follow or care about the intra-industry shuffling. No one believed that too much from them wasn't a good thing. "When Will I Be Loved" took off, tracing almost the same path of "Cathy's Clown," which had hit the top of the pop charts the week of May 23, displacing Elvis's "Stuck on You," and number two on the R&B chart behind Jackie Wilson's "Doggin' Around," and pushed "When Will I Be Loved" to number eight on the pop chart the week of July 18. "Cathy's Clown" also won them their fifth Gold record, and the B-side "Always It's You" broke off on its own run, hitting number fifty-six and climbing to number one in England. Following the same trend, the *It's Everly Time* album—which rolled out with a fashionable cover shot by rock photographer Tom Palumbo of Don and Phil in button-down business suits, Don playfully tugging at his tie—would sprint to number nine and number two in England.

That sparked demand for the rehash that was *The Fabulous Style of the Everly Brothers*—amusingly, the brothers on that cover clad in morning coats, or perhaps as Bleyer saw it, *mourning* coats—which rose to number twenty-three. However, after ten songs that had gone top ten on the country chart, "Cathy's Clown" missed it altogether, as had "Let It Be Me" and "When Will I Be Loved," a somewhat baffling sign that their market had outgrown the country nest, giving them less reason to cater to it—not that the country pipeline wasn't a helpful reminder to their first wave of fans who kept buying the Everly Brothers compilations, two more of which would arise in 1962 with *The Golden Hits of the Everly Brothers* and in 1963 with *15 Everly Hits*. Also, Wesley Rose kept going to the Bryants' spigot for country rock songs.

However, in light of the new trend, Don and Phil were starting to look elsewhere, which was a risk, as Wesley was still dead serious about keeping them on the Acuff-Rose feeder. When a new song written by Boudleaux Bryant, "Let's Think about Living," was given to them, they handed it off to Texan rockabilly singer Bob Luman, who had also been signed by Warner Bros. and had a top-ten pop and country hit with it early in 1961. The song, summoning people to stop thinking the worst things about living (perhaps a subtle reference by Boudleaux to Don Everly), dropped in some famous song lyrics including "Cathy's Clown has Don and Phil . . . where they feel like-a they could die," a neat little confluence of "Bye Bye Love," "Heartbreak Hotel," and "Be-Bop-a-Lula." And, in retrospect, the three years that The Everly Brothers had come since "Bye Bye Love" seemed like a full generation, so far that 1957 seemed like ten years ago. In many ways it was.

○ ○

While "Nashville Blues" may have sounded like they were planting a flag on their home turf, after signing with Warner Bros. the Everlys decided to go Hollywood after all. Moving to the fast lanes of the Southern California dream factory under the palms, in fact, had been on Don's mind. And Phil, who needed more open space to do his drag racing, needed no convincing. Still living with Ike and Margaret on Forest Acres Drive, across the road from his brother, he had been waiting for Don to make the decision, filling Don's head with images of beaches and the Sunset Boulevard music clubs, and even acting in bad movies like Elvis—or at least like their cousin James Best, who had become a character actor in movies and on TV, playing good ol' boys on sitcoms like *The Andy Griffith Show, in training for his apogee as* the dimwitted Sheriff Roscoe P. Coltrane on *The Dukes of Hazzard.*

What's more, Don was being pressured by Warner Bros. Records to go to where the action is. Indeed, the whole "Cathy's Clown" interlude was like the call of the wind and the wild. It had sold big, and would keep on selling, its sales level rising to around eight million, and decades later it was selected by the Library of Congress' National Registry of historic songs. For Warner, it was a gamble that paid off, likely saving the label from going under. Ask anyone at the company today why a wobbly label became an enormous, multi-imprint, international cartel and they will ineluctably mention the words "Cathy's Clown."

The future certainly seemed to be tangible in L.A. And the move was not impeded by any family loyalties, as both Don and Phil had very little to do with Ike and Margaret anymore as their world broadened. Moreover, neither did Don feel any particular need to stay at home with Mary Sue and Venetia or take them with him into the new frontier, where the older Venetia would be available for updated play dates. In fact, Venetia Stevenson was ready for him, having ended brief flings with Elvis and the veteran actor Audie Murphy, with whom she acted in a low-grade 1960 movie *Seven Ways from Sundown.* Naturally, he couldn't simply walk out on his family, neglected as they were. Instead, he shot the bull, one of his best gifts, telling Mary Sue he was going to L.A. to feel out the vibes and make sure it was right for the family to relocate there. He also gave credence to the scenario some hoped for, that he would live out his Hollywood fantasies, grow cynical of a place where dreams went to die, and come back home to find peace of mind. All of it was bullshit, and the tip-off was when he told Mary Sue why she shouldn't come with him.

"You're just not Hollywood, babe," he said.

The implication, of course, was that he *was* Hollywood, which few had believed, unlike Phil, whose laid-back, free-bird life bugged his older brother to no end. In truth, Don needn't have played the Hollywood card with her. Mary Sue had no desire to relocate three thousand miles away from her parents. She also had no illusions about the future. And what Don didn't know was that Mary Sue was about ready to pull the plug on the marriage, having had it up to here with his temper and cheating. Wanting to free herself and their daughter from the sham and the constant reminder of him with Ike and Margaret, she stepped away and began discussing terms for a divorce with a lawyer. Don would have preferred to stay married for propriety's sake and to avoid negative publicity, but he would not be able to escape this sort of wreckage of his personal life, though in La-La-Land, such wreckage was almost normal. And, once on the coast, he and Phil were like kids in a chocolate factory. They moved into airy flats in the same North Hollywood neighborhood, and while Phil bought more cars, Don wasted little time before blowing $80,000 on a yacht that he kept in the party-hearty slips of Marina del Rey, on which he began sailing with Venetia Stevenson as his first mate.

Warner Bros. Records, looking for a follow-up to "Cathy's Clown," sent "So Sad (To Watch Good Love Go Bad)" out onto the playing field, backed with the impish Little Richard cover "Lucille." The record went on a twelve-week run on the pop chart, "So Sad" going to number seven pop, number sixteen R&B, and number four in England. It also took them back briefly into country territory, at least in the trade paper *Cashbox*, in which it hit number thirty-one on the Top 50 country list; and as an aftertaste, "Lucille" went to number twenty-one on the pop chart. Don and Phil were living high, for sure. They were already taking acting classes paid for by the Warner overlords, living with other would-be and never-to-be stars at the Hollywood Hawaiian Hotel, a surreal Shangri-La that Warren Zevon would write about in "Desperados Under the Eaves."

Keeping up with the continuing Everly Brothers demand, Archie Bleyer released as singles two more of their vaulted songs, "Like Strangers"/"Brand New Heartache," which also leaped up the charts, to number twenty-two on the pop list. And another surefire hit fell into the brothers' laps early that fall of 1960. Ex-Cricket Sonny Curtis, who was drafted into the Army and taking basic training in Southern California, was on a three-day pass and walking through Hollywood when he ran into Don. Sonny told him he had written a new song called "Walk Right Back," which Jerry Allison said seemed ideal for the Everly Brothers. Sonny sang it right there for Don. As Curtis recalled, "I had only one verse written—and Don called Phil down, and they worked out a gorgeous harmony part. They said, 'If you write another verse. we'll record it.' I went back to base, and wrote a second verse, and put it in the mail to them, and next morning, I got a letter from Jerry telling me that the Everlys had already recorded the song before they got my letter—they had simply recorded the first verse twice! And that's the version that was released."

The song, a plea to a lost lover to "walk right back," clearly not something Don was prone to doing in his life, sent them back to Nashville and Studio B on September 17. The usual crew was waiting, with Wesley Rose producing and Chet Atkins's session cats to drive home the brothers' smooth harmony at a relaxed mid-tempo pace, with Don crooning poetically, "Think of the love that burns within my heart for you." It was Buddy Holly-esque in theme and delivery, especially the pullback line about being "so lonesome every day"—and Don and Phil would insist that the disk would read: "Arrangement by the Everly Brothers." Warner waited to release it while squeezing the last drop out of both "Cathy's Clown" and *A Date with the Everly Brothers*, which zoomed to number nine on the album chart and number three in England.

However, during this interim, the A-side of the intended record would be subject to flips and flops. Because the Curtis song was published by a non-Acuff-Rose company, Wesley preferred to go with a song originally recorded as the B-side, "Ebony Eyes," by Nashville writer John D. Loudermilk, a maudlin tale of a plane crash that killed the brown-eyed girl coming in to marry a soldier boy on his weekend pass, and as such, one of many entries in the "teenage death song" sub-idiom unleashed by the 1959 "Teen Angel" by Mark Dinning (and carried on by Pat Boone in his 1961 hit "Moody River," thinly copying the melody of "(Till) I Kissed You"). It was recorded on November 1 in Studio B and released as the A-side. But the single, released in early 1961, ran into the same moronic static "Wake Up Little Susie" had, deemed by some as too adult for the market, leading a few radio stations to flip the record and instead play "Walk Right Back," which made number seven on the pop chart in early April, while "Ebony Eyes," weathering its early doubts, soon after rang in at number eight pop and number one in England, despite the BBC also banning it. The nonsensical sideshow only helped push the sales of another two-sided Everly Brothers hit. And yet, this kerfuffle was pale beside the one that cropped up when the brothers turned next to the follow-up record.

Their choice was another song recorded at the November 1 session, "Temptation," the old evergreen cowritten by Nacio Herb Brown and Arthur Freed in 1933 and sung by Bing Crosby in the movie *Going Hollywood* and much covered by the likes of Artie Shaw's orchestra, Perry Como, Mario Lanza, and Billy Eckstine, and there was a country parody by Red Ingle. The Everlys' idea was to turn the old favorite into a rock and roll standard, in the manner of other fossils being refashioned as fogey rock—witness the doo-wop versions of Rodgers and Hart's "Blue Moon" (which even Elvis covered), Warren and Dubin's "I Only Have Eyes for You," and Ted Weems's "Heartache." It began not with a sweet guitar intro but an almost "Wipeout" drum roll kicking into the Everlys' chant of "Yeah, yeah, yeah-ah" and followed by "You came, I was alone / I should have known you were temptation." Swathed by Atkins's pungent licks, Buddy Harman's piston-like two-one backbeat, and female backing singers wailing their lungs out, the brothers went so high on the scale that they sounded like Frankie Valli.

They were so juiced by it that they unilaterally slotted it as the follow-up to "Walk Right Back." But that intention set in motion a joust with Wesley, who had grudgingly accepted "Walk Right Back" as an A-side but despite producing it had doubts about its viability, and no desire to have a song with a publishing history of its own take the place of a good Acuff-Rose song. The Everlys would get their way, but down the road it would create a power struggle that they could not possibly win.

Don Everly lived high all right. He went out and spent like a drunken rock star, partying on the yacht, hanging out with fellow wealthy young men—one being Phil Everly, who had his own big boat, an eighteen-foot cabin cruiser—and a klatch of ass-kissers. But the impending divorce from Mary Sue, which he knew would drain away much of his money, worried him. The acting thing had gone bust, both brothers admitting in interviews that either of them had the necessary skills to pull off any roles on screen, Phil saying it was hard enough for them to act like Everly Brothers, and that the only roles offered them were for inane rock and roll movies playing themselves. Moreover, for all the success of "Cathy's Clown" and "Walk Right Back"/"Ebony Eyes," half of Don's royalties were going to be on the chopping block.

Archie Bleyer still spoke periodically with Phil, whose relationship with Jackie Ertel had become a long-distance engagement, and during those conversations Phil expressed worry that his brother was coming apart at the seams. And Archie had a solution. Its name was Norman Jacobson. Though not known in the public eye, the then-sixty-year-old German-born physician was a Madison Avenue crutch for well-heeled actors like Marilyn Monroe, Lauren Bacall, Humphrey Bogart, Judy Garland, Ingrid Bergman, producer David O. Selznick, playwright Billy Wilder, and author Truman Capote—who knew Jacobson as "Dr. Feelgood" or "Miracle Max" for his quick-draw prescription pad. What they came for was a concoction that they euphemistically called "vitamin cocktails"—some vitamins, painkillers, and human placenta as the delivery system for the amphetamine Ritalin, a drug that could get you so high you'd believe you could conquer all ills, with the downside that it made you a prisoner of it. Any pain, any injury real or imagined, would magically vanish, but return with vengeance. As Capote once said, "You feel like Superman. You're flying. Ideas come at the speed of light. You go 72 hours straight without so much as a coffee break. Then you crash."

The side effects would be things like mood swings, hyperactivity, hallucinations, loss of appetite, nightmares, thoughts of suicide, and impaired judgment. The transitory trade-off was good enough, even for President John Kennedy, whose war-related back injuries were so debilitating and damaging to his youthful image that he secretly visited Jacobson's office for injections before the debates with Richard Nixon. JFK took Jacobson on diplomatic trips and had him visit the White House numerous times, saying privately that despite a stinging FDA report on those "vitamin cocktails," "I don't care if it's horse piss. It works." Nor did Jackie care; if the Netflix series *The Crown* can be believed, she caused a flap during a state dinner in England by insulting the Queen, later apologizing by saying she and the president had "a drug habit" that made her "off-kilter."

Referred to Jacobson by Bleyer, Don and Phil joined other musical luminaries like Leonard Bernstein, composer Alan Jay Lerner, Thelonious Monk, Maria Callas, Eddie Fisher, Paul Robeson—and Elvis, whose drug dependency included Jacobson's syringes to the butt. Don never got down to the specifics, but in the 1970s he said, "I was introduced to a doctor who said I needed vitamins. . . . He told me to inject myself and handed me a syringe." Apparently, Jacobson refilled the syringe by prescribing his cocktails cross-continent, and whenever the brothers took off on tour, Don would tank up on the stuff. For whatever reason, Phil seemed less into it, perhaps because he wasn't in the "leadership" role Don owned, and was less prone to depression and self-flagellation. Besides, chain smoking was Phil's stress relief.

For Don, it was a growing addiction. "People didn't understand drugs that well then," he said. "They didn't know what they were messing with. It wasn't against the law: I saw a picture of my doctor with the president, you know? . . . Ritalin made you feel energized. You could stay up for days." It was what made Dr. Feelgood a celebrity himself. That same year, when Yankee great Mickey Mantle began to break down late during his avidly followed pursuit of Babe Ruth's home run record, he clandestinely took Ritalin "vitamin" shots from Jacobson—who, hoist on his own petard, would fall hard after one of his patients died from acute amphetamine poisoning. Jacobson himself then became addicted to amphetamines. He lost his license in 1965 and died four years later at seventy-nine. And for four of his prime years, Don Everly came all too close to melting down as well.

○ ○

All he knew was that he was lifted, as the Jackie Wilson song went, higher and higher. There was PR work to be done for the singles and albums. There was constant hopping back and forth between L.A. and Memphis—though they ran into static when the mucks at the Grand Ole Opry told Wesley they were offended that despite numerous invitations, the Everlys had not come "home" to the stage at the Ryman. Feeling no great need to return to what they considered a past life, and never having been willing hostages in the Opry's pompous co-opting of country music, Don had issued a Magna Carta of the Everly Brothers to a British writer in 1960 that went like this: "We're not Grand Ole Opry, we're obviously not Perry Como, we're just pop music. But, you could call us an American skiffle group."

That pungent delineation effectively terminated their reserved place in the Opry's privileged membership roll, and they would take it as a compliment, for helping move the borders of the country genre further outward in the coming years. (As an aside, one had to be pretty damn good to be unimpressed by this banishment—some others who were outcast being Hank Williams, Johnny Cash, and Jerry Lee Lewis). Phil was more like a retainer in these judgments, not as interested in making grand statements of intent like his intellectual, more driven brother. That underlying need by Don applied to other facets of the act's success, especially the obsession of working their way out of the static cling of Acuff-Rose and Wesley Rose. Those contractual ligatures were seemingly inviolate and perpetual, but he was willing to take a stand against Wesley's role as manager with veto power, which to a big thinker like Don felt like indentured servitude; the income flow was nice, but it was a headlock around their necks. While Elvis obeyed the Colonel like a cocker spaniel, Don foresaw a future that rested on his vision, not those of mercenary men. Sitting within the power pocket of the re-charged Warner Bros. Records, he made the first salvo to dent the system, with "Temptation."

Justifying his faith in the old bauble, he would say, with tartness, "I woke up one morning and I'd dreamed [the arrangement for it]. That's when the shit hit the fan with Wesley. He hated 'Temptation'; I loved it. If he'd owned the publishing, he'd have loved it too." Further underlining the absolutism the brothers figured they had earned, literally, they also slated as the B-side of "Temptation" a cover of Mel Tillis's "Stick with Me Baby" from *A Date with the Everly Brothers*, a song published by Cedarwood Music, meaning A-R was shut out of both sides. If they had walked up to Rose and kicked him in the groin, it wouldn't have hurt him any worse. When Rose tried pulling rank with threats about legal action to enforce the contract, the brothers went full blast. They fired him as their manager. In turn, Rose, who would still publish their songs and still have a contractual hold on their royalties, fired *them* as managerial clients, an empty gesture that seemed childish.

The Warner upper crust had mixed feelings about all this mishigas. They too believed the Everlys had earned their way to greater control. But crossing Acuff-Rose might have derogatory consequences in terms of endangering the Nashville songwriting pipeline. Still, Jim Conklin went ahead on the record, going all in on marketing "Temptation." Indeed, as the disk was released in mid-May, Warner Bros. bought a very novel or very weird full-page ad in the May 22 *Billboard* with an offer to the public to invest in "stock" in the Everly Brothers. As if from a prospectus, there were no images of the brothers or records, only the famed "WB" corporate logo and the wishful creed "the first name in sound" beneath a text block that read:

New Issue: 2,000,000 Records
THE EVERLY BROTHERS
"TEMPTATION" [and] "STICK WITH ME" [catalog number]
#5220
ISSUED OVER THE COUNTER: Immediate Dividends.

The Warner honchos also took up Don on his newly conceived plan to test Rose's level of resistance by creating an Everly Brothers designer sub-label under the Warner corporate brand. Called Calliope Records, it had Warner's backing and distribution channels behind projected songs produced but not written or recorded by the brothers—although the real aim was to fool Rose by the brothers assuming pseudo identities that could deliver their songs to the market, which would be published by their newly established publishing company, Rooke Music. But as a door opener, the first product that came through Calliope, also in mid-May, was a very minor-league, and thus totally unnoticed 45 with public domain instrumentals on each side, Sir Edward Elgar's 1904 march "The Graduation Song, Pomp and Circumstance" and an old rag that Ike had them learn decades ago, "Black Mountain Stomp," both under the artist's name of Adrian Kimberly, with the credit on "Pomp" being "Elgar—Adapted by Adrian Kimberly" and, on "Stomp," "Adapted by Ike Everly."

In reality, there was no Adrian Kimberly. Both songs were in truth produced by Donald Everly at Warner's studio, located with all the fanfare of a broom closet on its movie and TV show production lot in Burbank, a floor above the machine shop. Studio B it wasn't, but it sufficed, and L.A. had its share of top session musicians, many of whom would within a year be the most

A decade before "Bye Bye Love," Don and Phil were being groomed for stardom by their father, Ike Everly, and their mother, Margaret, who put their sons—billed as Little Don (right) and Baby Boy Phil (left)—into a country singing family act. Ike had no idea his boys would far surpass his own career. (Author's collection)

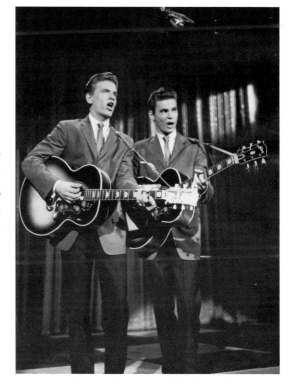

Don and Phil as the world first saw them: wiry, clean-cut, All-American kids with the best hair in showbiz, finger-plucking their guitars and singing perfect harmonies. At least the last part never changed. (Photofest)

Courted far and wide by the biggest rock-and-roll promoters, Phil and Don headlined the imperious disc jockey Alan Freed's rollicking and raucous Christmas holiday extravaganza at New York's Paramount Theater in the late 1950s. Here, they take in Freed's advice before going onstage. (Photofest)

Listening intently as a natty Buddy Holly dispenses wisdom in a New York hotel room between Freed shows, Don and Phil, having become tight with Buddy, would imitate the untamed Texan's wild excesses. When Buddy, who wrote a song for them, died in the famous tragic plane crash in 1959, Phil attended his funeral, but Don was so shattered he could hardly get out of bed. (Pictorial Press Ltd/Alamy Stock Photo)

The Everlys' path to massive stardom was greased by Chet Atkins, the guitar king of country music, who brought them to Nashville and landed them their first major record deal, with Cadence Records, in 1957. Atkins would play on nearly every song they recorded in the studio he built, Studio B, in Nashville, and they returned there to record with him even after moving to Los Angeles in 1960. (Photofest)

This 1958 shot of the Everly Brothers harmonizing as usual on a single microphone in Studio B shows how they dealt with the now fabled room's subpar acoustics. Atkins and his engineers fixed the flaws with such makeshift curatives as blankets hung on the walls to increase bass response and inventive mixing techniques. (Michael Ochs Archives/Stringer/Getty Images)

Don and Phil hang with Cadence Records president Archie Bleyer (right) at a company party at a posh New York restaurant on April 8, 1958, after becoming the first, and still only, act to have number-one hits on the pop, country, and R&B charts. They would dump Cadence in 1960 to sign a then-record $100 million deal with Warner Bros. Records, likely saving the company from folding. (Photo by PoPsie Randolph/Michael Ochs Archives/Getty Images)

After enlisting in the Marines in 1961, the hardest thing they endured during a year of basic training at Camp Pendleton was having their hair shaved off, though Don also struggled to curtail his Ritalin addiction. Often posing for publicity photos, such as this one of them inspecting their rifles, Don would also marry his second wife and the brothers appeared in uniform on The Ed Sullivan Show. (Pictorial Press Ltd/Alamy Stock Photo)

After numerous missteps with women, both Everlys were seemingly happily married when they posed at New York International Airport in 1963 en route to one of their tours of England—a year after Don had tried to kill himself there. Phil's bride—Jackie Ertel, Archie Bleyer's stepdaughter—holds a fur coat, while Don holds his and his wife Venetia Stevenson's daughter, Stacy Ember. Both marriages would have a limited shelf life. (Photofest)

The good vibes they had onstage could evaporate offstage. During their 1963 tour of England, they could barely look at each other while interviewed by the press, with Don patting down his hair and Phil—who was celebrating his birthday—staring forlornly at the floor. Already taking separate flights and staying in separate rooms, their feuding would soon blow the act up. (Trinity Mirror/Mirrorpix/Alamy Stock Photo)

The Everly Brothers' 1967 album Roots brilliantly recalled and broadened their love of the music of their youth and the glory of the land and the air to help form the new soft-pop, country-rock idiom that would dominate the early 1970s. The pity was that this album, while pointing the way for many other musicians, never got the credit (Vinyls/Alamy Stock Photo)

The signs of aging and living in a far different rock culture became obvious by the 1970s when the Everlys tried to look cool, suddenly appearing with long, unkempt hair and mod clothing seemingly from Goodwill. Looking like prisoners of war in this shot, their morose expressions revealed how tired they had become, and how close to breaking up. (Alain Le Garsmeur Everly Brothers/Alamy Stock Photo)

Following their messy breakup on stage in 1973, Don and Phil went their separate ways for the next decade, recording solo albums in the country-rock style they helped pioneer and finding new life partners. In this May 1974 shot, Phil happily posed with his second wife, Patricia Mickey, who was pregnant with his second son, Christopher. Don married his third wife, Karen Prettyman, in 1975. (Photo by Steve Wood/Express/Hulton Archive/Getty Images)

Don and Phil's alienation from their parents eased periodically such as when they played a set with Ike at the 1969 Newport Folk Festival and on their 1970 summer replacement TV series. For Ike, these rare moments were a taste of fame before he died in 1975 at sixty-seven from lung disease caused by having inhaled coal dust working the mines years before. (Michael Ochs Archives/ Stringer/Getty Images)

Fifteen years after their final studio album—though compilations kept popping up regularly—the Everly Brothers guested on Paul Simon and Art Garfunkel's 2003 farewell tour, which included the performance shown here at New Jersey's Continental Arena. Having been the folk duo's idols, they sang duets with them on oldies like "Bye Bye Love," which Simon and Garfunkel had covered on their 1970 album Bridge Over Troubled Water. *They also sang on Simon's historic 1986* Graceland *LP.* (Michael Brito/Alamy Stock Photo)

Don and Phil were among the first class inducted into the Rock and Roll Hall of Fame on January 23, 1986, at New York's Waldorf Astoria Hotel. In this group shot, to their left are fellow inductees Chuck Berry, Ray Charles, and Jerry Lee Lewis, and to their right, guest stars Billy Joel, Neil Young, and Keith Richards, who yuks it up with Don. (Photo by Ebet Roberts/Redferns/Getty Images)

After Phil died on January 3, 2014, Don made few public appearances, such as when he received an award from the Musicians Hall of Fame in 2019. Living a sad final act, he was fighting Phil's estate over control of "Cathy's Clown" and apparently victimized by his fourth wife, Adela Garza, who was arrested numerous times. He died on August 21, 2021, bringing an end to the awesome and manic Everly Brothers saga. (AFF/Alamy Stock Photo)

utilized cadre in recording, enshrined as the "Wrecking Crew." Don also got tight with Neal Hefti, a former big band trumpeter, who as a Warner composer would write the theme of the *Batman* series and the *Odd Couple* movie and TV show, and who arranged the Calliope material with a brass section, banging drum rhythms, glockenspiel accents, and a choir of female singers gushing "no more pencils, no more books, no more teachers' dirty looks" on "Pomp" and gibberish like "ba-bum-da-leedle, bum dee da lee" on "Stomp."

It was harmless, and even had some real rock riffs. *Billboard* ran a puff item about the unveiling of "the Everly Brothers' Calliope label and the release of "Adrian Kimberly's" record designed to take advantage of the school graduation season." The mag also reported that the brothers would only be involved "in an artist-and-repertoire capacity by introducing some of their own recording concepts as well as bringing new talent to the fore," stating that their "exclusive WB recording contract does not permit them to appear on their own label." But it was indeed fooled by Don's ploy of writing under a pseudonym. And if Jim Conklin and the other suits were aware of the con, they went along with it. Even so, despite Conklin's optimism that the "Kimberly" record would be "a top seller" due to its "novel approach," it remained a mystery few cared to figure out, though it sold enough to make it to number thirty-four on the pop chart. In England, though, it was banned by the BBC as too political, at the request of Sir Edward's estate, as the song, under its original name "Land of Hope and Glory," was being proposed as a replacement for "God Save the King" as the country's national anthem, to Elgar's dismay.

For Don, the shot across Rose's bow failed. Rose was not conned, and he warned Warner Bros. he would fully enforce the exclusivity clause on all Everly Brothers records, including those under a pseudonym. The "Kimberly" records didn't cost Acuff-Rose much, but "Temptation" might. Defying Rose, the record was released in May 1961 backed with "Stick with Me Baby," and lagged in America, going to number twenty-seven on the pop chart ("Stick" having its own run, to number forty-one), though in England it hit the top of the chart. Rose couldn't do anything about it being released, but he could strike a vindictive note. An Acuff-Rose lawyer sent them an angry letter informing them that the Everly Brothers would be prohibited from recording and/or releasing the work of all Acuff-Rose songwriters, and—this was the kicker—that included *their own songs*, past, present, and future, written by either or both Everly brothers. In the parlance of the trade, Rose had kicked nuts. And just in case they didn't get the message, he had another warning about a song he knew the brothers wanted to release as a single, the Boudleaux Bryant "Love Hurts," although, like "Temptation," it had been produced by Rose and already released as a track on *A Date with the Everly Brothers*. Then came word that Acuff-Rose had filed suit against the Everly Brothers for breach of contract.

As Don remembered, "Wesley took 'Love Hurts' that we'd recorded and had in the can, and he covered us with Roy Orbison [whom Rose was also managing]. The arrangement was ours, and it was written for us. We couldn't release it as a single because we didn't know if Acuff-Rose would license it or not because we were in a lawsuit with them. It got that bitter."

Just whom Rose believed he was hurting by these interdictions is hard to see. Orbison only used "Love Hurts" as the B-side of his number-one classic "Running Scared" that year, which of course meant Acuff-Rose profited. But if it had been issued as an Everly Brothers single, it might well have cleared much more. But this was how big shots like Wesley Rose played the game: to win, at all costs. Yet, as it would turn out, both sides came out losers.

○ ○

In mid-1961, not only was Wesley Rose closing in on Don but so were the consequences of his philandering. The idea that he would someday move back to Nashville and be a good house-husband and father came to an end in April when word of the troubled marriage broke in a story in the *Nashville Banner* by Red O'Donnell, who asked, "What gives with Don & Mary Sue Everly?" Then, on May 22, the L.A. court writer for Associated Press reported what would be picked up in papers across the country for days—that Mary Sue Everly had filed damaging divorce papers with the L.A. Superior Court. She accused the "rock 'n' roller" of abandonment and "cruelty, "alleging he had "choked her and kicked her in the stomach on one occasion," a stinging claim most newspaper dispatches omitted. To be sure, she had every reason to be terrified of him. Both Everlys were gun collectors, who packed heat for their protection and kept guns around their homes. And Don was now injecting himself regularly with Ritalin, which had frightening emotional side effects. Worse, he had no hesitation blaming it all on Mary Sue and whoever came to her aid. One of Don and Phil's friends, Eddie Crandall, a manager of country music singers, was the boyfriend of Hank Williams's widow, Audrey, at the time. Crandall confided to Don that Audrey was in close contact with Mary Sue. Furious at her, Don said a few years later, "Audrey ended up advising my first wife on how to divorce me! What a shrew!"

Mary Sue wasted no time going to court and asking for a monthly payment of $1,750—$1,500 in alimony and $250 in child support for the now two-year-old Venetia. It was well within his means, she said, citing not only his fat Warner Brothers contract but his fully paid-for $800,000 yacht. Don could not reasonably contest it, not with his egregious behavior. Mary Sue also filed on grounds of adultery, alleging he had an ongoing relationship with Venetia Stevenson. Don was only glad that Mary Sue likely hadn't publicly thrown in his drug usage as well. But then Mary Sue was glad *he* didn't know that she had a secret herself, having a relationship with Ernie Tubb's twenty-six-year-old, country-singing son Douglas Glenn, whose country singing brother, Justin, had a recent hit called "Love Is No Excuse," which pretty much summed up both Don and Mary Sue's inability to stay together. Another would be Douglas's own hit, "Skip a Rope."

Don had his lawyer see the divorce through as quickly and painlessly as possible, though the family court judge let him have it between the eyes, ruling that he "was guilty of such cruel and inhuman treatment and conduct towards [Mary Sue], as renders it unsafe and improper for her to further cohabit with him and be under his dominion and control." Under the ruling he was given visitation rights for their daughter with the condition that Venetia Stevenson not be present. In truth, Don was relieved that he could carry on with Stevenson openly now, and he would move fast to pin her down in marriage. Nor did he intend on spending much time with his daughter, whom he almost never saw once Mary Sue then married Douglas Tubb, creating a bizarre labyrinth, Don being romantically involved with a woman who had the same given name as his daughter, while his ex, Mary Sue, became stepsister to Elaine Tubb, Don's erstwhile girlfriend who'd introduced him to Mary Sue.

He was certainly pleased that the child support was more than reasonable for a superstar, and that he would not even need to foot that once Mary Sue remarried. Nor did moving through this crater in his life throw him off track—or ease the pressures he never seemed to handle all that well. The continual touring and travel to and from Nashville for recording was what had gotten him hooked on Ritalin, on which by mid-1961 he was more of a dependent than his daughter was on him. In August, he and Phil were back in Studio B recording another Warner project, an album to be titled *Both Sides of an Evening*. The idea was to let the Everlys define their new selves their way, by having them tuck some old country and old Broadway into their catalog. The four days of recording with Atkins, Chance, and Harman added guitar man Hank Garland, pedal steel guitarist Walter Haynes, percussionist Lou Busch, and pianist Marvin Hughes—a coterie that lacked just one thing that had been constant before these sessions: Wesley Rose was out as producer. While there would be no specific producer's credit on the record, there would again be the telltale recognition: "Arrangement by the Everly Brothers." In light of their feud with Wesley Rose and the mutually ludicrous firings of each other as manager and client, this for all intents and purposes basically made them producers of their own work, at least for now, though it was really Don's expertise that was in play.

Under his direction, he, Phil, and the crew would lay down fourteen songs divided into "Side A: For dancing" and "Side B: For dreaming." On the former side were Tin Pan Alley memories like "My Mammy," "My Gal Sal," "Mention My Name in Sheboygan," "Chlo-e," Merle Travis's "Muskrat," the 1876

British brass-band favorite "Grandfather's Clock," and the traditional "Bully of the Town," which Ike Everly had taught them as children. The B side had had "Hi-Lili, Hi-Lo," "The Wayward Wind," Hoagy Carmichael's "Little Old Lady," Oscar Hammerstein's "When I Grow Too Old to Dream," Jimmy McHugh's "Don't Blame Me," and Nacio Herb Brown's "Love Is Where You Find It."

It was cool and clever, and would find a niche down the road when remastered versions were rereleased. At the time, though, Jim Conklin and his marketing people tried hard to sell this out-of-leftfield EP by making it available for one dollar on a seven-inch disk with samples of each song under the stand-in title *Souvenir Sampler*, which contained a coupon on the back for a full refund of the dollar if the album was bought. But as a follow-up to "Cathy's Clown" it fell into a roadside ditch. As well, when *Sampler* went onto the market in August it conflicted with *It's Everly Time*, which itself was sniped when Archie Bleyer released another oldies compilation, *Rockin' with the Everly Brothers*. Warner also released a mini-album with "Don't Blame Me," "Walk Right Back," and "Lucille."

To be sure, the easy availability of their records was not a big change, as they had averaged a new hit every four months or so for two years. But this time, while the jam-up of albums kept the royalties coming, it took a toll. The so-so tally of "Temptation" in America and the failure of *Both Sides of an Evening*—which also spawned minor hits with "Muskrat" (number eighty-two) and "Don't Blame Me" (number twenty)—weren't deathly but certainly were downers. Now, with no songs from the Nashville trough and in need of a big hit, they had suddenly reached a crossroads.

CHAPTER TEN

Crying in the Rain

Although Wesley Rose had been wise to the name game Don had played with Calliope Records, the Everlys kept the sub-label running in the hope that it could uncover new talent, its alleged original intent. And it would be through this lower-case channel that they found a way to revive themselves. Again, Sonny Curtis was helpful to them. During his time in the post–Buddy Holly Crickets, the group had been supplemented by a songwriter and pianist from Texas, Glen D. Hardin, who had moved to L.A. and played gigs at the Palomino Club, a hangout for relocated country performers and an important venue vital to the rise of West Coast country rock. One could hang at the bar with Johnny Cash, Buck Owens, and Willie Nelson, all of whom Don and Phil grew close with, and Sonny introduced them to Hardin, who later would be in Elvis's backing band in the 1970s (and who arranged "Let It Be Me" when Elvis covered it).

Hardin had a host of songs to sell, one called "Cornbread and Chitlings," a takeoff of The Kingston Trio's 1959 folkie "Raspberries, Strawberries," Hardin making it about the ins and outs of dirt-poor Southern life, cooking, and mountain dew. Phil took a liking to it and went looking for an act to record it on Calliope. In retrospect, the band that did was a can-you-believe-this anomaly, a one-time accretion of what would be three pop music giants, Glen Campbell, Carole King, and Gerry Goffin. Campbell, of course, was perhaps the finest American guitar player ever, even back then a rising part of the L.A. studio session crowd while trying to launch himself as a singer. He also hung at the Palomino and rubbed elbows with Phil, as did King and Goffin, the married songwriters from Brooklyn who were Brill Building staff writers for Aldon Music, run by the famed music publisher/manager Don Kirshner. The couple sometimes came to the coast to play demos of their songs to L.A. producers, one of which, "Take Good Care of My Baby," recorded by Buddy Holly soundalike Bobby Vee, went to number one on the pop chart that summer of 1961.

When Phil heard a song of theirs called "Melodrama," they gave it to him in exchange for allowing Carole to wing it on the Calliope label, a kick for her, since her and Goffin's primo pop writing would keep her quivery soulful voice otherwise silent until her earth-moving *Tapestry* came out in 1971. Phil assembled this trio of Hall of Famers-to-be into a temporary group known as the Keestone Family Singers, with two of the future's most familiar voices joined by Phil's already famous alto. This violated the contractual edict about the brothers not singing on any Calliope record, but it seemed a mere technicality when Phil produced both songs at Warner's studio in late summer, the A-side being "Cornbread and Chitlings," which Phil coated with banjo and fiddle lines and Campbell on lead, doing spoken-word proto-raps (if one wants to be kind) in a Tobacco Road drawl about there being "somethin' in the air down there in Texas."

Most of it was a jumbled hoedown with only Phil's voice identifiable. "Melodrama," which despite its pedigree was just as lighthearted, a novelty damsel-in-distress song similar to the Coasters' "Along Came Jones," about characters from the *Rocky and Bullwinkle* cartoons—Dudley Do-Right saving the damsel from Mean Snidely Whiplash. If heard today, it would make anyone swear it couldn't possibly be Carole King behind it, including Carole King. It also may have caused some copyright issues with the cartoon people—that is, if anyone heard it. Phil didn't need to worry. Virtually no one did.

○ ○

Carole King, though, would have a far greater impact on the Everly Brothers, who desperately needed quality writers given Rose's sanctions and threats—which seemed to have crippled them when Warner Bros. Records could only dip into the *Both Sides of an Evening* album and release the throwbacks "Don't Blame Me" backed with "Muskrat" in early autumn. The returns were meh. "Don't Blame Me" reached number twenty pop and "Muskrat" number eighty, while Archie Bleyer was still cashing in on the "old" Everly Brothers catalog by rereleasing "Bye Bye Love" and "Wake Up Little Susie" on one single and "Let It Be Me" and "('Til) I Kissed You" on another. While Don and Phil earned some more royalties on them, as they did on all the Cadence compilation albums—making Wesley Rose's prohibition on them recording new songs they had written seem aberrant— the contrast between old and new seemed only to favor Archie and worry Warners. But fate was kind to them. When King and Goffin were back in New York, they agreed to a one-off switch of songwriting partners and King, with Howard Greenfield, cowrote "Crying in the Rain" for the Everly Brothers, whose usual tableau of miserability with a country rock twang was delivered by two Jewish songwriters from New York City.

It stood on perfectly equal ground with all those previous Nashville tearjerkers. Upon being sent the demo, Don and Phil knew they would have to record it, and fast, before someone else did, someone big. For songs of this quality, they hightailed back to Nashville and Studio B, to reconnoiter again with Atkins and the crew. And for the B-side, Don also took another shot at conning the excommunicated Wesley Rose (or was it the Everly Brothers who were excommunicated? Opinions differed). Pulling out an older song of his, "I'm Not Angry," he would stick the name "Jimmy Howard" on it as the songwriter, a name no one seemed to know anything about, for a good reason: Like Adrian Kimberly, Jimmy Howard didn't exist, though it was also used on another quickly recorded album designed as a sequel to *Both Sides of an Evening*. This offering of Broadway show tunes and country cut-ins more market-worthily titled *Instant Party!* had as the lead track "Step It Up and Go," a cover of the 1939 song "Bottle It Up and Go" by Delta bluesman Tommy McClennan, whom the Everlys ghosted in order to apply Jimmy Howard's name to it.

That album could have been summed up by one of its songs—the Comden-Green "The Party's Over"—rather than Cole Porter's "True Love." Others included Mort Dixon's "Bye Bye Blackbird," Bob Merrill's "Theme from Carnival," "Oh! My Pa-Pa," Wayne Shanklin's "Jezebel," Johnny Mercer's "Autumn Leaves," and the country-oriented "Ground Hawg," listed as "Adapted by Ike Everly." The LP went out in a nifty gatefold, the cover showing only their faces as the top of exclamation points peeling back to a large photo album with a great portrait of them and a booklet of comic book-style images framing each song. But while it charted only in England and an AllMusic retro-review pronounced it "a low point in their artistic fortunes," Don thought he'd gotten away with the Jimmy Howard con, prompting him to try it again with "I'm Not Angry," the publishing rights to which he assigned to Leeds Music, a major worldwide publisher.

As with the credits for the *Both Sides of an Evening* LP, Don and Phil would prominently put "Arrangement by the Everly Brothers" on both sides of the single. Trying a novel approach on the intro of "Crying in the Rain," they had Chet flick a coiling jangle-pop feel as Harman played quiet, bongo-like drum rolls coated by thick echoes laid on by Bill Porter on the engineer's board. With no choruses, the brothers' vocals on the verses were loud and barbed, their echoes nearly swallowing up the room at bravura levels, Don's solos shaking the walls. Intuitive and convincing as they always were, they seemed as emotionally tied to a set of lyrics as possible, as if squeezing out every last drop from their souls. King and Goffin of course would soon write the ultimate song of love as a battleground, "Will You Still Love Me Tomorrow," but this one also bled pain, in the "heartache," "pain," "misery," and "sorrow" of rejection that could only be hidden by crying in the rain, a fanciful wish to "wear a smile and walk in the sun" again. The amazing thing is that it sounded so *manly* in its bleeding heart. By comparison, "I'm Not Angry" was a more caustic take on rejection, short and flippant, tears replaced by snark inside a thumpy "Peter Gunn"–like beat and more than a little cruel, in the hope that the straying woman's house would be haunted and her car stalled "until you wanna be with me." In light of this wish list, it was almost comical to hear them sing, "I'm not angry, I'm just sad."

However, learning of the "Jimmy Howard" credit on the latter, Rose knew he was being had when the record came out in December. With no more warnings, he turned up the heat on his lawsuit, and with no serious response from the Everlys' lawyers, the court quickly awarded Acuff-Rose exclusive rights to the song and any current and future ones written by either or both Everlys—which codified that Acuff-Rose would pull the same publishing royalties on the single as Kirschner's Aldon Music on the A-side. While Don and Phil would still be splitting those royalties with each publisher, the Rose prohibition on Acuff-Rose writers—including themselves—was still ironclad. (Though the Jimmy Howard credit would not be replaced on the record, or on *Instant Party!*) However, there was nothing that could keep the brothers from slagging Rose publicly. Even years later, Don was trying to explain the chain of events this way: "When we went to Warner, everything was fine. Then we recorded 'Temptation' but Wesely Rose stopped it because he didn't have the publishing . . . so we got into this brouhaha, and he cut us off from all the Acuff-Rose material."

Don, in a personal fit of pique, would relegate "I'm Not Angry"—*ha!*—to the trash bin rather than have it earn a penny for Rose. He all but excised it, never putting it on a compilation album. It was a meaningless gesture, and Rose's now-legally confirmed embargo made the load on their shoulders grow heavier. As did Don's dependence on Ritalin. He was either shooting up or popping those "vitamins" regularly. He seemed euphoric at times, but then the crash came, and he was volatile, moody, standoffish, rambling, and lost so much weight that he seemed skeletal. Phil worried about him. "What we needed was to take a long vacation, to get off the merry-go-round," he said years later. "There were too many people making too much money off us, keeping us going. Things were too confused. We should have taken a long rest. But in those days we couldn't." He also acknowledged that, with so much swirling around them, there were "tensions between Don and I. . . . Well, we're just a family that is like that, I guess. Everything that was happening then contributed to it." But as if by some hidden power, they did get what they needed, a rest, courtesy of the U.S. military.

○ ○

In the pit of cold war tensions, young men like them were required to serve limited stretches in the military. They had registered by law with their draft board, and rather than be subject to the draft, they enlisted in the Marines, though they clearly received special treatment. Their hitches would be served together in the same camp, and would only be for six months for rudimentary basic training. On November 25, they were inducted and sent just a couple hundred miles away to Camp Pendleton in San Diego, the West Coast depot of the Marines' Eighth Battalion through which two hundred thousand Marines passed during World War II and the Korean War. And yet six months under the hot sun in fatigues was a godsend. Not even Elvis had it so good, serving half a world away with the Army in Germany for two years before returning home in March 1960. It was still several years before America became entangled in Vietnam, and they were mainly poster boys in their dress uniforms in newspaper and magazine photos, with a modicum of time spent going through the rigors of loading Howitzers.

But even this light load was beneficial to Don, who had to withdraw from Ritalin. And Phil, relieved of racing his cars and greeting the sunrise after a night cruising the bars on Sunset, also seemed renovated. Both Everlys looked fit and fed, and needed to do nothing in the way of recording as almost concurrently "Crying in the Rain" was released. What's more, not only were they being permitted to use the base as a PR prop, but the commanders even cleared the way for Don to marry Venetia Stevenson in the base chapel on February 13. It was kept small, most of the attendees being other Marines, but received a good bit of media attention. Phil of course was best man, but Don, who was alienated from Ike and Margaret, had no other relatives on the guest list. Venetia, whose parents were there, looked striking as always in a long white gown and lace headdress and Don looked good enough to be a Marine recruiting poster.

The base allowed them a quick honeymoon in San Diego, but they had more plans that involved merely being seen in those uniforms. The Warner PR department had set up another appearance for them on Ed Sullivan's show on February 18. Although Elvis had refused to do any performing until his hitch was over, Don and Phil leaped to be able to fly across the country on Sullivan's dime and be put up again in a posh hotel. On the Sunday night of the show, they were presented by Sullivan, who told the audience, "Here are two United States Marines, the Everly Brothers who have just finished their boot training out on the coast, so let's have a wonderfully warm welcome."

Actually, they still had three months left, and Sullivan's producers may not have even known Don was a newlywed. They entered the stage to the sound of the orchestra playing the Marine theme song, in full uniform, their famously wavy hair shaved into tight buzzcuts. Shaking Sullivan's hand, the impressed host said to Don, "You've put on twenty pounds, right?" "That's right," he said. "Well, you look great," the enthused Sullivan added, then, "Sing a number for Colonel Glenn," meaning John Glenn, the military man turned astronaut whose Friendship 7 orbital flight would blast off two days later. They then sang and strummed "Crying in the Rain" at a slightly faster pitch with a horn and violin accompaniment from the orchestra, again, a really bad idea which stole away the song's simple emotional pull. Sullivan had them back after a commercial to sing "their latest song, 'Jezebel,'" which actually was not their latest song but fodder on *Instant Party!* When it was done, Sullivan was standing just feet from them, to again shake their hands and urge the audience, "Let's have a fine hand for the fabulous Everly Brothers, let's hear it for them." Clearly, they were enjoying the attention, but if Don had gotten married to a dream girl and was physically healthier, he was still at least psychologically addicted to Ritalin, and was no doubt counting the days before he could go back to it as if he were returning to a spurned lover.

○ ○

The Sullivan shot upped the ante on "Crying the Rain," which by the week of March 3 peaked at number six on the pop chart, their first top-ten hit in a year (as well as going to number six in England). It was a crucial restorative for the Everlys—in gratitude for Don Kirshner's obeisance, they sent him a fifty-pound bag of peanuts, his favorite food—but neither a hit record nor six months of clean living went very far for Don. After he and Phil had been honorably discharged on May 24, they were back home in L.A. and Don was back on Ritalin, a habit that would nearly ruin both his and his new wife's lives. There was trouble between them from the start, with Don flying off the handle and going psychotic at times, frightening her and trapping her in a familiar conundrum of abused wives. She clearly cared for him and believed she might be the only chance he had to save himself from self-ruin. But that would require him to quit Ritalin, and whenever it looked like he had, he'd fall right back into hell.

There was an associated problem, too, in that more than a few potentially valuable writers were wary of offending Acuff-Rose by aiding the Everlys. Still, the first ones Don and Phil embraced had their own security blanket, having written extensively for Elvis—a trio of New Yorkers, Bill Giant, Bernie Baum, and Florence Kaye, whose work for Elvis included "(You're the) Devil in Disguise" and the soundtrack of *Roustabout*, *Viva Las Vegas* (though not the title tune), *Kissin' Cousins*, *Spinout*, and *Girls! Girls! Girls!* The song they gave the Everlys was "That's Old Fashioned (That's the Way Love Should Be)." It began with a marching-band intro and thumping trumpet riffs that peeled off into a proud endorsement of, if not virginity, at least waiting for the good stuff while strolling "beneath the silvery moon"— though good for a laugh was Don singing "I'm the kind who loves only one." Of course, they pulled it off, even if they were unlikely spokesmen for turning the clock back to the ethos that actually made "Wake Up Little Susie" controversial.

The record went out in May, backed with a new song recorded in Nashville in April, "How Can I Meet Her," written by more bullet-proof allies Gerry Goffin and another Aldon cohort, Jack Keller, which reversed field with the brothers in their more cynical mode, sneering at "that stuck-up so-and-so" of a girl, but confessing that they had one objective—"How can I meet her?" "Old Fashioned" rose to number nine on the pop chart and, in a sign that they might have a new sanctuary, number four on the Easy Listening (now Adult Contemporary) chart, created by *Billboard* as a safe harbor for comforting, "square" music in the feverish rock age. "Old-Fashioned" was a perfect fit, and its success sparked "How Can I Meet Her" to number seventy-five pop over the summer. The case could be made that they were the "new" Everly Brothers—the Brill Brothers.

Indeed, "Meet Her" even had harmonica frills and hip but safely "nonthreatening" semiotics that would have been ideal for one of the inane beach-blanket-bingo movies that commenced in 1963—and would have surely been helped if Don and Phil took *those* kind of parts and came on screen in Speedos. In any case, they were hanging in quite well as mostly all their 1950s contemporaries withered. *The Golden Hits of the Everly Brothers*, released during their time as Marines came in at a respectable number thirty-five on the album chart, and a second Goffin-Keller tune that came in July, "Don't Ask Me to Be Friends," another possible subliminal message for Wesley, ran up to number forty-eight on the pop list, and number sixteen on the Middle-Road chart, the second name for it after Easy Listening. Beautifully dreamy, with strings added to buoy an emotional journey into love's betrayals, it was also notable as Phil's first vocal solo on the bridge.

Also back in the swing were their tour dates, their first since the 1960 trip to England marred by Eddie Cochran's death, their objective being to revive the global appeal end of their act. A month-long tour was set, promoted by Arthur Howes, and the demand for them had not flagged a bit. With Venetia becoming pregnant in August, Don hoped that taking Venetia with him to her hometown of London would help shore up their marriage. So in early October, after heading to Nashville to record a now-obligatory Christmas album braising holiday standards with country sauce, they were on their way. As they left, though, the world was holding its breath, bracing for what would be weeks of agita as the Cuban Missile Crisis turned perilous. Beyond the obvious peril that lurked, for Don and Phil the tour could end at any given moment, since as first Marine reserves they could be called back into active duty. But then, dealing with Wesley Rose seemed like a battle zone to them as well.

CHAPTER ELEVEN

Cuckoo's Nest

The Everly Brothers arrived in London separately, an augury of the future. Phil arrived first, on October 9. But Don, in another ominous sign, missed two flights before he, the five-months-pregnant Venetia, and the brothers' new agent, Mitch DeWood, a young former production assistant for Ed Sullivan and cousin of Andy Griffith, got in late the next day. While waiting for him, Phil sat for an interview with the British journalist Maureen Cleave of *The Evening Standard*, who in the October 13 paper offered the acute observation that the Everlys "have an Asiatic mold of face" and "look like Puck as sculpted by Epstein" and seemed "rather fragile"—adding that Phil "made me think of Holden Caulfield," notwithstanding that the laid-back Everly was less cornered than his older brother, although he, like Don, could make female reporters—like all females—want to either fall for or mother him.

He could also mix a bit of pseudo existentialism into his normal goofiness. For example, he rapped about collecting expensive paintings by artists whose names he didn't know— one was "Shazman or something," perhaps meaning Cezanne. His favorite painting, he said, was of "a dark sky with a taut tree, and in the tree is a little man with a beard and a cane. It's ghastly. I still kind of like it, though. I have three of his." But then he went on, "I love singing. It's the same excitement as opening Christmas presents when you were a child. [But] if I cease to be a success is my life over? Am I dead? I am not dead. I can dig a ditch." However, his great fear, he said, was that "Maybe I'm getting more adult."

He was prescient in that respect, as the next couple of days would prove. Both Everlys were more than a little rusty from their long absence. They began rehearsals at the Prince of Wales Theatre with a threesome of L.A. musicians hired as backup players on the tour, guitarist Don Peake, bassist Joey Paige, and drummer Charlie Blackwell. Yet the atmosphere was rancid. According to Paige, Don had "mentally broken down" when the band tried to rehearse in L.A., and that was what caused him to miss his flight while getting his head together. Now he was woozy and seeming unaware of where he was and what he was doing. Phil tried to take control, saying, "Let's try 'Crying in the Rain,'" but they got only a few bars into it when Don, according to one news report, "let his Gibson crash to the ground and rushed across to his wife Venetia, weeping" as the musicians "sat in stunned silence."

Phil quickly ended the rehearsal and as everyone went back to their hotels—Don and Phil in separate ones—the tour seemed to hang in the balance. Arthur Howes was quoted as glumly saying, "Everything has been against us" and back at the Warner Bros. compound half a world away, there was a cloud over the Everly Brothers' status, not to mention changes in the company's hierarchy that might not have been as favorable to the act after two years of still stable but declining success. Jim Conklin was pushed out in 1961 and replaced as label president by former Capitol Records boss Mike Maitland, who needed his top act to act like one. Don Everly, as the newspapers reported, had suffered more than a rehearsal panic; in reality, he had, according to reports, "passed out" and subsequently been rushed to London's Charing Cross Hospital, from where he discharged himself after six hours.

The following day, Sunday, he was reportedly taken to another hospital, Middlesex, and as at the first hospital, had his stomach pumped and was rehydrated. As these serious but still sketchy details arose, Venetia, who had come to England as a salve to ease the tumult Don had caused back home, gave a statement to reporters, saying she had watched in the hotel room as Don lay on his bed and "gradually slid into unconsciousness," whereupon she frantically called for the ambulance that took him to Middlesex. But then, after he was released, the two of them fled, taking a limo for Heathrow Airport, leaving Phil high and dry. Mostly, there was only confusion, in that Phil had not been kept apprised of what was going on and had only read about it in the papers. The Everlys' traveling party downplayed the whole thing, with Venetia further clarifying that Don had been waylaid by "food poisoning" and "physical and nervous exhaustion."

However, it took the rabid Brit press only a few hours to reveal some of the truth. The AP's London bureau did some sleuthing and ran a wire story with the headline "Singer Treated for Pill Overdose: Don Everly Stricken in London." It was reported that Don had "a reported overdose of sleeping pills," confirmed by a hospital record reading: "Donald Everly—overdose." Even this, though, was incomplete. Don himself was walled off by Venetia and DeWood and tour security people. In the car, said one report, "Everly rested his head on his wife's shoulder in the rear seat and pulled up his coat collar to hide his face from photographers." At Heathrow, a reporter was able to ask him what had happened. "I can't say," he mumbled. "I don't know."

More walling off came from TWA, its officials, according to another account, having been "told to keep Mr. Everly's departure a close secret, One of them said: 'We have special instructions.' . . . There were no Customs or emigration formalities for the dark-haired singer [and] the reservation department was told that he was ill and might need a wheelchair. All Mr. Everly would say as he leapt up the steps of the jet flight was: 'I wanna go home. I don't feel good.'" Some dispatches actually seemed to make light of it all, one headline reading "Everly (I wanna go home) Brother Flies Out." And Phil, fidgety to begin with when answering questions, didn't really know what to say when he woke up and the reports got to him. Thrown by the rumors that Don had made a suicide attempt at the hotel, Phil couldn't even fully deny it. Hemming and hawing, he said, "I can't understand this. I can't imagine why he'd take sleeping pills. There's no reason." Then, getting on script, he added, "Of course, he's been working awfully hard."

As the mystery deepened, rather than canceling the tour, Howes left it in Phil's hands, contingent on the reaction of the audiences and the effects at the box office. Howe surrounded him with backups like British-Australian country singer Frank Ifield, American blues singer Ketty Lester, and the British chorale the Vernons Girls. But the entire load fell on the brother now on his own. The opening was at Granada East Ham in Newham. The house was filled, and Phil took the stage beside Joey Paige, who would play acoustic guitar and sing Don's parts. With an easy charm, Phil told of Don's absence because of working too hard and that he was doing well back home. He would feel more comfortable each night, later saying, "I don't know what I was thinking on that first night—I was too mixed up. But that second night, at Hull, was one of the most wonderful experiences I've ever had. The audience was really with me and this, more than anything, made me grab hold of myself and determine that I wouldn't pull out of the show."

Howes green-lit the rest of the schedule, and though an appearance scheduled for the brothers on the BBC's *Sunday Night at the London Palladium* was canceled, for many fans the attraction was seeing the Everly brother who remained. Indeed, if there was a positive to that tour, it was that Phil need not feel like he was the number two Everly, and moreover, bolded by the fact that he was saving the act. Meanwhile, the brother who split would go through more hell. After landing at Idlewild Airport, he was described as "ashen-faced" and rather than continue on to L.A., Venetia "rushed him into the public health facilities at the airport. He was heard to ask, 'Where's the ambulance?'" Venetia then had him taken to a hospital in the city, as DeWood repeated to the press that Don had "severe physical and nervous exhaustion," and a PR representative, Connie de Nave, echoed the food poisoning explanation, saying he was "so weak he could not fight it off."

At Manhattan Hospital, though, the story turned darker, though kept under wraps. Exhaustion and food poisoning could not have caused him to do what became clear in time—try to end his life, twice. Knowing the truth, Venetia, no doubt putting her pregnancy under great strain, made the decisions on what should be done. That turned out to be placing him in a psychiatric ward, where he would undergo electroshock therapy to ease his mind, which had been tortured by the effects of Ritalin, more so because Don had likely doubled up on it, guzzling Ritalin in pill form via cross-country prescription by Dr. Jacobson, knowing he couldn't bring the stuff to England under British law. Being given shock treatment, though, was just as much of a public stigma. The process, portrayed in movies as a prehistoric torture for deranged people confined to "cuckoo's nests," would, when Don's treatment became known in the future, lump him for many with Jack Nicholson's R. T. McMurphy, strapped down, electrodes placed around his head, shocked into never-never-land.

However, these crude images were fantastical. Electroshock, which was in time renamed electroconvulsive therapy (ECT), was often conflated with the now-avoided lobotomies, in which the brain's frontal lobes were partially severed, which left some patients dead or institutionalized. Conventional ECT, which declined as antidepressant drugs did the job better, is regarded as safe, and still given at times to children and even pregnant women. Still, treating Don this way was highly debatable, when curing his Ritalin habit might have been the way to go; nonetheless, his attempted suicide put a sharper focus on immediate therapy, the medical opinion at the time being that he was an immediate danger to himself. And so Venetia, who was already scarred by his abuse, signed the papers authorizing ECT treatments, which required up to a dozen "shockings" within a week, carried out in two New York hospitals. He came out of them weak and weary, but seemingly more at peace as he and Venetia flew home to L.A. where he'd be confined to bed rest. Though few beyond the inner circle knew it, half of the Everly Brothers would be incommunicado for several months, when his very life was at stake.

○ ○

Phil, of course, was coping with another crisis as the English tour went on without Don. Every day, the entire world was obsessed as the Missile Crisis deepened and on October 22 John F. Kennedy ordered a blockade of Cuba. In Croydon for the next gig, Phil said, "If Kennedy calls, then we'll have to go—even if it's in the middle of the show tonight!" Some reservists like him and Don had already been told to be at the ready; another, Jerry Allison, who was also on tour in England with the Crickets, was ordered to come home and rejoin his Air Force unit. The tour made it to the end on October 25 at the ABC Theater in Exeter. School kids in America were being instructed on how to duck and cover under their desks, but everyone could finally let out a deep breath eight days later when Khrushchev finally gave in and pulled the Russian nukes.

By then, Phil was back in L.A., checking on the recovering Don and needing to ascertain whether his brother would be able to perform again, and if not, how Phil would elevate himself as a solo act. He had mixed feelings about it, as had Don, who had never wanted to sing with Phil and always had it in his mind to branch off into a solo career but knew how solid and profitable the Everly Brothers were. And so for months they were stuck in stagnation, the only records on the market that fall of 1962 being vinyl memories, Warner's *Golden Hits* package reaching number thirty-five and Archie Bleyer's reissue of *Songs Our Daddy Taught Us* called *Folk Songs of the Everly Brothers*, from which came a re-released single of "I'm Here to Get My Baby Out of Jail," hitting number seventy-six on the pop chart. Cadence would also issue the Everlys' Christmas album of timeworn tunes.

Fortunately for the Everlys and Warner, Don's misadventure in London never did stir up much tar in America, where the story was fairly ignored. Unlike Elvis, who seemingly couldn't belch without it making the front page, the Everlys could escape scrutiny by dint of their clean-cut identity—hell, weren't those boys in the Marines just months ago? When pressed to comment about his still enigmatic lost-weekend pull-out in London, Don would skillfully evade the harsh truths by shrugging it off as a personal blip that was caused by an addiction to Ritalin that he swore he had conquered; the word "suicide" never came up, nor that he had swallowed sleeping pills by the handful in London to accomplish it. There were only ruminations about being "strung out" and having "got so far out there," which actually were pretty brave, such as, "I remember getting to the point where I didn't wanna live [and said] 'Let me out,'" and, "I was so high; it didn't matter whether I went on living or not." Another time, he blamed his distress on the cure—"Shock therapy didn't do me any good. [It] was a pretty primitive treatment at the time" and that it took away so much of his memory and normal brain activity that it "knock[ed] me back for a long time. I thought I'd never write [songs] again" and "I didn't know what I was doing."

By his estimation, it would take three years to get Ritalin out of his system, and at least a year more for his memory to rebuild. But in a larger scope, the Everly Brothers' career had no time for the pain and didn't allow for much downtime. With music changing rapidly, decisions had to be made on new songs to sing, tours scheduled, lives lived. That could only make matters worse.

Phil seemed to believe he couldn't wait for or delay growing up. While Don was dormant, he moved onward. Being engaged to Jackie Ertel didn't seem to be binding for a time as he openly approximated Don's fascination for pert daughters of storied British actors by taking up with Ann Marshall, whose parents were the dashing Herbert Marshall, who costarred in 1940s movies with Bette Davis and Marlene Dietrich, and his second wife, model Lee Russell. Phil and Ann were seen prancing around Hollywood, and one gossip item had them being *very* serious, reporting on May 9, 1962, that "Herbert Marshall's daughter, Ann, is engaged to Phil Everly." However, Ann would later say that Phil had already dumped her by then, on Valentine's Day, no less—her twentieth birthday—upon which he returned to Jackie. On August 21, another gossip item reported that "recording exec Archie Bleyer's daughter, Jackie, and Phil Everly, of the Everly Brothers singing team, are getting hitched."

On January 12, 1963, they did, at an affair hosted by Bleyer in New York at the Episcopalian Church of the Transfiguration, also known as the "Little Church Around the Corner, on Twenty-Ninth Street," which had been referenced in Joyce's *Finnegans Wake* and later came up in Woody Allen's *Hannah and Her Sisters.* Phil's mood was swelled being in the spotlight, alone, glad-handing industry executives and greeting visitors. Don felt good enough to make the cross-country trip to serve as his best man, though he seemed pale and emaciated and had to rely on Venetia, who had to tie the cravat on his tux for him. He then walked the bridesmaid down the aisle, his face blank. Archie, who hadn't seen Don in years, told guests he was worried about him, with reason. What's more, Phil took on the role of making deals, for example, pushing Gibson to go to market with a signature Everly Brothers guitar. But on a personal level, they were becoming strangers. There would be PR photos taken of them with their wives, but otherwise they went their own separate ways, no longer taking joint vacations and riding horses around picturesque country trails. For all practical purposes, the Everly Brothers were something like independent contractors.

The worst part of Don Everly's midlife crisis at age twenty-five was that he was apt to destroy not just himself but everything around him. The Everly Brothers as an act hung by a thread, and so did Don's marriage. During his recovery, he was no easier to live with. The woman who had saved his life twice was in his crosshairs. He blamed Venetia for subjecting him to electroshock. On his own, he began seeing a psychiatrist to reclaim what he felt he had lost, but his slow recovery seemed not to dispel the deepest darkness or the possibility of a relapse into taking Ritalin. That was the living hell he had made for himself.

A historical lens reveals that three of country rock's preeminent performers seemed frightfully in sync. Along with Don, Elvis and Johnny Cash suffered addictions to cocktails of amphetamines, barbiturates, and opiates prescribed by their own Doctor Feelgoods. Mirroring Don's admissions of being the eternal outsider, Elvis once said, "No one knows how lonely I get. And how empty I really feel." And Johnny recalled playing the same loser's game: "Over a period of time you get to realizing that the amphetamines are slowly burning you up. Then you get paranoid; you think everybody is out to get you. You don't trust anybody—even the ones who love you the most." It took him several breakdowns, arrests and decades of rehab to finally kick it, while Elvis of course did die in the loneliest way, alone, at only forty-seven, in his opulent bathroom in Graceland. Whichever path Don went down, he faced a rough haul, as did Venetia, who was always just a tick of the clock from his next blowup, even as she neared her delivery date.

If the birth of their first child, a daughter named Stacy Dawn, on May 5, 1963, seemed like it might create a good diversion, it turned out that he did the same as he had when Mary Sue gave birth to Venetia Ember Everly—he had little to do with the child and grew more distant from her mother. Getting back to the music became a crutch that increased tensions. While they searched for songwriters who could help them achieve another miracle like "Crying in the Rain," they turned back to their custom label, Calliope Records, proving at least that they were still in the business by releasing a couple of arthritic instrumental standards, "God Bless America" and "Greensleeves," using the old pseudonym of Adrian Kimberly as the performer. However, on another release, a new song they had written, "Draggin Dragon," arranged by Neil Hefti and backed with a rendition of the Disney classic "When You Wish upon a Star," they tried recycling "Jimmy Howard" as the writer, but Wesley Rose legally obtained ownership of it. None of the singles rose above obscurity, and Calliope was folded away, never to release another record.

Out of options, the Everly Brothers moved unsteadily ahead, facing a year when the Beatles were gaining a head of steam. Don and Phil, who could fit themselves into any musical genre and still harmonize like nobody's business, finally recorded under their own imprimatur, going back to Memphis for a January 27, 1963, session, covering "(So It Was, So It Is) So It Always Will Be," composed by former CBS orchestra leader Arthur Altman, who had written pop country hits like "All Alone Am I" and "I Will Follow Him," and the much-recorded evergreen "All or Nothing at All." "So It Was" seemed like a perfect harmonic gift, seasoned by a flamenco-style guitar. Don also wanted to use a song he'd written and recorded in June of 1962 but not released, "Nancy's Minuet." But since Rose's rules ruled it off limits, he made a concession to Acuff-Rose. He would use "Minuet" as the A-side, otherwise he'd kill the song altogether. Rose, who was eager to solve the mutually destructive feud, gave in.

"Minuet" was no throwaway, either. It began with dark-hearted electric guitar chords and a heart-beating drum, as if a seductive finger were beckoning one to a shrouded place. The first line was sung in a lower-scale harmony and cleverly referenced the biggest Everly hit of all—"I'm dancing round and round, acting just like a clown." In fact, this theme, that a man will act like "a foolish marionette" for true love, was an adult theme that reflected less teen-idol fare and conformed to a realization that both Everly brothers had come to: they desperately needed love. Don even added some harpsichord-style moodiness. However, when released in February, it created confusion among the DJs, who were unsure the song was rocking enough and whether the brothers had become too dark. Fans must have been of the same mind, as the poor early sales led DJs to flip it over.

That didn't work, either. "So It Was" made it only into the second hundred pop songs, though it did cause some noise in England, going to number twenty-three. Yet that had meaning in itself, and immense irony, signaling that the seat of operations for their resuscitation, even salvation, would be where Don Everly had tried so hard to end his own life.

CHAPTER TWELVE

London Calling

The next single that would test their viability, released in May, had as the A-side "It's Been Nice (Goodnight)," a song they'd recorded in 1961, composed by the lordly songwriting team of Doc Pomus and Mort Shuman and sung by Freddy "Boom Boom" Cannon in a British political satire movie *Just for Fun* in February. Working on the British angle, Phil told the English press that "It's our answer to the critics. We've been accused of doing too many sad songs recently," and proffered it as a bouquet to English fans for their loyalty, which would spark a tour there in the fall, for Don a return to the scene of the crime. The single, with the B-side "I'm Afraid," a hell of a metaphor for them at this stage, also stiffed, hanging around outside the Hot 100 before dying, though it was another ray of hope across the sea where it went to number twenty-six. That they had hit the wall in the States was now a growing context, which a Brit paper took note of in a story headlined "Phil and Don Everly Put Up a Fight," the fight not against each other but their semi-rejection at home. Warner Bros. Records, still selling enough Everly Brothers units to turn a profit on them as a mainly post-country act, saw the only opening for them back in that former zone, and thus their next album took them backward as a way to take them forward.

The album, *The Everly Brothers Sing Great Country Hits*, was recorded in October 1963 at Studio B, with Chet Atkins and company, the twelve cuts mixing their gorgeous harmonies and soft-rocking tinctures into the mainframe of Don Gibson ("Oh, Lonesome Me," "Just One Time," "Sweet Dreams"), Hank Williams ("I'm So Lonesome I Could Cry"), Hank Locklin ("Send Me the Pillow You Dream On"), Frankie Brown ("Born to Lose"), Hal Blair ("Release Me"), Johnny Cash ("I Walk the Line)," Carl Belew ("Lonely Street"—a hit for Andry Williams in 1959 and also recorded by Archie Bleyer's orchestra), and the folkie 1950s country song "Silver Threads and Golden Needles," which when recorded a year before by the Brit folk group the Springfields, fronted by the wondrous Dusty Springfield, became the first single by a British group to reach the top twenty of the American pop chart.

The work did indeed turn a corner for them, hitting the right tone and finding a niche in rock for traditional country tunes in the prism of an otherwise fading country idiom. Their take on "Silver Threads," with Chet unleashing a torrid solo, was one of the building blocks of what would soon become identifiable as country rock, transferable to studios outside of the South. A trip through the album's backwater-blues track list had detours like the cowboy-gait and finger-snapping melody of "Walk the Line" or instilled the feeling of riding the rails the way Hank Williams did about being a "lonesome whippoorwill." And though the album didn't set off any sonic booms, not enough to chart, future record generations would regard *Great Country Hits* as "some of the most beautiful in the Everlys' output, and the arrangements are models of creative simplicity" and "as beloved as anything by the Louvin Brothers or even, say, the Brown's Ferry Four in its sheer beauty and simplicity."

As such, it was a tangible steppingstone, and set a semipermanent fallback position for the brothers and for rock in general within a few years. And making a new album with this sort of depth and vision certainly reinvigorated them, leading them to get out on the hustings again and to choose new songs to record. By summer, they had recorded two that were written by another Brill Building wedded couple, Barry Mann and Cynthia

Weil, "The Girl Sang the Blues" and "Love Her." Neither was spectacular. The first was a slice of jingle-jangle pop about a sexy barfly who "sang a song of love and looked at me" but after being signed to a record deal left him lost in a crowd of "a million guys." The second, a "Let It Be Me"–like ballad, had their soaring vocals lurching higher and higher, the lyric pining for an odd but inescapable woman to whom "I keep on comin' back like a magnet," as blaring strings seemed to scrape the paint off the studio ceiling.

Released together as the A and B sides, the Everlys and Warner Bros. Records hoped for a Christmastime swell for the songs, as prosaic as they were. And Don and Phil leaped back into the old grind. Over the summer of 1963, the brothers played a full schedule of gigs through the Midwest, prefacing the new trip to England, to which was added dates in Paris and Germany. The venues in America were, as always, the sort of county-fair, vanilla-flavored throwbacks such as the Box Elder fair and the rodeo in Logan, Utah. The sights, sounds and definitely the smells were much like they were when the Everly Family used to appear at locales like this with Little Don and Baby Boy Phil in their little cowboy outfits.

If it seemed cruel that this renewed phase of bus rides through Nowheresville had left Venetia Everly to tend to their new child without him, and she used that time to do exactly what Mary Sue Everly had when Don moved out on her to go Hollywood. With the freedom to act on her feelings of being abused, she hired a lawyer and filed for divorce. And again, it got into the papers, perhaps not by accident, with déjà vu embarrassment for Don. A United Press International item reported that Venetia had "asked for reasonable alimony and support for the couple's daughter Stacy Dawn," and follow-up stories stirred in details such as that Venetia, like Mary Sue, alleged that he had "hit and kicked her several times." Another had it that "she was so frightened of him that she had to lock herself in her room and call somebody to get him away from her."

As the divorce proceeded, Venetia moved with Stacy to her showbiz parents' palatial home in L.A. But then, after his profuse remorse, she agreed to move back and drop the divorce. It would never be an ideal coupling, and Don later called it a "miserable marriage," blaming his lack of any real closeness on the daughter of British aristocrats constantly putting *him* down by treating him like a feckless "country boy." But they would hang on for the rest of the decade, having two more children—another daughter, Erin, born in November 1965, and a son, Edan Donald, in August 1968. For Don, it was at the least a blithe projection of stability in a highly unstable world in which things never seemed to get any easier. But it was a fake pose. And things would only get worse.

○ ○

The autumn 1963 tour of England began on September 29 at the New Victoria Cinema in London, a day after they made a quickie stop at the Star-Club in Hamburg, a dingy hovel with broken plumbing and thuggish audiences that had become semi-famous as the proving ground where the Beatles honed themselves into a reputable band, originally as a rag-tag backup act for Little Richard. The gig went well for the Everly Brothers and, as it happened, Richard would be in England days later milking his own post-peak popularity there; on October 5 he would join the Everlys' tour. Arthur Howes had also signed Bo Diddley and a disheveled band of art-school refugees called the Rolling Stones, and this lineup carried through the November 3 finale at the Hammersmith Odeon, with not an empty seat to be had at any of the near daily shows, and on some days two shows a night.

Though Little Richard was, well, Little Richard, hogging his stage time and making the tour seem like it was his, Don and Phil, who of course had done well covering his songs, had no problem with him stealing shows. But by agreement the Everlys were the closing act, even if Richard complained to Howes about it. As they were not content to be left in the dust by a raucous Richard, they put on tremendous shows themselves. They also made room on the stage for a mass jam session, thrilled to harmonize with their hero Bo Diddley. On this motorcade, the Stones were like back-seat passengers, though Mick Jagger could brag about "bowling along to the Ev's dressing room and sort of join[ing] forces, just for kicks. Can you imagine it? One night we were all singing numbers like 'La Bamba,' and going mad with tambourines and maracas at the same time! It really was fantastic. They really are artistes. The first thing that strikes you about them is their professionalism."

This was the sort of adoration that was common no matter where they were, and the sales figures that it came with in England were bullish, another form of addiction for Don and Phil. Warner Bros. Records geared their Everly Brothers franchise virtually to England, where they walked to a different beat. Only months before the Beatles and Stones would break big in the States, the Everly Brothers were already established as something like the American delegates to the culture. Basically owning London, they and their entourage had their own floor of suites at the Mayfair Hotel, shopped for cool clothes not found in American shops, and were regular drop-ins at the in-crowd music hubs around town, treated royally by the hipsters and social butterflies who hung with the crowd. Because Venetia was home with their daughter, Don was on his own to shop around for groupies who didn't know what a "country boy" was but knew who a rich one was.

The significance of the Beatles was put into a sharper lens when, just weeks after the Everlys returned stateside, President Kennedy was murdered by rifle shots fired through the morning air that terrible day in Dallas on November 22. The world stopped in mid-step. Camelot was gone and the business of making music seemed irrelevant, useless. Albums geared for the Christmas season would go unbought, including the Everlys' holiday records. The Mann-Weil singles had no chance to get off the ground, "The Girl Sang the Blues"/"Love Her" didn't get off the ground, though "The Girl Sang the Blues" made it to number twenty-five in Britain. *The Everly Brothers Sing Great Country Hits* lost whatever steam it might have had, not making the chart. Even with the quite extenuating factor of a president's death shrouding leisurely life in America, Phil recalled that "nothing really worked" for them at home, making Don and Phil to construe the closing track of the album, Jerry Allison and

Sonny Curtis's "This Is the Last Song I'm Ever Going to Sing," as a possible prophecy, at least in America.

Of course, it wasn't, not even close. The odd dichotomy was that the Everlys were difficult to definitively judge either as has-beens, a favored oldies act, or one just a step from a new hit. True, their chart-topping days were over—but something about them didn't make it feel that way, explaining why top writers made time to provide them with songs. No other 1950s/early 1960s American act soon to be submerged by the British Invasion could boast the armchair of loyalty that they did, nor the remarkable resilience of their songs in England, where the rock world would be based for the next decade. And they had constructed a country rock province that would help sustain the American record industry and be the basis of the next decade's tastes. Moreover, if it wasn't clear that they were cool, their "Be-Bop-a-Lula" cover in director Jack Smith's cringeworthy, gender-bending, underground-breaking *Flaming Creatures* was proof of that, for better or worse, as was the scene in the 1965 Truman Capote cinema verité about nothing, *Poor Little Rich Girl*, in which their *Best of the Everly Brothers* plays on Edie Sedgwick's victrola.

But, true enough, England would be the pivot point of their career, just as everything changed. When the Beatles, who of course had revered the Everly Brothers, appeared on the same stage they had at the Ed Sullivan Theater on February 9, 1964, seventy-three million people watched. A new rock and roll flame had detonated, with Liverpool-based newcomers in boots and cereal-bowl-shaped hair being the avatars of a reoriented culture and a new world map. It sent American record companies into a panic. And the Everly Brothers could have said, "Told you so."

○ ○

In a sense, what they would do within the American market from now on was somewhat irrelevant, as long as they sold well enough to keep alive the promise of a renaissance. And this seemed almost a strategy as both Warner and Archie Bleyer kept vying with each other to see which could release the next compilation album. Warners even had them rerecord the cream of their Cadence hits in a chirpier, brighter style for the first album of 1964, *The Very Best of the Everly Brothers*. With eight of the twelve tracks owned by Acuff-Rose, Wesley Rose certainly had no objection, and even if the sanction on recording their own new songs remained in effect, it seemed to be the next tentative step toward a rapprochement. While it didn't make the album chart, *Billboard*'s review in August gave it a "Pop Special Merit," and the steady drip-drip of sales over time would make it the Everlys' first and only Gold album in America, and a Silver album in England. Their drought on the singles list at home didn't ease, though, as their next single, another Jimmy Reed cover, "Ain't That Lovin' You, Baby," died at number 133, though its flip, "Hello Amy," was one more hint of a coming detente with Rose, written by Don and published by Acuff-Rose.

As another summer of schlepping through county fairgrounds concluded, Warner went ahead in September on their first album of all-new material since the 1960 *A Date with the Everly Brothers*. Trying to fit them into the now-Beatle-ized music orbit, the title was taken from the track "Gone, Gone, Gone," written by Don and Phil, a clear marker that the detente was now complete; with neither side saying anything about the thaw, it was as if they wanted it to be seen as a natural state of affairs with no hard feelings in the way. The song was the Everlys' answer to the denser, clanging Brit rhythms, with a blues bottom that rode the Bo Diddley chick-a-chick-a beat and was further amped by the crash bam boom of drums, maracas and electric riffs encircling the brothers' more clipped and urgent, Beatle-esque slang about being "really gone, done moved on, 'cause you done me wrong." This Merseybeat checklist was applied to all the new tracks, which included Don's "The Facts of Life" and "The Drop-Out." But the most significant facet was the return of Boudleaux and Felice Bryant, whose "Don't Forget to Cry" was a grim, almost sinister sounding plaint of a love lost on a bumpy ride that felt like "a roller coaster on a carousel," while Boudleaux wrote "Honolulu." Another Acuff-Rose property was the associative "The Ferris Wheel" by Ron and Dewayne Blackwell, who'd composed the soft-rock 1959 hit "Mr. Blue."

And Acuff-Rose's John Loudermilk provided "Torture" and "It's Been a Long Dry Spell"—which would have been a boffo title for the album.

But the debit was that the balance of this Beatle-fashioned album was pieced together from songs recorded but unreleased, dating back to 1960—the Bryants' "Donna Donna" and "Radio & TV," and Boudleaux's "Lonely Island." This may have been due to a lack of enough good new material, but it also served as a means to keep the past Everly vibe in the mix. And the disconnect between old and new would lead to confusion among their fans, and retro-reviewers, a brutal one by AllMusic calling the album "A jumble of tracks from varying sessions that, despite some excellent moments, were indicative of the general directionlessness of the Everlys' career at this point." *Gone, Gone, Gone,* released in December, did not chart. But it still seemed to move the Everlys up, an inch, a notch, and kept them on a mild but tangible roll. Four singles came off the album, two of them putting them back on the Hot 100. "The Ferris Wheel" climbed to number seventy-two pop and number twenty-two in England. "Gone, Gone, Gone" did better, scaling up to number thirty-one, and number nineteen in Canada, number thirty-six in England.

Reviving the mania of the Everly Brothers in America clearly wasn't a simple chore, but it was aided greatly by the Acuff-Rose truce and a lingering affection that TV people had for them that few others could hope for. When *Gone, Gone, Gone* went out on the market, they did their first guest shot in years on a big primetime TV show, the premiere episode on September 16 of ABC's *Shindig!,* the first of the rash of mid-1960s live shows for young audiences, created and hosted by L.A. DJ Jimmy O'Neill and his girlfriend—the very peripatetic Sharon Seeley. Headlining with Sam Cooke and The Righteous Brothers, they emerged singing the old Sister Rosetta Thorpe blues buster "Up above My Head," clapping as they sang along, clad in sporty suits. Later, following Sam Cooke's dazzling version of "Tennessee Waltz," O'Neill, saying it was "one of their too-rare [recent] television appearances," introduced the Everlys, who ran through "You're the One I Love," a song by the Bryants that the Brothers had recorded but not yet released, then dove into "Lucille" as the closing credits ran and the cast jiggled and sang along. The pity was that, with arguably two of the greatest duos in music history, nobody had Don and Phil jam with Bill Medley and Bobby Hatfield.

They would make repeated returns to the show, three more times in 1964, the next one on October 14, sharing the bill with Roy Orbison and singing "Let It Be Me," then on November 18, flashing back to "All I Have to Do Is Dream" and "Bye Bye Love" to keep alive the basic ingredient of their appeal, which had pushed the *Very Best* album to its gold record status, and closed the show with their "Rip It Up" cover. These appearances also sparked their "second life," helping "Gone, Gone, Gone" peak respectably, the closest thing to a "comeback" they'd have on the charts in America. And this is how they would roll from now on, never penetrating the market as far as they wanted but perhaps more than they should have. It seemed like a fair deal, pleasing the rock kingdom that they weren't gone, gone, gone. But it was appropriate indeed that the B-side of "Gone, Gone, Gone" was "Torture," because that would always be their flipside.

In spite of what would be nine stops at *Shindig!* over 1964 and 1965, and two others at a wilder-eyed version of it, *Hollywood a Go Go*, there would be limited upside to the next five Everly Brothers singles—Don and Phil's "You're My Girl" backed by "Don't Let the Whole World Know"; a cover of Buddy Holly's "That'll Be the Day" backed by John Loudermilk's "Give Me a Sweetheart"; the brothers' "The Price of Love" / "It Only Costs a Dime"; their "I'll Never Get Over You" backed by Don and Boudleaux Bryant's "Follow Me"; and the steel-string cover of "Love Is Strange" that they previewed on *Shindig!* These offerings were part of a major change in the Everly Brothers' modus operandi. But, tired of the back-and-forth trips to and from Nashville, they hoped their evolution could unwind in L.A., within the corridors of the new rock crowd. The sessions that yielded those singles and two albums in 1965 were at United

Recording Studio on Sunset Boulevard. They had to sacrifice Chet Atkins but gained remarkable West Coast sidemen that included Glen Campbell, James Burton, and Sonny Curtis on guitar; Larry Knechtel on bass; Leon Russell and Billy Preston on piano; and Jim Gordon on drums.

They were also assigned to Warner Bros. A&R man Dick Glasser, an Ohioan with a wide-angle lens on pop music, having been in a band with Leon Russell, written songs for Dean Martin, the Ventures, the Kingston Trio, and Johnny Cash, and would down the road become director of MGM's country division in Nashville, producing Atkins and Glen Campbell. Glasser would coproduce the next six Everly albums, the first being *Rock'n Soul*. True to its name, it plucked from various vines, including their own, country, smartly proving that all three vines were on the same tree. Sprinkling informal touches into some songs, the feel would be similar to their downhome country albums, but with a wider focus across soul and country. On *Rock'n Soul*, side one consisted of their covers of Buddy Holly's "That'll Be the Day," the old soul of the Falcons' doo-wop hit "So Fine," Chuck Berry's "Maybellene," Martha and the Vandellas' "Dancing in the Street," Wilbert Harrison's "Kansas City," and the Ray Charles's "I Got a Woman."

Side two began with the only non-cover on the album, their rerecorded version of "Love Hurts," followed by Little Richard's "Slippin' and Slidin'," Dale Hawkins's "Susie Q," the Elvis version of "Hound Dog," Ray Charles's "I'm Gonna Move to the Outskirts of Town," and Charlie Daniels's "Lonely Weekend." Again, the work was superb, and the reaction to it palpable in the rock canyons on the coast, if not nationwide, while in Britain, there was the usual fervor. In the May 1, 1964, issue of the *Record Mirror*, critics Norman Joplin and Peter Jones reviewed *Gone, Gone, Gone* and *Rock'n Soul*, headlining the entire review page "2 Wild Albums from the Everlys."

Clearly, their transitional process was keeping them within a power nexus. The country rock they had polished was now a fused ingredient of L.A. rock. Consider the rise of the Byrds, who one critic memorably pointed out, "sounded like a bunch of guys who used to be the Everly Brothers and wanted to be the Beatles." The Everlys' work was aimed to be taken as seriously as The Byrds' electrification of Dylan folk, but never did turn that corner. Their work couldn't get far from the table; even years later, when their albums deserved attention, old cliches were sometimes hard to shake, as is obvious in another sour AllMusic retro-review that dismissed *Rock'n Soul* on grounds that "because of the overfamiliarity of most of the songs, it has to rate as one of the brothers' less interesting efforts, regardless of the high level of execution."

Still, as with almost all Everly Brothers' works, good or bad, it was another small step forward for them and for the idiom they owned, it being notable that the "That'll Be the Day" cover, the only single release from *Rock'n Soul*, struck out in America but hit number thirty in England. That status quo seemed affixed, and this justified a "part two" of panoramic country blues—*Beat & Soul*, which Warner rushed out in August 1965. This one had only one new song, granted it was Don and Phil's "Man with Money," a biting tale of a woman falling not for a man but for his bank account, and her lover being willing to even commit robbery to become a man. This of course was quite a reach for two young men with bulging bank balances. But, with funky twelve-bar blues to play with, it came up coolly, even amorally catchy. The set list merged "Love Is Strange," Robert Higginbotham's "Hi-Heel Sneakers," Ma Rainey's "C.C. Rider," Willie Dixon's "My Babe," Ivory Joe Hunter's "I Almost Lost My Mind," Rufus Thomas's "Walking the Dog," Doc Pomus's "Lonely Avenue," Chuck Willis's "What Am I Living For," Curtis Mayfield's "People Get Ready," and Bobby Troup's double entendre "The Girl Can't Help It," the title song of a movie comedy originally sung by Little Richard.

All in all, the idea was to add some countrified blues sting to their catalog. But a continuing debit was that only "Man with Money" came from the brothers' pens at the same time that the Bryants and other top writers were wearing out their éclat and time frame. "You're My Girl," "That'll Be the Day," and "The Price of Love" had all failed as singles at home, and "Man with Money" was only issued as the B-side of "Love Is Strange," which had a hilarious redo of the proto-rap bridge of the original that went *Hey Don. Yes, Phil. How would you call your baby home?* but made it only to number 128 in America, with "Man with Money" not charting on its own run. *Beat'n Soul* rose only to number 141. Yet, now that they were ensconced within the caste of top West Coast musicians who set the stage for the overarching country rock subdivision of the 1970s, they could ride out tepid sales with the slack to find the right door. As such, they pushed on, living out what seemed to be nine lives.

○ ○

The invitations from the variety and rock dance party shows were still open, and they dutifully made their way on April 13, 1965, to New York for NBC's *Hullabaloo!* The episode was hosted by the lounge singer Steve Lawrence, who after an old shot on screen of the Everly Family way back when said, "We'd like to thank Ike and Margaret for having two such talented sons," then, "Ladies and gentlemen, the exciting sound of the Everly Brothers!" They emerged in tuxes to sing "Lonely Weekend" and later, with Lawrence, "All I Have to Do Is Dream," with a walk-on by Sammy Davis Jr. Then, without taking a breath, they were back on a plane for Britain, where reporters still were obsessed with finding some static between them.

Two years before, a *Daily Mail* reporter had asked Phil if "the rumors" were true that the "act was breaking up." As forcefully as he could, he had said, "There is no dispute between Don and me. We are partners and we are going to stay like that as long as I live." That brief quote ran under the headline "'Everlys Won't Part'—Phil." Now, the *Evening Post* recycled the theme, writing that "Family feuds forgotten, the Everly Brothers are making albums once again." As late as 1970, Phil would be using the same one-liner "We only ever had one argument. It's been lasting for 25 years." It was almost a sign of their relevance that, unlike in the States where few considered this an important issue, the Brits were still harping on it, leaving Phil to riff, "You could just as easily say that the tension between us existed from day one, from birth. And will go on forever." But the guttersnipes were of course on to something. Although he tried mightily to hide his ire over being the "junior partner" of the Everly Brothers, accepting rare lead vocals as if they were breadcrumbs, in his mid-twenties Phil, like Don, had pondered the possibility of going solo rather than continuing taking different planes and generally avoiding each other out of the studio and on tours that could include some hefty paydays in far-out destinations such as Tapanilan Urheilutalo in Helsinki, Finland.

Not that anyone could have sensed this dissonance in public. The 1965 trek through England, lasting through the spring, summer and early fall, was arranged by no less than the Beatles' manager Brian Epstein, with backup acts managed by Epstein such as Billy J. Kramer, Cilla Black, the Marionettes, the Alan Eisdon Band, and Lionel Blair and His Kick Dancers. There was also a trio called Paddy, Klaus, and Gibson, the latter two, bassist Klaus Voorman and drummer Gibson Kemp, having been in early Beatles lineups. Voorman, who would illustrate the Beatles' *Revolver* album and later be in the Plastic Ono Band, was known to be dropping acid with Epstein during idle hours, and had to step in and play with the Everlys when their bass man, Dale Hallcon, had to take a few days off with the flu.

Playing sold-out shows backed by a touring band that also included Sonny Curtis and Jim Gordon, the reviews were almost delirious. After a show at the ABC Cinema in Chesterfield, the October 30 *Derby Evening Telegraph* review was headlined "SHEESH KAPOW! Everlys a Knockout!" The concerts would only be part of the Everlys' be-everywhere, do-everything existence. Interspersed with the shows were TV appearances on *The Eamonn Andrews Show, The Scene, Top of the Pops, The Five O'Clock Club, Ready Steady Go, Thank Your Lucky Stars, Gadzooks! It's All Happening, Ready Steady Go!* again, and *Thank Your Lucky Stars* again. Sometimes it seemed as if they were on perpetual standby at the BBC. And while singing the oldies was mandatory, they received the same audience zeal when they branched off into lesser heard songs like "The Price of Love" and "People Get Ready." And England was transforming *them*. Their Brylcreemed permanent waves were now shagged into cereal-bowl mop-tops, Don letting his bramble into a bush of tight curls, while Phil chose a straight sweep across his forehead.

They didn't need to alter their tight Camelot-era suits, pencil ties, and Tyrolean boots on stage, given that the Beatles had adopted that same sort of sartorial crispness, and the also crisp half-bows they took after each song. But they soon were following the Fab Four into the pastels and groovy patterns of the swinging sixties. On a side trip to Dublin, they posed for the hip Irish magazine *New Spotlight*. One photo taken had them on either side of mini-skirted blonde singer, Eileen Kelley, Don in a red corduroy reefer jacket, blue-and-black horizontal-striped shirt, and blue-checked pants, Phil in a blue, red, and white tartan suit from head to toe, hand clutching a lapel. But that photo never ran with the article about them, surfacing only in the 1990 book *The Swinging Sixties*. However, a more intriguing photo in the magazine was a black-and-white image of a playful fist fight between Don and Phil Everly, under a sarcastic caption reading "Brotherly Love."

CHAPTER THIRTEEN

Chained to a Memory

Almost reluctant to be back home, the Everly Brothers could maneuver about practically unnoticed. Phil was out and about more often than his hermetic brother, who was usually sleeping off a bender or side shot of Ritalin, unshaved, eyes half-closed and bloodshot, more a Skid Row bum than a rock star. Phil, who by contrast had a perennial beach-boy veneer, would pop up at a Sunset club, pick up a microphone and vamp some song or another with the house band, holding a burning cigarette. And he too became a father when on September 9 Jackie gave birth to a son, Jason, while Phil was away completing his still-pending Marine hitch. But Phil's marriage and fatherhood were not much better than Don's. When Lou Adler, the eccentric owner of Dunhill Records who produced the Mamas and the Papas and Johnny Rivers, and later Carole King, married the former *Donna Reed Show* actress Shelley Fabares, Phil was one of Adler's best men in the wedding party that included Annette Funicello, Jan and Dean's Jan Berry, and some high-priced Hollywood agents. Without Don at his left elbow, he seemed genuinely happy, unlike when he had to force a smile in publicity shots with his brother.

Their income depended on those forced smiles and simpatico on stage, and they were there when one of the first rock and roll "cause" concerts happened on June 23, 1965, called the Freedom from Hunger benefit at the Shrine Auditorium, a three-hour fest put together by *Shindig!* producer Jack Good. There, the Everly Brothers were on the top tier with Johnny Cash, the Byrds, Sonny and Cher, Gary Lewis and the Playboys, Jackie DeShannon, the Chambers Brothers, and Willie Nelson. One review regaled them as "without a doubt one of the best American acts, or in the entire world for that matter. . . . The two Everlys have influenced many of the top English groups, and after seeing them perform 'live' it is certainly easy to see why!" Living in the core of the recording and TV arcs, they could hopscotch to and from *Shindig!* and *American Bandstand* at a moment's notice, and jet to New York for the big mainstream shows. On January 28, 1965, they hit ABC's *Jimmy Dean Show*, singing a medley with the garrulous country singer, who also presented them with honorary certificates as Kentucky Colonels. During their snippet of Don Gibson's "Sweet Dreams," when they sang the line "I should hate you the whole night through," Don and Phil gave each other a playful side eye. Dean noticed. "Did you do that on purpose?" he asked. They all laughed, but their contentious partnership was no laughing matter.

To those who were aware of it, the row between them was kept down low. And they were adept at explaining it away with well-practiced lines, which Don especially could boil down into multipurpose aphorisms, able to summarize the entire transition of The Everly Brothers in two sentences: "We went into the Marines. I had some personal problems around about '62, then I woke up and the Beatles were here." It may have been a private joke that their last single of 1965 was called "It's All Over," a highly depressing, heavily echoed song with Phil's soft alto on lead contrasting with the lyrics about a failed love, one passage going: "Didn't even cry / I just stopped living When you said goodbye." More than ever, the titles and lyrics of grim Everly Brothers songs could be interpreted as broader personal confessions.

○ ○

They were too productive and relevant enough to avoid the tenuous time passages that had relegated Little Richard, Chuck Berry, Jerry Lee, and even Elvis, though he had several comebacks left in him. But while the Everlys' lingering past still propelled and profited them, attrition in the business ended the free ride that had kept on enriching Archie Bleyer when he rereleased old Everly Brothers songs. The aging Archie had gotten lucky when impressionist Vaughan Meader's *The First Family* album on Cadence Records parodying the Kennedys in Camelot sold a record 7.5 million albums. But Phil's father-in-law (for now) was forced to liquidate Cadence and sell its skeleton to Andy Williams, who had split from him in 1961 to sign with Columbia and now wanted to gain control of his back catalog. That was something the Everly Brothers *should* have at least tried to do for themselves rather than leaving it in the prehensile hands of Wesley Rose. Still, they were pleased that Andy had no interest in rereleasing their backdated songs, which weren't as sellable anymore and surely didn't help them cultivate a new image.

Nashville, too, was intent on altering its sound, welcoming a new crowd. Bob Dylan, who had covered "Wake Up a Little Susie" in 1962, came to town in mid-decade to record *Blonde on Blonde*, *John Wesley Harding*, and *Nashville Skyline* and massive singles like "Lay Lady Lay" and his duet with Johnny Cash, "Girl from the North Country." As for Rose, after winning the cold war with the Everlys his power was at its peak. As he had with the brothers, Rose advised Roy Orbison to jump to a bigger label when his Monument contract ran out in 1965 and he signed his own $1 million deal with MGM, with Rose as his producer. But as the old-time country set was being subsumed, the new set of romantic, often blitzed country "outlaws" took over, led by Willie Nelson, Johnny Cash, and Waylon Jennings. Meanwhile, country royalty moved upward. Chet Atkins was made vice president of RCA's country division, toured with Black musicians, and signed the first Black country performer, Charley Pride.

Of course, one of Chet's legacies was that the base country rock that he had mastered with the Everlys became a new and profitable idiom based not in Dixie but L.A., catching fire when the Byrds—not one of whom was a Southern man—covered Dylan with a twelve-string Rickenbacker and Everly Brothers-like harmonies. The door opened, Southern boys, Northern boys, and a few Canadians like Neil Young streamed to the coast. By rights, Don and Phil Everly deserved to be at the head of the class, and they never stopped trying, releasing two new albums for three straight years through 1967. These were wildly inconsistent, however, with Don and Phil unable to write more than a couple of tracks per album and thus still needing to rely on outside writers to make bold statements for them.

Their first LP of 1966, *In Our Image*, released in April, seemed to be aiming for a country rock vision of John Lennon's plaintively introspective "In My Life," and included the previous hit single "The Price of Love" and the flip side of another single, "Love Is Strange," Phil and Don's "It Only Costs a Dime," a clever shuffle-beat plea to a woman who never calls, even though "I know you got the time." They also wrote "I'll Never Get Over You," their most overt "British" sounding record besides "Gone, Gone, Gone," though the hectic tempo and arrangement with harmonica preening and thick echoes drowned the vocals, which were after all the heart of any Everly project. Don solely wrote "It's All Over," which had a twist, putting Phil on lead vocal, buttressed by a harpsichord, getting down to the abyss of love—"Didn't even cry / I just stopped living When you said goodbye." Three more Brill Building songs made it onto the disk, Bernie Baum and Bill Giant's "Leave My Girl Alone," Mann and Weil's hip-swiveling "Glitter and Gold," and Keller and Greenfield's "Lovely Kravezit," the theme song of the movie *The Silencers* that they made sound a lot like "Cathy's Clown."

There was also another song from their old ally Sonny Curtis, "I Used to Love You," "(Why Am I) Chained to a Memory" by Broadway show tune writers Eddie Snyder and Richard Ahlert, and country songwriter Marge Barton's "June Is as Cold as December." The curiosity piece in retrospect is a Motownish romp, "(You Got) The Power of Love," by Delaney Bramlett, then a session guitarist and regular player at the Palomino and member of the *Shindig!* house band, whose singing career with his wife Bonnie and Eric Clapton was soon to begin. The track would leap off the record, its bluesy organ and piano runs and rushed cries of "you got the power baby" and "you put me in the groove" sounding now not unlike "hip" 1970s sitcom themes such as on *Maude* or *Good Times.*

It was an admirable effort, well performed and well aimed, its "electric" character ear-worthy for its time, if a bit too loud and, well, needy, even for them. Warner seemed not overly interested in spending much to promote the album, likely because there was no killer hit on it, and was content to count sales of it in England—which turned out to be as paltry as sales in America. The single releases of "It's All Over," "The Dollhouse Is Empty," and "(You Got) The Power of Love" flopped on both sides of the pond (though Cliff Richard's poppier, more bubble-gum cover of "It's All Over" would make it to number nine in Britain two years later). However, England would stay in their purview, even if they never would have another prominent hit there. And it was where one of the great, if not widely known, collaborations would occur.

○ ○

That happened in May, when Don and Phil were touring the island in search of sales for *In Our Image.* Along the way, they were sought out by the Hollies, the harmonious pop rock five-some cofounded by Allan Clarke and Graham Nash that had scored several hits in England, their tight, lush harmonies groomed by Nash's adoration of the Everly Brothers. He had waited outside a music hall to meet them when he was fifteen, recalling in 2017 that even at twenty-one meeting them again nearly knocked him off his feet.

"Who the fuck would've NOT been a fan of the Everly Brothers?" he said. "'Bye, Bye Love' changed my life. So now, six years later, me and Allan ran into them on the steps of the Meridian Hotel in Manchester. Not long after, we were at a sound check before we performed at the London Palladium with Pete Seeger when Phil Everly called the hall. I got on the phone and he asked if we had any songs they could record. We did, and would have written some on the spot if we didn't. And the very next day we were in the studio recording with the Everly Brothers."

Clarke, the feisty lead singer with the thundery alto voice, couldn't make the session at Decca Studio in Westhampton, but the other Hollies did, guitarist Tony Hicks, drummer Bobby Elliott, and bassist Bernie Calvert, who rounded up a few other somewhat notable players—the pre–Elton John Reggie Dwight on keyboard and the pre–Led Zeppelin Jimmy Page and John Paul Jones on guitar and bass, who were ungodly session cats in England, as were others who filled in when needed—Andy White on drums, Arthur Greenslade on keys, and bassist Terry Slater. Being introduced to Don Everly, Jones recalled years later that Don was the "real" guitar player of the two Everlys. "He didn't play lead, though, he just had this special rhythm thing." Added the illustrious Page: "They had a three-hour session and spent two and a half hours on this [one] damn thing and then they pretty much said, 'Alright, that's it, let's do the B-side,' and Don Everly picked up his guitar and just started roaring away with fantastic rhythm and I thought, 'Wow, this is great.'" While he didn't remember what song it was, "I remember really playing like mad on it."

But the Everlys were short on time and could produce only six tracks over three days, half of the intended track list. The other six would be done back home weeks later in L.A. with Dick Glasser and a crew of James Burton, Glen Campbell, Jim Gordon, pianist Don Randi, and guitarist Al Casey. The album, *Two Yanks in England*, would boast eight songs on which Clarke, Nash, and Tony Hicks were credited as writers—"So Lonely," "Signs That Will Never Change," "Like Every Time Before," "I've Been Wrong Before," "Have You Ever Loved Somebody," "Don't Run and Hide," "Fifi the Flea," "Hard Hard Year"— though because of their own industry entanglements they were listed with the collective pseudonym of "L. Ransford," Nash's grandfather's name, as a still cautious Wesley Rose had to find out in order to make sure it wasn't another Don Everly circumvention ploy, detente notwithstanding.

The album was filled out by two songs by Phil and Don, "Kiss Your Man Goodbye" and "The Collector" (cowritten with

Sonny Curtis), one by American producer Mark Barkan "Pretty Flamingo" (a hit at the time for Manfred Mann), and Ska musician Jackie Edwards's "Somebody Help Me," a soon-to-be hit for the Spencer Davis Group. In keeping with the musicians' basic instincts, most of the tunes had a distinct Brit feel, to the point where Don and Phil's vocals were sped up to sound younger and more high-pitched, and staccato guitar riffs, dramatic pauses and tempo shifts plugged in as if on a checklist for each song. Melodic and jangly they were, and technically solid, yet any listener could have heard the songs and wondered: Where the hell are the Everly Brothers?

The Hollies judged their songs good enough for the band to record thereafter on their own, and "Have You Ever Loved Somebody?" was covered by the Searchers, and "Fifi the Flea" by the New Jersey garage band the Sidekicks. But, excruciatingly, none of the songs were judged by Warner to be right as singles, save for the only single to be released from the album, "Somebody Help Me" backed by "Hard Hard Year," which came and went. Only in the Netherlands was a single released, "Fifi the Flea," oddly listed as being performed by "Don Everly Brother," and on the B-side "Like Every Time Before" by "Phil Everly Brother." The album bombed in America and England. Worse, few even knew it had been out there at all, or that these two yanks in England were reversing the dynamic of the British Invasion. Indeed, that question—Where the hell are the Everly Brothers?—was now the subtext of their ever more troubled lives.

Joey Paige, the bass player who was an on-and-off member of their traveling band, remembered the brothers' deteriorating relationship as "strange," given how easily they could gauze over their internal problems when they made history stand still on stage. "Sometimes," he said, "it was good, sometimes it was bad. Other times it was intolerable." Paige would find himself having to mediate their stew of arguments, even picking the outfits to wear on stage and which songs to perform when the brothers even fought about that burning issue. Paige, shading it as best as he could, said there was a "lot of conflict" and a "lot of love" between them, and clarified that Don was the "dominant" brother, keeping Phil strapped into his role as the "little brother."

Those moments of conflict could be blurred by the warmth and applause of the audience of a big TV show. After coming home, on August 1, they made their way in New York to the youth-oriented *Kraft Summer Music Hall* replacement for the vacationing *Andy Williams Show,* which put them in propinquity to the future of the culture, the show's head writer being George Carlin and a guest on that show was Richard Pryor. They were caught in a time capsule, for sure. On that clunky show, which was geared to college audiences, "youth" was represented by the Five King Sisters and two ex-New Christy Minstrels, the brothers seemed almost like uncles but when they did a medley with the show's cast, with Pryor almost embarrassingly intoning the "He's a bird" part of that song, they made the show watchable. On that count, they never missed.

The albums didn't either, not usually, and never for a lack of artistic achievement. Having moved from a dependency on singles to albums, the next, *The Hit Sound of the Everly Brothers,* dropped in March 1967, sending them out on tour again. Graham Nash ran into them by chance when the Hollies and the Everlys were scheduled to play in Toledo, Ohio. The Everlys had the stage the first night, and Phil called Nash and invited him to attend. By then the Hollies had their first two top-ten hits in the United States, "Bus Stop" and "Stop, Stop, Stop," and Nash on that very tour would meet Stephen Stills and David Crosby and soon leave the group and move to L.A. But the memory of that night in Toledo still makes him dizzy. "So I go down to the sound check and Don looks over and says, 'What are you gonna sing with us?' And I'm dying inside. I'm dying. This is my life's dream! But I'm trying to be cool, and I go, 'How about "So Sad." How about that?' Then it's . . .' That key OK?' I have a cassette of me singing 'So Sad' in three-part harmony with the Everly Brothers, who made the music that changed my life."

Hit Sound again showcased how deep the Everlys could reach. Two months of recording started at United in December 1966 with Wrecking Crew guitarists Glen Campbell, Larry

Knechtel, Al Casey, Lou Morrell, and Don Lanier, bassists Ray Pohlman and Chuck Berghoffer, percussionist Gary Coleman, and drummer extraordinaire Hal Blaine, with engineer Eddie Brackett on the board, who won a Grammy that year for Frank Sinatra's "Strangers in the Night." They would hammer together another "concept" album of radically different touchstones from the wells of soul ("Blueberry Hill," "Good Golly Miss Molly," "Sticks and Stones"); the Brill Building (Burt Bacharach and Hal David's "Trains, Boats and Planes," David's "Sea of Heartbreak," and Irwin Levine's "The Devil's Child"); folk-pop (Jimmy Webb's "She Never Smiles Anymore)"; country (Hank Snow's "I'm Moving On" and Don Gibson's "(I'd Be) A Legend in My Time)"; rockabilly (the Buddy Holly breakout "Oh Boy,") blue-collar rock (the Animals' redo of the traditional "The House of the Rising Sun")—and a real challenge, Nick Ashford and Valerie Simpson's "Let's Go Get Stoned," the wittiest call to get high ever, previously recorded by the Coasters and Ray Charles.

Vast as this tableau was, and as well performed, it was all well within their brand, with the gifts of new studio knick-knacks like multitracking—two dozen, compared with the four tracks used for the early Everly recordings—guitar feedback, instrument isolation, and vocals done separately from the in-strumental track. This may have had something to do with their 1960s work being more distant over the radio, and those precious harmonies less up-front and compelling. And Warner again found it devoid of worthy singles with only one track released, "She Never Smiles Anymore" backed with "The Devil's Child," recognizing the immense upside of Jimmy Webb. who had only one song released up until then, and still several months before he struck gold with Glen Campbell's iteration of "By the Time I Get to Phoenix." And "She Never Smiles" figured to be a perfect fit, with gypsy-like violins similar to those in Mary Hopkins's recording of Paul McCartney's "Those Were the Days" tinting a ballad of lost love, the Everlys' high-pitched vocals adding a layer of sweet cream. But Warner switched it to the B-side to put the play on "Devil's Child," as a plea for attention from now-very-open-minded baby boomers. The song surely was an attention getter, possibly the first in a long line of rock songs to define a witchy woman, here luring them into "a whole lotta sin," and vulnerable to being shot in the face and stabbed with steely knives. Open-minded, indeed.

If Warner believed this very against-type angle was the Everly Brothers' means of going "adult" in the *Sgt. Pepper* era, it became more of a gravel path, as it went nowhere. Which was too damn bad. In the long view, this takeout of history remains a remarkable anomaly, one that might figuratively be called "Everlys on Acid." For Don, the way things were going, that might have even been the case.

CHAPTER FOURTEEN

I'm Finding It Rough

Hit Sound was the only Everly Brothers album to be released in the pivotal and divisive year of 1967—when the country had all but split in half, with *Sgt. Pepper's Lonely Hearts Club Band* and the Monterey International Pop Festival in mid-June unveiling the more whimsical than actual "Summer of Love" as America escalated the disastrous jungle war a world away. Every border that rock had obeyed in the past was cast aside, seemingly along with the Everly Brothers, who were now a loss leader rather than industry leader. Yet, to their credit, they hung in, taking swing after swing at the gates. While the oldies circuit padded the pockets of Chuck and Richard and Ricky, Don and Phil avoided those nostalgia exercises, which could make still young men feel old.

Of course, they still played the oldies, with the understanding that the songs had not gotten old at all but were part of the brick and mortar of the culture, prompting Don's nugget of pearly wisdom that great rock should never have to beg to be heard again. But they clearly would have been out of place at Monterey—and God knows, two summers later at Woodstock. They existed in their own unique time warp, looking ahead and back at once. Later that summer, they did a guest shot on *The Mike Douglas Show*, with Douglas surprising them by inviting onto the stage

Ike and Margaret, who had been secretly brought to Philadelphia. Their sons were appropriately startled and hugged them. Ike and his boys then sang "I Saw the Light." For that inlet of time, it was old-home week, notwithstanding that their relationships with their parents had turned cold. It was sweet and sentimental, the very turrets of their success. But these qualities had gotten carried far from their contemporary existence.

Don later put it this way: "Being the Everlys in the '60s was a handicap. We didn't fit between the Holding Company and whoever." This was a sure measure that when it came to the psychedelic anime of rock all around them, they didn't try to pretend to fit, nor did they hold it against the Monterey producers, Lou Adler and John Phillips for not inviting them to be in the same rostrum as Jimi, the Who, the Byrds, Otis Redding, Jefferson Airplane, Janis Joplin, and Moby Grape. Folk rock was duly represented by their more hip and depthful doppelgangers Simon and Garfunkel, and the fire of rock lit by Jimi Hendrix. The pressure was on for even ingrained acts. The Grateful Dead's set at Monterey was a fiasco, with Phil Lesh later admitting the heat they took from the crowd meant they had "blown" their shot at the inner circle. The Everly Brothers had no desire to be a victim of mindless group-think, derided by hipsters who were raised on their music.

Indeed, only a month after the festival that redefined rock, Warner released *The Everly Brothers Sing*, meant to gauge their place in the system. It was a potpourri of modernism while regressing back to old comforts, a formula they couldn't get quite right yet. The new avenue toward the late-1960s pecking order was their reliance on Terry Slater, the British bass man whose writing reflected a soft rock poeticism. He played on Campbell's first massive hit, John Hartford's "Gentle on My Mind," and when he presented Don and Phil with several compositions, they chose "Bowling Green," "A Voice Within," "Talking to the Flowers," "Mary Jane," and "Do You," virtually turning the album into a Slater-conceived project.

The Everlys' only contributions were leftovers from previous albums, "I Don't Want to Love You," and a second call for "It's

All Over" from *In Our Image*. And country rock was otherwise short-shrifted. Two of the remaining tracks were overtly Brit-induced, a cover of Procol Harum's "A Whiter Shade of Pale" and "I'm Finding It Rough," by Irish symphony-pop writer Patrick Campbell and British studio hand Chris Thomas, who had worked on Beatles and later Procol Harum sessions and later with Pink Floyd and the Sex Pistols. The final tracks were rock and soul, a cover of Cannonball Adderley's hit "Mercy, Mercy, Mercy," written by Joe Zawinul, "Somebody Help Me" by Jamaican ska and R&B singer Jackie Edwards, and "Deliver Me," by Daniel Moore, whose songs had been recorded by Joe Cocker, and later Three Dog Night, Bonnie Raitt, and The Band. In light of all the future industry bumblebees whom the brothers gave flight to, they were perhaps pop music's biggest equal opportunity portal. And the door finally cracked open for them, with "Bowling Green."

Slater, who, like most Brit musicians, idolized both the Everlys and Brian Wilson's songwriting and tonalities, transposed the hazy simulacrum of "California Girls" to the Kentucky hills, even hailing "the prettiest girls I've ever seen" as—arguably—Kentucky's prime commodity, along with the simple pleasures of sunshine, moonshine, and girls who wear "dresses cut country tight" and make a man "lucky If he's seen a Bowling Green night." They laid their dreamy harmony—another turnabout irony, as Brian Wilson had built the Beach Boys' vocals on this very harmony—onto a jingly, flutey, "feeling groovy" beat with a chorale of "bah-bah-bop-bop-bah" and "ching" as scat accompaniments to Al Capps's slide guitar line within a cacophony of percussion, guitar, and keyboard runs.

As weird as it was to use Bowling Green as a catchphrase (though it did recall the traditional song "I Wish I Was In Bowling Green")—weirder still, a copywriter's credit was given to Jackie Ertel Everly, whose only other such experience was singing background on a couple of Chordettes songs for her stepfather. It certainly was infectious, hitting number forty on the pop chart in early July, missing the chart in England but, rather startlingly, going to number one in Canada; why, no one really seemed to know. The song would also be on Glen Campbell's eponymous 1969 album. In the broader lens, *Sing*, arranged by two real L.A. pros, Gene Page and Billy Strange, was clearly an improved version of the late-1960s Everly Brothers, or at least a *different* Everly Brothers.

But what was most noticeable was that it needed some good old country *relaxation*. Anyone who assumed "I Don't Want to Love You" was a callback to their innocent qualms about inescapable love must have been floored when Rod McKuen began singing the song—or at least what *sounded* like Rod McKuen—languidly musing about morning and the sound of laughter and tears and the pillow cold in fear, seeking the "path to tomorrow" that would "lead me nowhere," while they and backing singers moaned and wailed and the beat shot into a frantic tide repeating the title refrain. On "Mercy, Mercy, Mercy," they keened with scratchy, bluesy confidence to the point of and hoarseness, against the woodwind accents of Jay Migliore and horns pumping out the famous jazz melody but without any jazz or the usual charm that would be better provided by the Buckinghams' cover of the song that same year. "A Whiter Shade of Pale," with only Phil singing, was bracketed by a stately organ similar to the original but in a key too low for Phil's voice to keep from cracking.

Each track brought a surprise within slightly psychedelic borders, The tinny guitar lead on "Finding It Rough," despite being within a six-string fusillade by no less than Campbell and James Burton, would indeed leave fans to find it rough, as would the fuzz guitar feedback on Slater's "Mary Jane"—the obvious allusion to marijuana then, given away in the first verse that whatever happens in love and life, "I don't care no more / I've got my Mary Jane." Even the album cover, designed by art director Ed Thrasher, was striking; the brothers, dressed in different jackets, don't stare into the camera with glaring eyes as much as stare it *down*, their old altar-boy humility lost in some sort of inner bitterness, Don's mouth pruned, his left hand bent into a fist propping his chin. It failed to chart, which was seemingly the norm now, and "Bowling Green" getting to number forty, while decent, was not a hall pass into rock's new chromatic spectrum.

○ ○

Still, in a world of crossfire ironies, Don would soon "fit" with Jimi Hendrix, and would be no stranger to dropping acid or getting banged silly on weed. Years later, he recalled to *Rolling Stone*'s Kurt Loder that he had met Hendrix over the summer of 1968 at The Scene, one of the Greenwich Village folk-rock clubs, during the time the Everly Brothers were in town for a June 28 gig at The Latin Quarter.

> I had never been to Greenwich Village before, so Steve [Paul, who owned The Scene] and Jimi took me on a tour. Here we were, Steve wearing a bathrobe, the three of us smoking a joint in the back seat of his limo. I was still worried about getting busted, but they didn't seem to be. We went to the Bitter End, and there was Joni Mitchell, whom I had already fallen in love with via [her] records. My life changed. I wanted to play these places, too. I wanted to be a part of this music scene. I became friends with Jimi, liked him a lot. He invited me to sessions, even came around to the Latin Quarter to see me, can you believe it?
>
> It was all very strange. I took LSD—the best, Owsley's orange sunshine—but I was wearing tuxedos at the same time. We'd be playing a country show one night, then the Fillmore West the next, with the Sons of Champlin or somebody. Played the Bitter End, too, finally. Met Bob Dylan there one night. We were looking for songs, and he was writing "Lay Lady Lay" at the time. He sang parts of it, and we weren't quite sure whether he was offering it to us or not. It was one of those awestruck moments. We wound up cutting the song about fifteen years later.

These sorts of reveries did not include Phil, whose Republican ideology turned him off when he would hear Don engage in new-age parlance, saying things like "I'm on very good terms with my cosmos. I have an understanding, you know, with this body and with this mind." Not that Phil was any kind of saint; his adulterous flings were just as varied as his brother's. And while their arguments about the war and politics had them yelling and screaming at each other in private, to keep the peace, "protest" was not in their song repertoire. The brotherly meme wasn't only good for business; it *was* the business. But the Summer of Love was also the summer of anti-war declarations within the music sphere—as Stephen Stills and Neil Young of Buffalo Springfield noted, battle lines were being drawn on the streets of Hollywood—and Don was turning more leftward. As he explained it,

> We played Saigon once, a benefit for the Tan Son Nhut orphanage. That night we sat on the roof of this house and watched them napalming stuff outside the city. We played a lot of hospitals in the Philippines, too, full of Vietnam casualties. That's when it began to dawn on me that something was dreadfully wrong with that war. I became very political in my mind, totally anti-Nixon, but there didn't seem to be much I could do about it. We were working nine, ten months out of the year; we were really out of touch with what was going on in the world.

Yet, through Don's eyes, just as much trouble was wrought by the record industry. Despite that bloated contract, he had never believed that the suits really had the act's best interests in mind, and now he saw a new system that had merely given way to more corporate powers and power games, with big decisions being made by snot-nosed kids. "Everyone suddenly got real young," he would recall, "and if you were over thirty, they didn't trust you." The bottom line was carved in cement, and for both brothers, it was the record companies that could *never* be trusted. But Phil, for his part, had a broader foil than his brother and the industry. He detested the peace movement in general, even blaming *it* for the act going into decline, by leading performers to think they had to make a collective political statement in songs. Resisting that, as he once said, took a general toll on the Everly Brothers:

> The Sixties weren't my cup of tea. I never bought that philosophy that, you know, we're all brothers and that'll solve everything. And I never believed that music dictated the times. I always thought it reflected them. We were against the

grain in that period, and there was a lot of confusion about our direction. Maybe we were just losing the freshness of it all, losing interest.

○ ○

That seemed a fair appraisal for an act that would have no albums released from July 1967 to December 1968, and just two middling singles in the latter year. They did record some songs, and one that Don spent much time on was a projected single called "Even If I Hold It in My Hand (Hard Luck Story)," written by Nashville songsmiths Carlyle Hughey and William H. Smith. For Don, it may have been a way to unburden still unresolved issues that had led to his suicide attempt; though the subject was technically lost love, it maundered into some depressing terrain with frontally terrifying lines, the most harrowing being "There's even a doubt and a fear this gun will kill me / Even when I hold it to my head." It had a powerful bass line by Glen Campbell and a mildly tangy psychedelic effect. Yet it was shelved until finally released as a newly mixed version on the 1994 *Heartaches and Harmonies* box set, with the curious liner note "Don and Phil have no recollections of cutting this track," and as a rough take on the Bear Family 2006 *Chained to a Memory Box* package that stripped the Campbell part. Even so, one retro-review calls it a "minor-chord-mini-masterpiece."

All it really is, however, is a lost track from a lost act that had two years and two albums left on its contract, with no one rushing them back into the studio. They mattered far less to the suits, who had their cushy jobs in no small part due to the Everly Brothers having bailed out Warner Bros. Records, which had grown quite fat itself. In 1966, having diversified into Warner/Reprise, Frank Sinatra's custom label buying the company, and being part of the Warner brand ever since, the entire conglomerate was then bought for $32 million by Seven Arts Productions, which a year later bought Atlantic Records. In 1969 the whole Warner shebang would be again sold, to National Kinney Corporation, which would become Time Warner and the music division would acquire Elektra and Nonesuch

Records in the early 1970s, when it would be Warner-Elektra-Atlantic. Today, as Music Group Corp., it stands as the third-largest cartel in the industry, after Universal Music Group and Sony Music Entertainment.

Back when all this was effervescing, and label president Mo Ostin was feeding himself on profits, the Everlys were respected, even loved, but just pawns. Warner had already licensed some of its Everly Brothers catalog, leasing *In Our Image* to Columbia's low-budget sub-label Harmony Records, which retitled it *Chained to a Memory*. Indeed, the grapevine had it that the brothers wanted out. Also, they had hired a Hollywood manager, Jack Daley, to do what Wesley Rose had a decade before, sort out offers from other record labels. Biding time, they released three non-album songs to fill the gap. The first, a cover of The Four Preps' "Love of the Common People," an arid Mamas and the Papas-style folk-pop tune with a big, sprightly backdrop and a message elevating family above false gods—"Living on a dream ain't easy / But the closer the knit the tighter the fit."

It reached number 114 pop (and number four in Canada), but the follow-ups were only mild curiosities, John Loudermilk's similarly preppy "It's My Time"—on which Don sounds eerily like Neil Diamond—and "Milk Train," by commercial jingle and bubblegum pop writer Tony Romeo, who soon after would pen *The Partridge Family* theme song "I Think I Love You." Even more eerily, on "Milk Train," Don and Phil sounded as peppy as David Cassidy. Clearly, they would put far more time and thought into the next studio album, intending it as their 1960s epitaph, a statement of purpose and mission achieved in ten years of growth, a farewell song helping to format an idiom they had made so viable. It was, at long last, a well-thought-out project. And what a song it would be.

CHAPTER FIFTEEN

"Life's the Illusion"

The album would be titled with one word that cut through all the pretension of rock and roll bands posing as societal and cultural hand grenades, and got back to who they were. After throwing out "mod" songs that had done little for their status as contemporary artists, Don and Phil re-upped their country bona fides under the broad interpretation of that one word—*Roots*. Their notion was to tailor country old and new into the same *permanent* roots for the rest of time, just as it was permanently rooted in their minds and their art. It was another ambitious format for them, but this time they needn't alter who they were. Old was old, new was new, but it was all the same root of their soul, affirming the form of country rock *they* created, and applied to songs not technically country but about the soil and the air above the American continent as wide as the eye could see. And this suddenly became a big deal not only to them but to Warner Bros. By the time the session crew assembled in April 1968 at United Studios in L.A., the project would be guided by two engineers, John Neil and Mike Shields; arranger Perry Botkin Jr.; and string conductor Nick DeCaro, who had arranged "Guantanamera" and in the 1960s, Barbra Streisand's "The Way We Were" and Gordon Lightfoot's "Sundown." There would also be a new producer, Lenny Waronker, who had big-time written all over him.

Son of a classical violinist who had played in the 20th Century Fox Orchestra and then founded Liberty Records, he had worked his way up in the Liberty A&R department before being hired as an assistant to Mo Ostin, born Morris Meyer Ostrofsky, who had run Reprise Records and in 1963 took over both labels when Reprise bought Warner Bros. The label was then run as a two-headed creature, Warner-Reprise, with signings that included the Kinks and Jimi Hendrix, and Waronker was one of a legion of young rock-obsessed L.A. hipsters en route to being made president of Warner Bros. Records in the 1970s. Another in this brigade of Dead End Kids was a beguiling Brit, Andy Wickham, a non-musician who was every musician's idea of cool, his rap imitative, his connections deep in the Canyon. When Ostin ran across him at the Monterey Pop festival, he hired him as a bird dog, or as he was called on the scene, Warner's "company freak" or "house hippie." He was so omnipresent that he could be seen during sessions, mingling with the talent. And by doing so at the Everly Brothers' *Roots* sessions, Wickham would be credited as an assistant producer.

Waronker took the album as a personal challenge. He persuaded Don and Phil to include songs by two young writer/ arrangers he had recruited for Warner, Ron Elliott, leader of the soft-pop group the Beau Brummels, and Randy Newman, a satirically gifted childhood buddy of his in L.A. The only Everly-written track would be a rerecorded, slicker and countrier version of "I Wonder If I Care as Much" from their debut album, which would be intro'd as side one, track one by using an old. crackly tape of a 1952 Everly Family radio show. This would contextualize old and new, reaching back across the Everlys' genesis, and then further back to the old Brakeman himself, Jimmie Rodgers, by covering "T for Texas," the classic boxcar tale of "sleepin' in a hollow log" and swearing revenge, ready to "shoot me a rounder oh that stole away my gal." The track list then jumped ahead to Merle Haggard's "Mama Tried," which was so good that Merle would release his own version by the time the album was completed, and to Glen Campbell's "Less of Me," on which he played slide guitar wrapping around the brothers' vow to "Think a little more of others and a little less of me."

It flickered to and fro like this, and Waronker hit it right. Ron Elliott's entry, "Ventura Boulevard," was a gorgeous dream on a bed of DeCaro's high strings swathing vocals wishing for a metaphoric "hayride" or "slow walk," and the best explanation of where the current-day Everly Brothers stood—"Everyone thinks I've been gone for too long / I only went for a ride." The last cut of side one was the traditional Kentucky "courting" song "Shady Grove," which has been sung through the years with around three hundred different verses and even by a different name, "Matty Groves." A picking, banjo stomp with native-style vocals, it was credited on the album to "P.O. Wandz," a pseudonym for Terry Slater, with backing vocals by Jackie Erte Everly and Venetia Everly and ending with a few seconds more of a long-ago Everly family radio broadcast.

Side two began with Newman's "Illinois," an effusive bow to the state's prairies and meat-packing ends, the glow being, as Don and Phil well knew, "the lights of Chicago when daylight is ended and night has begun"—a work so knowing that it's astonishing that it wasn't adopted as the state anthem. It was followed by Slater's "Living Too Close to the Ground," a kind of fly-high "Free Bird" precursor—"Listen and hear each word, stop or you'll miss the birds" by "living too close to the ground." Indeed, with vocals that never hurried and dug cell-deep for meaning, each song on the album seemed to rise off the ground and expand into an ethereal haze one could feel all around them. Don's vocals especially were like nothing ever heard from him, intentionally underplayed, even trembling. Returning to the country masters, the George Jones–Ray Price "You Done Me Wrong," which was intro'd by another short clip from the radio, with Ike sending his boys into the song, which they often sang as kids, though here they graced it with a rock-flavored timpani and sugar-cane horns and mandolins.

Elliott's second track, "Turn Around," a jingly tale of young love with the guy beckoning his summer fling to stay as winter approaches and the "Midnight wind is blowing awfully hard," sung as a Pure Prairie League-type country croon. The penultimate track, Haggard's "Sing Me Back Home," which had been a hit for Merle a year before as the title tune of an album, was again prefaced by the old radio fare, with Ike and Margaret warbling "That Old Rugged Cross" before segueing into Don and Phil's quietly intense, brilliantly harmonized redo of "Sing Me." The playout track was a Slater-arranged medley of "Shady Grove" and "Kentucky," ending with a final outtake from the radio clips.

Roots was, and is, an outstanding work, a top-to-bottom triumph that became an obsession, the weeks of recording parting only briefly when Venetia got closer to her delivery date and gave birth to Don's first son, Edan, on August 25. Warner immediately pressed the album, with a cover shot of Don and Phil by Frank Bez wearing blinding white shirts, slacks and shoes, Phil sitting on a rock and Don standing over him, foot on the rock, both squinting into the sun under a breathtaking blue sky. The record went out in November, with a Billboard review labeling it "haunting and well performed," with "much sales appeal here." Or at least one would have thought. Waronker, pushing his project, approved a two-full-page ad in the magazine with the covers of Warner's new albums under the new-age phrase "The New! The Now!—The What." Roots was the first listed, ahead of those by the Association, Dean Martin, Richard Pryor, Petula Clark, Randy Newman, and Sammy Davis Jr. As it got around, there was nearly universal positive buzz—Robert Christgau's Village Voice notice, with none of his normal acerbic tone, called it "their autobiographical studio tour de force . . . thoughtful, even-tempered, and unique."

In Britain, The Guardian's Geoffrey Cannon, went all geeky, writing that "The songs develop a linear flow, which is not fugal, but logical, in that you know every note the moment it is played, but not before: the same quality as that of Bach's Brandenburg concertos [that] gains a momentum and identity entirely its own." Less fusty, in a 1972 Rolling Stone retro-review Bud Scoppa—who had dissed their previous LPs as a "descending level of self-parody," and their stage shows "a stale, lifeless night club act"—judged Roots "a surprising and complete return to their former artistic prowess [that made them] sharp on stage again, not forever trapped in their own pasts."

The sticking point was one that Waronker hoped he could sidestep—that there wasn't a suitable single compatible with the times to propel even this magnificent work. True, the late 1960s could bless an act based solely on an album, and the Everlys' "concept album" should have been a good example. But an act that came into being almost completely on singles did not have that luxury. Ostin and Waronker tried hard to find a way out. "Turn Around" had seemed like the best bet, but Elliott preferred to save it for the fading Beau Brummels, who put it on their 1969 album *Bradley's Barn*. And so by the end of the year, the only chart *Roots* was on, or would be on, was a list called "Low-Price Pop," along with works by Eydie Gormé, Lou Monte, and the Riviera Strings. Warner tried to save it by belatedly releasing "T for Texas" as a single after the new year, but it went under quickly. As for the album, its brilliance was forever undercut by the public's stubborn resistance to spending a few dollars on Everly Brothers albums on grounds that they had grown up with "Bye Bye Love" and "Cathy's Clown" and nothing else really mattered quite enough. And so even though Warner sank decent money into promotion, the end of the story was the same. If one could get to one of those county fairs or rodeos to hear them perform the oldies, or catch them on TV, *that* mattered enough.

On the other hand, for musicians who knew a good thing when they heard it, *Roots* would be one of rock's most glaringly over-looked works, one that musicians would swear to the gods by, and would be one more primer worthy of deep study. Among the rockers who arrived in L.A. as it morphed from surf to country rock, all were devotees of the Everlys—The Byrds, Dil-lard and Clark, The Flying Burrito Brothers, Linda Ronstadt, Joni Mitchell, Emmylou Harris, Crosby, Stills and Nash, Poco, and whoever else Andy Wickham signed during acid-drenched nights in the Canyon. Even the Stones soon slipped into their "country" phase, during which Keith Richards said, "We loved the songs of Felice and Boudleaux Bryant—the Everly Brothers stuff they wrote . . . that melancholy, high-lonesome shit," he said. "We were always looking for the next heart-tugger, looking to pull that extra heartstring."

Don and Phil may have been sandbagged by their own legacy, but they still had a wide berth. They would close out the decade with two more loose singles, Terry Slater's "I'm On My Way Home Again" / "Cuckoo Bird" and a cover of James Taylor's "Carolina in My Mind," backed with "My Little Yellow Bird," both of which went nowhere. And yet they had a full touring schedule, roaming through Canada, jumping to England and Ireland, bouncing back to the States for the stop at the Latin Quarter where they met Jimi Hendrix, then on September 15 as part of a ten-hour show in the huge tureen of the Rose Bowl in Pasadena called "An American Music Show," a pre-Woodstock-style festival also featuring Joan Baez, the Byrds, Big Brother and the Holding Company, the Mothers of Invention, Buffy St. Marie, Wilson Pickett, and Buddy Guy. Then came a hop into Vancouver, and when the calendar turned, all across the United States, the crowning moment being their first landing at a place they once would have snorted in laughter about playing—Las Vegas, performing for soused, chain-smoking, middle-aged people taking a break from the craps tables. The venue was the Versailles Room at the Riviera Hotel, where they dutifully did their thing on twenty-eight straight nights, two shows a night.

Then, with only one day to travel across the country, they were on stage at The Bitter End for sixteen consecutive nights— the second-to-last show only minutes after they had appeared on the June 15 *Ed Sullivan Show*, their first appearance there in seven years, not to sing anything current but rather the almost tauntingly nostalgic "Walk Right Back," Wake Up Little Susie" and "Bye Bye Love." On their tour they were accompanied by their tight rhythm group, Robert Knigge on bass, Sam McCue on guitar, and Tiny Schneider on drums, and they were with them two weeks later back in Vegas at the Landmark Hotel for fourteen straight nights. These excursions seemed to be based not only on money in their pockets but attracting a substantial offer from a new label. However, both were in their thirties in

1969 and similarly torturous meanderings a decade ago had driven Don to the Ritalin cocktail madness and near suicide. Ominously, he seemed to now to be just as wasted.

He had begun to drink heavily and was no stranger to acid, pot, and pills. Frequently, he forgot lyrics to songs on stage and grew incoherent when addressing the audience. Two other songs were recorded as possible singles—Sonny Curtis and Jerry Allison's "Carolyn Walking Away" and Terry Slater's "Lord of the Manor"—but were held back because his vocals were raspy and off-key, though at Don's insistence the latter's down and dirty tale of a fop and a maid in a white-glove mansion made it into the stage act, its creepy indifference to right and wrong usually leaving the crowd uncomfortable, though it did allow him the ironic tonic of noting that fans "won't hear our new song unless it's on FM underground." Accordingly, Phil found himself having to prop up the act at times, taking over on some of the challenging lead guitar parts and carrying the between-songs banter, shooting Don the same looks of disgust and anger that Don had for years rained on him. If they could have slowed down and taken stock, they would have seen that the guard rails around the act seemed to be slipping away, and trouble was waiting to get in. Some big trouble.

○ ○

One positive development was that the historical asides on *Roots* had given Ike Everly a way back into the business. Unfreezing their relationship with him, they accepted an invitation from the founder of the Newport Folk Festival, George Wein, to appear at the festival's Rhode Island home on July 19, 1969, the last edition of the ten-year-old festival, and Wein, a master historian who venerated Ike, was all for him performing with them. The gig was a kick for Don and Phil, whose marriage of folk and country rock had been validated even as their own sales had slipped, and they eagerly looked ahead to being at the same venue where, in 1965, a crucial moment in the rock evolution occurred when Bob Dylan was booed off the stage by folk purists when he played electric-rock backed by the Paul Butterfield Blues Band. The 1969 edition spanned four days, featuring acts as varied as Johnny Cash—who introduced his protege Kris Kristofferson—Big Mama Thornton, and Muddy Waters.

The Everlys' Saturday-night closing set would draw the biggest crowd, around eighteen thousand, but they also did a laid-back Saturday afternoon "workshop" appearance, shades covering their eyes, along with Ike, who flew up from Nashville. Now sixty-one, he had thick white hair and little to say, nodding as his sons told stories of sucking up his tutelage long ago. He then played and sang three of his go-to songs, "A-Blues," Merle Travis's "Blue Smoke," and the retitled folk song "Ike Everly's Rag," which had been recorded by Travis. His boys then did a set avoiding all but two of the oldies while going with country folk—"Going Down the Road Feeling Bad," "I Am a Pilgrim" (both of which had been covered, by the Grateful Dead and the Byrds), "Nellie Gray," "Bass Fiddle Rag," "Don't Let Our Love Die," "Born to Lose," "You Done Me Wrong," "Dirty Guitar Blues," "Down in the Willow Garden," "Oh So Many Years," and "Ground Hawg."

The two oldies were "When Will I Be Loved" and the show-closer was, what else, but "Bye Bye Love," with which they would also close the more showbizzy Sunday-night set, also sharing some prime time with Ike. The show, which for some in the audience brought the Everly Brothers out of hiding, was a howling success, sending them off with cheers. One prominent reviewer, Jan Holdenfield of the new music mag called *Rolling Stone* could feel deep soul even in their pop songs, writing that they "brought extraordinary urgency and desperation to a medley of 'Let the Sunshine In' and 'Hey Jude' [which was] no longer a happy hippy hymnal but rather a heartbreaking plea." Happily, a long-lost, and at times inaudible bootleg of the two sets became available and were put on the internet a few years ago. (That year's festival was in fact a historical landmark as well, that concluded when Wein interrupted James Taylor's first important American gig to joyously announce that the Apollo 11 astronauts had landed on the moon.)

Don meanwhile had decided that the Everly Brothers' final Warner project would cross off the bucket list the last remaining goal—their first live recording set, which would be a double-album because, as Don recalled, "We owed them two albums, so we decided to get them both out of the way in one go." He also had thrown a figurative rabbit punch at Phil shortly before Newport, broaching the possibility that they should each do solo projects as a needed break. As with such suggestions in the past, Phil was hesitant to stray from his strong point, the harmony that cushioned the act while letting him, as he put it, avoid the "heavy lifting" that Don did. He may not have even believed Don was serious about it and would risk taking a hard fall as a solo.

But Don in the fall signed a conditional, two-album solo deal with Lou Adler's Ode Records, with the first album to come out in 1970. The deal was permitted under the Everlys' Warner contract and Mo Ostin rightly considered this as Don's main interest, for which the live album acted as fodder during their last months with the label. On February 6, 1970, the concert from which the album was recorded was staged at the Grand Hotel in Anaheim before a jammed ballroom crowd. Seemingly making the set list up on the spot, they ran through—almost literally, their impatient selections seeming as if they had an appointment elsewhere—two dozen or so songs, either complete or piecemeal. From this buffet, Adler would knit together twenty-one tracks, with Don's sometimes muddled verbal intros on "Mama Tried," "Kentucky," "Bowling Green"—leading to the upbeat oldies, and covers of "Maybellene" and "Rock and Roll Music." The curveball was a semi-cover of *Abbey Road*'s side-two medley, "The End," followed by their own medley of "Aquarius," "If I Were a Carpenter," their song "The Price of Love," "The Thrill Is Gone," and "Games People Play."

The rest of the tracks were knitted from their ballads, a cover of Jimmy Reed's "Baby What You Want Me to Do," some other oddball medleys, "Lord of the Manor," and "Love Is Strange," a lineup that an AllMusic retro-review describes as "a bizarre Beatles obsession that included appending the coda from 'Hey Jude' to 'Susie Q' and even turning 'Let It Be Me' into 'Give Peace a Chance' at the end." It was, to be sure, slapdash and sloppy, a wet noodle. Even the liner notes had some incorrect song titles,

"Let It Be Me" listed as "Let It Be." There was some mild discussion at Warner about junking the project. Yet, as things turned out, Ostin would be able to button the album when the brothers were chosen by Johnny Cash to be the summer replacement hosts for his popular, sometimes surprisingly countercultural Saturday night ABC variety show, for a ten-week run in July, when the album would be released.

Cash, a longtime friend of Don and Phil, was one of those musicians knocked out by the *Roots* album, and when they spent time together at the Newport Festival, he invited them to not only appear on his show but to take its reins for the summer. The guest shot on February 4, two days before the live album was recorded, was notable for finally bringing the Everlys back to the stage of the Ryman Auditorium. Cash, who was openly liberal and antiwar, had helped to rebrand the Grand Ole Opry, putting country and rock stars on the same stage where they once had been forbidden from comingling, for some of them their only national TV exposure. This was how remarkable the Cash show was. On that episode, Johnny sang "Folsom Prison Blues," Dusty Springfield sang two songs, Cash and esteemed actor Kirk Douglas dueted on "I Walk the Line," and Cash and Rod McKuen "Doesn't Anybody Know My Name?"

When he brought on the brothers at the start for a quick hello, the three of them were quite a sight, Johnny in his black tux, Don in a peacoat with big silver buttons, Phil in brown with a long, frilled vest. Then, when they performed, Johnny intro'd them by playing on his guitar the famous opening of "Bye Bye Love," which, he said, "Don taught me." Now wearing puffy-shirted English-style suits with white ruffled collars and looking like well-dressed daffodils, they were on the same spot where they'd played in 1958 in informal suits and received gold records from Archie Bleyer. Then came the all-purpose fallbacks, "All I Have to Do Is Dream" and "Wake Up Little Susie," reminding audiences about why they were still so attached to the Everly Brothers. Cash also paid homage to Ike Everly, who, with Margaret, was also on the show, a rare chance for them to spend a little time with the sons who had flitted in and out of their lives. In a segment called "Roots," Ike warbled "That Silver Haired

Daddy of Mine" with the boys. But those few minutes, while homey and rustic, betrayed the increasing tension between Don and Phil. The set for the segment was an old log-cabin living room, fireplace burning in the background. Around a dozen guests, including Roy Orbison and Carl Perkins, sat on and around a long couch, the brothers at opposite ends. When Cash brought them up to sing "Kentucky," Phil never once glanced over at Don, a little thing that meant a lot. In a later segment, the three Everly men, with Cash and his country-singing brother Tommy Cash, ran through "Looking Good to Me." That could only be called wishful thinking,

When they began their interim show on July 8, it was called *Johnny Cash Presents the Everly Brothers*, and the album was called *The Everly Brothers Show* to solidify the connection between the two. Unlike the regular Cash series, ABC kept the budget low and taped two shows at a time at ABC Television Center, the old Vitagraph Studio, in Hollywood. Johnny would guest-star on the first show, on which the Everlys would sing "Wabash Cannonball" and "I Walk the Line" with him, as well as "Detroit City" with guest stars Kenny Rogers and the First Edition, and "Ruby Tuesday" with Melanie. Don and Phil would sing four Everly Brothers songs and Phil soloed on "The Last Thing on My Mind," which may have expressed how he felt about harmonizing with Don, though these segments were the basis of the show, which ran smoothly, the brothers' meshing easily with musical notables who had country in their blood like Linda Ronstadt, Arlo Guthrie, Marty Robbins, Neil Diamond, B. J. Thomas, even Stevie Wonder and Ike and Tina Turner. They kept feeding their Beatles' addiction, too, in one show singing "Lady Madonna" and Don doing an emotional solo on "Ticket to Ride." They also brought Ike back to be on the finale, the three again jamming with Cash. It was all fabulous, and pre–*Midnight Special* and *Don Kirshner's Rock Concert*, these shows were really the place to be. Some at ABC considered spinning off their own show. But not only was the live album a nonstarter, the network was about to pull the Cash show, giving it one more year before casting it into the trash bin of TV's "rustic" shows, leaving only *Hee Haw* among the nitwitted 1960s country boilerplates.

Don would blame the lack of a continuing Everly series on ABC, for treating the show as nothing more than a "money-making scheme." But now, with the chore of being an Everly Brother done following a September date at the Schaefer Music Festival in New York, Don could turn to his solo album, *Don Everly*. By now, publishing rights were no longer an issue with Acuff-Rose, which granted both Don and Phil individual rights on new songs, which would be administered by numerous companies, including Bowling Green Music, a partnership they established with Terry Slater. And Don had high expectations. The sessions were held at the A&M Records studio—the same place where they'd shot the TV show—with Lou Adler agreeing to produce the debut LP. The crew included Ry Cooder on bottleneck guitar, Sneaky Pete Kleinow on steel guitar, "San Francisco" Scott McKenzie on twelve-string acoustic, and Don on rhythm, as well as Chris Ethridge on bass, George S. Clinton on organ, Curtis Amy on tenor sax, Spooner Oldham on keyboard, Jim Keltner on drums, jazz bassist Max Bennett, jazz percussionist Milt Holland, and three female backing singers, including the two Clinger Sisters.

Impressive as that was, though, of nine self-written songs, he likely would not have used any on an Everly Brothers work, and one, the weepy ballad "Omaha," had been recorded before by him and Phil in 1968 but not released. The opening track was a "mod" cover of "Tumbling Tumbleweeds," the Bob Nolan song made famous in 1934 by The Sons of the Pioneers, which now was sped up in a hash of whining pedal steel and an undulating, seemingly druggy vocal sounding not unlike Lennon on "I Am the Walrus." By contrast, on his cover of Don Gibson's 1955 country ballad "Sweet Dreams," his bluesy, emotionally charged voice was more like Patsy Cline, perfectly bending to the vibe of the pedal steel. The first track of side B, "When I Stop Dreaming," was a cover of a Louvin Brothers song. And on the whole, his milky country-rock flavor does render the album with a Roy Orbison–J. D. Souther-style lonely-hearted vulnerability, peppered with effects one reviewer had called the "cosmic country" of *Roots*. "Eyes of Asia" was a pedal-string singalong. "Safari" was an interesting departure, country meeting reggae. "February 15th" was an intense plea for one more day to discover that "all I want to know is inside of me." "My Baby" had him on a louder, Allman Brothers-like road, with some free-form orchestral flights as he set out on "new highways with your back on my bed." "Thinking It Over" was his grievance about a subject he was expert in—bad marriage, telling his other half, "Things are getting sticky dear / It's who's gonna stay," the song, perhaps by design, semi-incoherent.

Filling it out, "Don't Drink the Water" was a semi-joking chugging rocker very closely mirroring the melody of the Clapton/Delaney and Bonnie "After Midnight"—perhaps a sly metaphor about his own descent into booze, the hook being "Don't drink the water, drink the wine." Also with a serious side was "My Friend," a misanthropic warning to fuck-ups like him to "walk away or run" because "life's the illusion." Overall, it was good L.A.-based country rock, with a real edge. But the old Everly Brothers sizzle, un-self-conscious depth and tight-fisted vocal control weren't there. It was obvious why Don had no male singer harmonizing with him, and he even had Adler refrain from adding post-dubbed echoes. Yet without that "third Everly voice" that came alive when he and Phil sang, his thinner vocals almost seemed shallow when the steel and pedal guitars were amped up. In other words, it didn't mean a thing without that Everly swing. And Don himself was, well, a little shaky. Years later, Kurt Loder posited in *Rolling Stone* that the album, "perhaps reflecting Don's state of mind at the time," was "a somewhat woozy effort, recorded with the assistance of much booze and reefer."

When released in November, a review in the British music media described the LP as "a merger between acid-trip and post-acid consciousness [and] the Everlys own brand of country-pop," and in one of the few reviews in America, *Billboard* judged it "a winner in every respect." However, Adler had no real attachment to an album he had produced for his own label, spending almost nothing pushing it and more focused on producing

Robert Altman's movie *Brewster McCloud* and soon, Carole King's debut album for Ode, the mighty *Tapestry*. He and A&M president Chuck Kaye determined the only single from *Don Everly* would be "Tumbleweeds," its least relevant number that, as with the album, didn't have a chance at charting and created a problem for Don when he heard that Bob Nolan had called the radio station and told them, "Take that piece of shit off the air."

Recalled Don: "I really felt bad. I just wanted to twist it around a little bit. That was one of the big disappointments in my life."

But more stringent was *Phil's* reaction, which was that the album felt to him like "cheating on a marriage." Years later, he said, "I felt tremendously let down by Lou Adler. I don't know what prompted Donald to do it. I never did understand, and I never understood Louis doing it because I considered him one of my closest friends and we've never had any kind of relationship since."

Another Everly album failed to make the charts, and the added downer for their fans was seeing images of Don on the album cover, where six Polaroid-style pictures of him were laid across the cover like playing cards, with him smiling underneath an urban cowboy hat, wearing leather pants and white cowboy boots, a look he hadn't appropriated since he was Little Don and openly engaged in damning the Grand Ole Opry theatrics. More jolting though was a still shot of him on the inner sleeve with a prickly five o-clock shadow, hair uncombed and falling into squinting, bloodshot eyes while sitting in front of a tie-dyed wall covering. This was the Don Everly of 1971, lost in a haze.

Still, the Everly Brothers had not split up, and needed to have people know it by joining forces to convince record labels they deserved a contract. And Don could clean up when he needed to, such as when the Everly Brothers joined forces again for what would be their last *Ed Sullivan Show* appearance on February 28, when they walked onto a psychedelic-themed stage and sang "Bowling Green, then returned with "Mama Tried," a slowed down version of "All I Have to Do Is Dream," and "Bye, Bye Love." They also made it to the *Dean Martin Show*, an interesting scripted moment coming when Dean, doing his fake drunk bit, called them the Smothers Brothers and Don and Phil did a neat little take-off of Tom and Dickey, Phil with a stand-up bass and Don, sounding much like Tommy, whining, "Mom always liked you better"—which he may have actually believed, and must not have believed was funny at all.

They also jetted to England to be on a TV show hosted by Petula Clark, did a *Midnight Special,* and another round in Las Vegas at the Landmark Hotel. That was followed by a gig at Caesar's Palace that was to be shared with the Smothers Brothers. But Dick Smothers tells a fabulously ironic story about what happened that reveals how on the edge the Everlys were.

> The Everly Brothers were probably the most important post-war singing brothers act that ever existed. But they hated each other. And they decided they didn't want to go on. They were mad at each other. And you just didn't do that to a Vegas showroom. They have ways of persuading you to go on. And so Tommy and I decided to have dinner with them, as we were almost exactly the same age, and tell them, you know, how they could get along with each other. Tommy took one guy aside, and I took the other. And Tommy and I almost broke up and didn't go on! But we got them to go on.

That was how infectious, or infecting, the Everly Brothers could be when their dirty laundry conflicted with their public image—and it was just a short step away from *being* their public image.

CHAPTER SIXTEEN

The Zen Chant

Don's stance on leaving Warner Bros. Records had him danc-ing on the head of a pin, inferring that the decision was purely his and Phil's. They were, he said in an interview, looking for a label that was "the right one" for them, and "Warners of course wasn't it, or else we wouldn't have left." In truth, Mo Os-tin had already made that decision for them. And the pressure to find the "right one" was especially pressing given that their personal lives had gone all to hell, with financial consequences. By 1970, the Don and Venetia soap opera and Phil and Jackie's quieter failure ended—remarkably, both in March. The divorces, both being finalized that year, would cost them a bundle under California's community property laws—in the millions, Don not spared this time when Venetia, unlike Mary, had no intention of asking for a mere pittance.

Not waiting for the shoe to fall, Don had walked out on his wife and children and taken up with the latest flame, which, with his penchant for kooky love triangles, was none other than Ann Marshall, eight years after Phil had dumped her on Valen-tine's Day 1962. Whether or not he had any desire to rub it in on Phil—or whether *Ann* did—Don was not shy in showing off the statuesque brunette, or for that matter, any lithesome woman he took up with. When he did a press interview for the Johnny Cash replacement series, the writer noted an "attractive young woman in purple pants" sitting with Don, who "paused to kiss her. Having trouble concentrating, he would rush off without explanation to another room to do who knew what, leaving the woman to sit alone, knitting." This apparently was Ann, and when Venetia got wind of it, she took the two kids and moved out of their North Hollywood home, severing them from him.

Don and Ann made the scene around L.A., and became friends with bad boy actor Dennis Hopper, who had scored a huge hit as costar, director, cowriter and producer of *Easy Rider*, one of the first movies with a hard-driving rock and roll soundtrack, and his girlfriend, the Mama and Papas survivor Michelle Phillips, who was divorced from John Phillips. When they married in Taos on Halloween in 1970, Don and Ann went along, and Don bought the marriage license. That marriage lasted all of eight days, which coincidentally might have been about how long Don would stay in love with any woman.

Thus, anything the Everly Brothers could earn from any source was sorely necessary, and as it turned out, they did made the charts again in 1970—but only because Andy Williams did what he insisted he wasn't going to do, putting out an album of their big Cadence oldies that same October on Barnaby Records, which Paul Anka had formed, named after his dog, along with other albums by former Cadence acts including Anka, Lenny Welch, and the early Jimmy Buffett. The hottest album, *The Everly Brothers' Original Greatest Hits*, culled twenty tracks of A and B sides and filler. It reached number eighty and number forty-four on the country album chart. That was good enough to release a second Barnaby album of lesser songs early in 1971, *The Everly Brothers End of an Era*. This would give Warner Bros. the idea to do the same in 1972 with the stock of Everly Brothers material they had, in a double album called *The Most Beautiful Songs of the Everly Brothers*, released mainly in England and Germany.

The last single that Warner released before the contract ran out was "Yves," a song written by Scott McKenzie. It, too, missed the charts. But in 1971, the free agent Everlys were thrown a life preserver when, after returning from another tour in England in September, their agent Jack Daley had finally closed a deal that would keep them in the same tunnel in which they could coexist in a grim gun-to-the-head sham of brotherhood while seeking that highly elusive renaissance.

○ ○

It was no bargain basement deal. Rather than a small label, they were signed by RCA Records, the second-oldest American label next to Columbia. Dating back to 1919, it was a cog of the immense Radio Corporation of America, headquartered for decades in the 30 Rockefeller Center tower that is still home to NBC. Of course, Don and Phil knew RCA well, having been rejected by the label back in the early days and having recorded their biggest songs at RCA's Studio B with RCA's Nashville wellspring Chet Atkins. And despite again rejecting them in 1960, RCA—which would within a decade be a subsidiary of Sony Music Entertainment—had never lost interest in them as its country music division kept growing beyond Elvis with newer stars like Dolly Parton, Charley Pride, Eddie Rabbit, and Jerry Reed.

As well, a younger generation invested in country music was settling in at the label under the watch of new label president Rocco Laginestra and managing director Kenneth Glancy, who would take over two years later. In 1971, when Elvis's thirtieth studio album *Elvis Country (I'm 10,000 Years Old)* went Gold, RCA's country-rock fold was deep, with fixtures like Gib Gilbeau, a pivotal early figure in the movement as leader of the Nashville West band with Gene Parsons, Clarence White, and sometimes Gram Parsons—all of whom would be in the revamped Byrds—and Sneaky Pete Kleinow, the sometimes Everly Brothers sideman who with Guilbeau would later form the revamped edition of The Flying Burrito Brothers. In between, Guilbeau's Swampwater band recorded two Cajun-rock albums and served as Linda Ronstadt's post–Stone Poneys backup band.

Don's wry rationale was less layered, and admirably honest— "They paid a lot of money, which enabled us to judge their enthusiasm." The details were not publicly known, but if the advances weren't on the level of the Warner contract, the four-year deal had roughly the same royalty structure, their output stipulated as one Everly Brothers album and one solo album by each brother per year, a condition Warner had summarily rejected, and something important for Don, who still wanted to transition from the brother act even if on a lesser tableau. And this time, Phil, who had not given much thought to solo recording, was also thinking more about the same kind of provisional, sanity-restoring escape route. Daley also expanded their brand as a business entity, establishing an independent, profit-sharing management company, Company of Artists, with Daley as CEO. He made some quick signings, representing lower-level acts like Riley Wildflower, who'd been with the spiritual-folk band The Gentle Soul, for a time with Jackson Browne, and singer-songwriter Malcolm Hayes. Each act's management fees would be lumped together and invested in projects that theoretically would benefit them all. As vague as it sounded, Daley also made promises that the Everlys would write songs for the others.

With the RCA deal set, the label honchos brought in big-time producer Paul Rothchild to work with them. Rothchild was one of the Canyon's most respected behind-the-scenes figures, having produced the Doors' first five albums, the Paul Butterfield Blues Band, and Janis Joplin's last album and single, "Me and Bobby McGee," as well as handling Crosby, Stills, and Nash's first record deal. Then thirty-six, the Brooklyn-born Rothchild was a wiz on the board, inventing methods of equalization and Dolby applications that brought rock into electro-pop, and as with everyone else in the business, he idolized the Everly Brothers. The deal was reported in the August 21 issue of *Billboard*, and soon after the Everlys and Rothchild went into RCA's Sunset Boulevard studio, where, among many others, the Rolling Stones, Creedence Clearwater Revival, Jefferson Airplane, and the Grateful Dead had hunkered down in surroundings built to the specifications of Chet Atkins's Studio B; and where the first 4-channel, 8-track quadraphonic tape cartridge system was installed in 1971 (though quad didn't catch on and was soon abandoned).

Recording the first Everly album on the label in late August was a major studio event. Rothschild filled the teeming room with the cream of the L.A. sidemen, including bass man Chris Ethridge, keyboardist Spooner Oldham, jug band guitarist Geoff Muldaur; R&B guitarist Wayne Perkins; psychedelic guitarist

Danny Weis; drummers Jim Keltner, Russ Kunkel, and Johnny Barbata; and pedal steel guitarist Buddy Emmons. There would be drop-ins by Graham Nash and David Crosby on backing vocals. Rothchild even employed jazz trombonist George Bohannon and tuba player Tommy Johnson. Places were made for guitar giants Clarence White, Waddy Wachtel, and Ry Cooder on certain tracks, and also in the pack were Delaney and Bonnie Bramlett, who had written for the brothers and whose song "All We Really Want to Do," was to be the leadoff track. The string section was arranged by the veteran session man Jimmie Haskell. And then there was a twenty-four-year-old savant, Warren Zevon, who could play, well, *everything* and had been all but adopted by Don and Phil, first as a backing singer and then as the musical coordinator on their tours.

The brothers, who were hard enough to get together as it was, had few new songs of their own. The only one composed by both, was a retread, "Green River," not the 1969 Creedence Clearwater Revival hit and album (or the American operation in Vietnam) but one they had recorded originally in 1968 that went unreleased. There was one by each of them alone, Don's self-explanatory "I'm Tired of Singing My Song in Las Vegas," and Phil's "Up in Mabel's Room," written with Terry Slater for *Roots* before being discarded. Thus, the album would ride on songs mainly written by heavy hitters like Kris Kristofferson, who contributed his "Breakdown," and Delaney and Bonnie's "All We Really Want to Do" was the underlying theme of the album. There were also covers of Jesse Winchester's "The Brand New Tennessee Waltz" and Rod Stewart's country ballad "Mandolin Wind." John Sebastian's "Stories We Could Tell" would become the title of the LP.

"Green River" was a throwback to the "Kentucky" and "Bowling Green" testimonials to the hills, their airy vocals meshing into a scenic orchestral cascade that included Cooder on bottleneck guitar. But the two newer ones were really solo efforts that defined who they were. Phil's "Up in Mabel's Room," a title borrowed from the 1944 movie comedy, was a simple, back-porch-strumming slow stroll, while Don's "Las Vegas" was a three-minute exercise in cynicism and distemper with a hint of Rick Nelson's "Garden Party," Don picking on the hopeless souls who "turn the wheel and let it spin" even if "you'll never win," a clear metaphor for his own lost soul, and while he avowed in it, that "I'm not coming back again," that was a vow he would not keep.

Of the other tracks, "Stories We Could Tell" was recorded at the ex-Lovin' Spoonful frontman's home studio, with Sebastian singing backup and playing guitar and harmonica. Nashville's guitarist and keyboardist Dennis Linde wrote three songs, "Ridin' High," "Christmas Eve Can Kill You (When You're Trying to Hitch a Ride to Anywhere)"—with Don sadly musing about the hype of the season corrupting the human soul, including his own, to wit, "The sound of one man walkin' through the snow can break your heart / But stopping doesn't help, so on I'll go"— and "Three-Armed Poker-Playin' River Rat" which was a shit ton of hard-rockin' ramblin'. Winchester's updated answer to the old standard "Tennessee Waltz," later covered by The Walker Brothers and Don Henley, dug deeply into country's unrelieved heartbreak, the brothers' perfect harmonies unwittingly recalling Don's own history—"I left Tennessee in a hurry dear, the same way that I'm leaving you . . . for love is mainly just memories."

"All We Really Want to Do," with Delaney on guitar and singing backup with Bonnie, was a good-time rock statement that, for all the ironies and resentments in the world, "All we really want to do is sing a good old song to you." On "Mandolin Wind," they quickened the cadence and glided through with a piquant slide guitar line. On "Breakdown," they injected high and lonesome emotion into what could have been an autobiographical lyric, given the mocking lines about being "stranded souls standing cold at the station" and the weary "Boy, you've sure come a long way from home." There was even some room for a snicker, "Del Rio Dan," written by psychedelic rock and jazz bassist Doug Lubahn, Holly Beckwith, and Jeff Kent, a send-up of the all-too-familiar country rock stereotype of an Old West "outlaw" and "devil's friend" in a "Stetson hat and a snakeskin band," who "is good, he is bad, bound to do what he can."

In the end, the album was a diverting mélange of contemporary country rock and cosmic country blues. Yet, Rothschild was not wild about the product that had consumed five months of meticulous mixing, arguing between the brothers over its direction, and additional recordings, "Up in Mabel's Room" being recorded as late as January 2, 1972. Finally, in March, *Stories We Could Tell* was released, its cover a bleak diaphanous black-and-white shot by photographer Norman Seeff of the pair while on tour in a white room of some sort, Don seated, Phil standing and wearing a large Russian hat, the words "Georgia Fugitives Hot Water" obliquely scribbled on a wall behind them. Although a review of the album in *Billboard* touted "Breakdown's" "great single potential" (this was not universal; Robert Christgau's review was that it was "humdrum" compared with *Roots*), the only release would be "Ridin' High," which like the album was lost and never found. Rather than take another shot with them, Rothchild moved on to the likes of Bonnie Raitt, Joni Mitchell, and Neil Young. And the Everly Brothers seemed very much alone.

With the sour taste of another well-done but ignored album, things began to get dicey for Don, who seemed to have had it with L.A., the smog, the cliques, the drugs, the greed, never mind his avid place in that crowd. A cliched ad campaign by RCA for *Stories* on a huge billboard high over the Hollywood Freeway that read: "They made your parents fall in love—imagine what they can do for you!" made him wince, and feel aged. By the end of the year, he would move to a farm north of Malibu. His political antenna crackling, he began taking environmental stands in interviews, ragging about other widespread ads for cigarettes and that "manufacturers have taken to re-siting their factories where there are no people to complain. In a remote New Mexico area one plant releases as much smog per day as Los Angeles does in a year."

For his professional and personal woes he blamed soul-wasting egos and fake friendships. Without consulting with Phil, he demanded that the next Everly Brothers album return to Nashville, Chet Atkins, Studio B, and implied that this was the first step for him moving back there in permanent exile from the rock capital he had helped build but believed had betrayed him. Not by coincidence, he felt the same about romance once. Ann left him on her thirtieth birthday—on Valentine's Day 1972, exactly ten years to the day that Phil had dumped her, perhaps as some sort of revenge on both Everly brothers who had twice woven her into their unsettled lives. As she confessed to *Vanity Fair* in 2007, "Phil left me on my 20th birthday, and I left Don on my 30th birthday. I sent their mother a telegram: happy mother's day,+ and thank you for not having a third son."

Venetia, just as with Mary Sue before her, got as far away from Don as she could, taking their children—with no small irony to Nashville as well, before he made his move, where she would forgo acting and work as a children's clothing designer. Rumors would float for years that Don hadn't even seen his kids since they were infants, apparently his own choice. One article reported his lame excuse: "He says his children did not notice [any difference], he was always away in any case." His next paramour was Karen Prettyman, a willowy, dark-skinned Nebraska native whom he met when the Everlys did a *David Frost Show*, on which she was a production assistant. One newspaper story called her "a severe-looking but tender-natured girl, of both Cherokee and Apache descent."

Towering over him, they made an unusual couple, but they clearly fell hard for each other, to the point where she left the Frost show and moved across the country to live with him. She was in the early stages of multiple sclerosis, falling ill for days at a time, and Don resolved to pare back his touring to be with her, which put the act on a short string. When she felt up to it, Karen traveled with Don and sang backup vocals at times. But worries about her health made him more seriously consider moving out of L.A., which would effectively terminate the Everly Brothers. To Don, this was what real love was, seeming like an amulet after the blighted marriages, calling his union with Venetia "miserable," one problem being that Venetia "made me feel like some country boy. Before I met Karen, I'd begun to think I was going to spend the rest of my life alone." His need for music and solitude had even led him to perform incognito once a week at a honky-tonk club far from L.A., where "nobody knew me. I'd sing for free beer."

Phil's own lonesome road had led him to *his* next wife, Patricia Mickey, whom he also met on a TV gig, Dean Martin's show, on which she performed in the scantily clad Golddiggers dance troupe. Phil obviously knew what he wanted in a woman, and he and Patricia danced to the altar on July 15, 1972. But while he didn't know what Don was up to, the two almost never being in contact, their adjutants knew to book them on tours and TV shows, and to arrange separate planes, limo rides, and lodge them in separate hotels. The amazing thing is how well they could still mesh on stage. The differences between them were too obvious to cover up, though, and they began to use it as a sort of one-liner, as if in reality the feuding was just part of sibling life. Phil's line about the one argument lasting twenty-five years becoming standard.

Actually, their easy humor even about such things was a plus. They were actually as funny as the Smothers Brothers when Tom and Dickie riffed about mom loving Dickie better. This was a quite effective defense mechanism when asked about serious issues in general. Asked their opinion of protest songs, Phil, who detested all of them as liberal caterwauling, puckishly said in light derision that "Wake Up Little Susie" was his favorite such song because "We protest having to sing it." Another time, he goofed on the song as "Susie, the zen chant." And though Don had deeper thoughts about political dissent on and off records, he kept it secreted in deference not specifically to Phil but because any such differences would be used as proof that they in fact detested each other. Instead, he went with a facetious cop-out about not being involved in rock and roll "protest"—"We're against [getting up at] early hours," he said, "We protest that." But it was too hard to cover up strong feelings sometimes. Phil, the unlikely rabble-rouser, couldn't keep from ragging on Everly Brothers' fans who were glued to the past instead of accepting them for what they were doing now.

"I think that if people are so happy remembering things from yesterday," he said, "maybe there's something wrong with today."

As for talk about the Everlys overstaying their time in the sun, Phil denied having any worries about what would happen "when the bubble breaks," saying that the dispassionate Ike had primed them to ignore things like "fear and guilt, that's what we were disciplined by." Yet even he couldn't hold back the truth when interviewed by Philip Norman of *The Sunday Times*, telling him, without irony, "You're witnessing the end of one of the greatest sibling rivalries of the 20th century." Indeed, the title of Norman's article—"The Everly Brothers: Growing Apart"—was dated. They had passed that point long ago.

○ ○

By the time the next RCA album was rushed into the pipeline in the summer of 1972, Don had told RCA and Phil that it needed to be recorded in Nashville. This was a personal statement of principle, to chuck off Hollywoodization and get back to being real. Chet Atkins made it a reality when he agreed to produce them and collate the best side men in town. The sessions at Studio B would be kept to a tight gathering, the guitars all being acoustic, played by Chet, Bobby Thompson, Dale Sellers, and Pete Wade, Paul Yandell on banjo, Hal Rugg and Weldon Myrick on pedal steel, Pig Robbins on organ, Dave Briggs on piano, Johnny Gimbel on fiddle, and Ralph Gallant on drums. Still, the LP, given the aw-shucks title *Pass the Chicken & Listen*, had the same shortcomings as their recent albums. Don and Phil contributed not a single song of their own, which was reason enough for them to finally record "Not Fade Away," the song Buddy Holly had written for them but which by now had been covered by tons of other acts.

They also reclaimed ties with Boudleaux and Felice Bryant, though only with a five-year-old song "Rocky Top," and not only enlisted Kris Kristofferson again, recording his song "Somebody Nobody Knows," but also his discovery, John Prine, whose Midwest existentialist country-folk was prickly and socially trenchant. His past in Kentucky mirroring the brothers' own led them to cover "Paradise" from his debut album, which Don took as a command—"Daddy won't you take me back to Muhlenberg County down by the Green River where Paradise lay." Other selections on *Chicken* were Mickey Newbury's "Sweet Memories," a hit in 1967 by Andy Williams, Waylon Jennings and Willie Nelson's "Good Hearted Woman," Guy Clark's "A Nickel for the Fiddler," and two by Gene Thomas, "Lay It Down" and "Watchin' It Go." They handled all of these without sounding as if they even needed to rehearse. As Don would say about it, "We sing differently, everybody's different when they're in front of Chet Atkins. The best thing to say is, if you've never bought an Everly Brothers album, buy this one, because it's the best one we've ever done. It was also the most fun for me."

Maybe so, but the fact that it was another well-executed Everly Brothers album with little original inspiration from the Everly Brothers pushed it into the bog of other such albums. And this might have been foretold before a note had been recorded. A few years later, Phil would relate that he and Don were so at odds over the songs that, on the ones that made it in, "We were saying 'okay' instead of 'yes.'" Even as they were promoting the album in England, they bridled over the fact that a minor RCA executive who had lent a marginal hand with it had the credits amended to read: "The Everly Brothers co-produced by Chet Atkins and David Kirstenbaum." "Can you imagine some young guy telling Chet Atkins what to do?" an offended Phil asked during an interview. "It wouldn't mean a thing if it said, 'co-produced by Freddy Fudpucker and David Kirstenbaum!'"

"Maybe they thought they'd like to do something for the boy," Don interjected.

"Do nothing for the boy!" Phil shouted. "Nobody ever did anything for us!"

Not incidentally brooding, as well, that many of the masters of their records had gone to their exes in the divorce settlements, Phil said, "I thought maybe I'd advertise for [buying them] through the fan-club. In a few years we're going to be really collectable, Donald."

"We can take it steady [only] for the next five years," Don guessed about the extent of their financial security. "Maybe they could do a film special on us, you know? Like they do on species that are disappearing," just as the Everly Brothers seemed to be doing.

○ ○

With another summer of touring, during which one of their back-ing musicians was a pre-Fleetwood Mac Lindsey Buckingham, Don seemed to have gone back to pre-medicating to stave off the punishing effects of endless travel and performing. He even confessed in an interview, "I like beer, champagne. Vichy water, I would drink quarts of that. Anything with bubbles." Whether or not the bubbles steeled him, or loosened him enough not to care, he inched toward the edge. A side effect was that he would throw Phil off kilter on stage, forgetting or fumbling words of songs, turning up the hostilities. A 2002 *Las Vegas Sun* article related that the Everlys were signed to play The Sahara Hotel in Las Vegas early during that summer of 1972, but during a rehearsal "the siblings got into a bitter shouting match, then turned on their co-headliner Nancy Sinatra, shouting at Frank's daughter, leaving her visibly shaken." This may be specious—there is no record of the Everly Brothers appearing in Vegas then, and the only Nancy Sinatra gig there was in January with Lee Hazlewood. Even so, stories like that are alarmingly common.

Don may have been piss-faced when he called Phil in the fall and informed him that the next tour would be the act's farewell, that he'd had enough of the Everly Brothers. He said the legal papers would be mailed, then hung up. Phil couldn't be sure that Don meant it, was sloshed, or just needed to vent. He had good reason to assume this. Sundering the act would mean the RCA deal would be breached, and advances would need to be returned. The continual touring, TV shows, all the good-time Everly vibes would be over, and solo work would be catch as catch can. But just in case, it occurred to Phil that it might be worth his while to record his first solo album right away. In March of 1973, he went into the studio with Warren Zevon, who arranged the LP's ten songs, two of which were written by Phil and seven by Phil and Terry Slater.

It was an understated, even light-hearted dalliance—the title, *Star Spangled Springer*, a very Phil-like play on words that made no real sense, but made for a comical album cover of a sardonic looking beagle in a suit. Like recent Everly Brothers albums, the room had some eye-popping names. Duane Eddy not only played his famously growling guitar but produced the album. The side men included Zevon on keys and on backing vocals Phil's new wife, Patricia. Less concerned with singing perfect harmonies, he laid down some grit worthy of a soul singer but mainly glided through the tracks with a peaceful, easy feeling, a welcome change. The work is today notable mainly for its opening track, a cover of Albert Hammond's "The Air That I Breathe," which Hammond had recorded without success and before the Hollies would make it an enormous hit in 1974. Phil's version was a sweet, emotional rendering with a backdrop of dreamy strings.

Clearly, he was after a non-Everly sound reinventing him as a 1970s pop star. "Sweet Grass County," another landmark to the hills, was trippy pop and the ballad "God Bless Older Ladies (For They Made Rock and Roll)" a light-jazz fillip. Two songs written for Patti, "It Pleases Me to Please You" and 'Lady Anne," both had her backing vocals (though the latter had an odd choice of name, given the brothers' separate flings with Ann Marshall)—while "La Divorce" too seemed to be less comical than a slam at Jackie, apparently the "you" in the song about her not caring "if I took my hat from the rack in the hall and walk through the door," which is basically what he did when he left her. There was also some Phil-style balderdash, like the incoherent "Poisonberry Pie" and Snowflake Bombardier," and a bow to his right-wing loyalties, "Red, White and Blue," standing up for totems of patriotism even as Vietnam was ending in shameful defeat. If there was a theme to the whole thing, it was an unspoken truth—I'm not Don.

Yet, like Don's work, few would notice the album when released in June, or the singles from it, "God Bless Older Ladies (For They Made Rock and Roll)"/"Sweet Grass Country" and "The Air That I Breathe"/"God Bless Older Ladies (For They Made Rock And Roll)." But the charts were far less meaningful to him than just standing toe to toe with Don's more ambitious solo work, and that going solo was an option that he could work again. As he had figured, if Don was serious about sundering the Everly Brothers, that option was near. Very near.

CHAPTER SEVENTEEN

The Bubble Breaks

Phil's album was completed before the Everly Brothers' 1973 summer tour that moved through Canada and then back down to California in early July. Don had not followed through on getting Phil to sign the dissolution papers to break up the act. But then, before a weeklong, three-concert-a-day gig at the John Wayne Theatre Knott's Berry Farm just east of L.A. in Buena Park July 8–14, he peremptorily decided that this gig would be the end of the line. He gave Phil two weeks' notice, and Phil had no choice but to accept it, though once more he couldn't tell if Don would hold to it, or whether he was just drunk and might forget about it when he dried out. But there was a backstory to this decision beyond the brotherly static, Karen's health. Her multiple sclerosis caused chronic flare ups and she had been confined to a hospital bed for weeks, with the prognosis dark. Three years later, Don would tell British newspaperman Stan Sayer:

> Karen had spinal meningitis. I sat at her bedside realizing the only person who mattered to me was slipping away from me. And all the while my advisers were saying to me: Hey, c'mon, we have a tour going soon. Then, miraculously, Karen recovered—fully. That changed my mind about what was really important in life. She was still in the hospital when I made my decision. . . . I needed something like that to find a whole new set of values.

Whether or not his boozing was his salve for this, it was so out of hand that Jack Daley had to cancel their July 6 concert at the Fresno Convention Center, on grounds of "illness." But he was back on his feet and coherent enough to make the gig at the park where free concerts drew thousands to the rustic tourist grounds seen in countless cowboy movies and TV shows for decades. And he had not forgotten his decree to terminate the act, telling the *Los Angeles Times* music writer Robert Hilburn after the penultimate shows on Wednesday the 13th, "It's over. I've quit. I've been wanting to quit for three years now and it is finally time to just do it. I'm tired of being an Everly Brother. I still like to sing 'Bye Bye Love' sometimes, but I don't want to spend my life doing it. I've got to find something else." The headline of the story was "Closing Book on Rock History Chapter."

The shows went well enough, and the next night, the park's entertainment director, Bill Hollingshead, expected an emotional and dignified finale of the Everly Brothers' sixteen-year saga—if it happened. Because, despite the *Times* story, many in the capacity crowds of 2,200 that would jam three times into the bandshell that night didn't know about the breakup. Hollingshead's Plan B was that it *wouldn't* happen, and he had geared the publicity to underplay the breakup angle as a safety measure in case Don blanked out. Without anyone really knowing what he would do, before the first show he spent his time in a backstage trailer bending the elbow—and perhaps ingesting other things. Years later, in the *Rolling Stone* profile by Kurt Loder, he casually referred to Ritalin still being one of his addictions into the 1970s. But whatever he was on that night, he was in no shape to go on stage. When he did for the 7 p.m. show, he looked pale and stumbled around, fumbling lyrics and chords. He was a sloppy parody and Phil couldn't save the ruined gig with humor. With the crowd buzzing, after the fifth of a ten-song setlist, an irate Hollingshead told the house announcer to tell the crowd the show was over.

With everybody watching this befuddled, Don seemed not the least disturbed. He rubber-legged off the stage as the backing musicians and Phil stood looking at each other. Phil lingered for a few minutes, saying nothing. Then, not having been advised what to do by the security people, he began to leave the stage, but not before he suddenly let a quarter-century of pent-up emotion rush out in a symbolic explosion. Lifting his guitar high over his head, he slammed it down far more violently than Hendrix or Townshend ever had, with shards and strings flying in all directions. He walked off holding a shaft of wood in one hand, never trying to get an explanation from Don, then went home with Patti, assuming the Everly Brothers were over.

The audience hung around, still buzzing, before they were asked to file out and make the seats available for the 8:30 crowd, which Hollingshead had held off on allowing in until he could figure out what to do. Not knowing what he'd find when he pushed his way into Don's trailer, he was astonished at how sanguine he seemed. Appearing sober, he told Hollingshead he could play the second and third shows without Phil and called together the backing musicians, running through a few songs and having different members handle the high harmony parts. Convinced, and knowing Phil was gone, Hollingshead hurried out to the stage area and changed the marquee signs to read "The Don Everly Show." The next crowd, who'd been let in on what happened by the departing audience, filed in, confused but not particularly fazed.

Surreal as it was, and still is in retrospect, the first-ever Everly Show proceeded, and damn if it didn't rock. Looking happier than he had for perhaps years, he and the band roamed through a country rock and pop anthology, excluding all Everly Brothers songs. They ran off Waylon Jennings's "Good Hearted Woman," Merle Haggard's "Sing Me Back Home," the Stones' "Honky Tonk Woman," and "Lucille," and as Hilburn reported the next day, "Considering the strain of the evening and the impromptu nature of the show, things went surprisingly well. . . . The audience—often restless in the free amusement park concert setting—seemed pleased." And Don dropped a remark that would be forever quotable. When someone in the crowd shouted, "Where's Phil?" he answered with a smirk, "I don't know, have you seen him?" Then, as if needing to explain nothing more, he told them, not at all with regret or ire, "The Everly Brothers died ten years ago."

He carried on alone for the third set, as well, and when he came off, he was relieved, still feeling no need to regret his self-induced spectacle. Hanging in the trailer with Karen and the bandmates, and not drinking, he offered up the only regretful thing he would say, that the breakup "turned out to be more emotional than I had thought. Someone said it was a little like getting a divorce and I guess it was." As for the future, "I haven't got a clue [as] to what I'm going to do. I really like the idea of getting a new start."

All that really counted was that his narcissistic, Holden Caulfield-ish behavior had gotten him what he had long wanted. The long slog was over, with a bizarre asterisk, but it was over.

The rest of the Everly Brothers tour, with its pending dates in England, was canceled, and the RCA contract put on hold until it was clear Don was not coming back into the act. However, the half-crazed story was not a major, or even minor, headline. There were stories about the loopy finale, almost all of them brief takeouts of a UPI wire story that took the details from Hilburn's story, but only in Britain was there any sort of perspective. To most, it was cause for shrugs—and, in lieu of sympathy, the promoters of the Fresno concert that the duo had canceled sued them in August for over $1 million in damages, which was the only time *Billboard* mentioned the Knott's Berry debacle at all. There would be no new work, nor appearances, by either Don or Phil until a year later. Neither would have much to say about the end of the act, and few asked. Months later, Phil gave in, telling the *Times*, "It was like getting out of school. Don made the final decision to quit, but it was something that had been coming for some time. It was simply a case of growing in different directions—musically, philosophically, politically—and add to that the normal, All-American brother-to-brother relationship, compound it by being together almost constantly for 15 years and you have a general idea what went on."

It took twelve years for Don to have his say, in the *Rolling Stone* dual interview, explaining that his "died ten years ago" crack was "a flip statement. I was a half in the bag that eve-ning—the only time I've ever been drunk onstage in my life. I knew it was the last night, and on the way out I drank some te-quila, drank some champagne—started celebrating the demise." He added that he thought of it as "a funeral" and that

> people thought that night was just some brouhaha between Phil and me. They didn't realize we had been working our buns off for years. We had never been anywhere without working; had never known any freedom. We were just strapped together like a team of horses. It's funny, the press hadn't paid any attention to us in ten years, but they jumped on that. It was one of the saddest days of my life.

Phil's only addendum was: "It was silly, you know? But Donald had decided. It was a dark day."

In the longer lens, the breakup removed many traces of the Everly Brothers for the next decade, which saw a general calm-ing in America with Nixon resigning in disgrace, the end of the cursed war, and hippies morphing into middle-aged business-men and women. For Don Everly, Karen's illness and his dis-taste for the industry left him with no choice but to recommit to a new lifestyle, the only connection with the Everly Brothers being to count his royalties. The end of the act coincidentally brought Jack Daley's Company of Artists to an end, its few art-ists either hooking on elsewhere or finding real work. The excit-able visions of an Everly Brothers multi-dimensional combine vanished into dust.

Don construed this seeming denouement as the right time to commit to moving back to Nashville. And this decision may have actually saved his musical future, as country rock had once more shifted back toward the South, with the rise of The Allman Brothers and Lynyrd Skynyrd. Added to that, the lack of L.A.'s choking pollution would be better for Karen. All of it made him antsy to pack up and go. As he would say, "In '74, I passed back through [Nashville]. I saw Wesley and my mother and father, and looked around. L.A. was chewing me up, and I said, 'I'm moving back.'" As he mapped out escape plans in his head, Phil continued mining the landscape of L.A. He quickly landed a TV gig, accepting an offer by Don Kirshner to host a biweekly half-hour tag-on to Kirschner's much-watched syndicated Friday night anthology *In Concert*, forerunner of ABC's *Don Kirshner's Rock Concert*. Debuting in January 1974, it was a mainly sit-down affair with Phil singing and having thoughtful discussions with acts like Hoyt Axton, B.B. King and Kenny Rankin—but not Don Everly. Phil was his usual relaxed, sometimes goofy self but he only lasted six episodes before the format changed to revolving hosts.

While still kicking around L.A., Don's senses cleared enough for another musical entree, moving on to his second Ode album, recorded not in L.A. or Nashville but London, though it was overseen by Tony Colton, later one of Nashville's biggest producers. The backing crew was led by Albert Lee, the cool Brit who had learned to play guitar listening to American bluegrass and would play lead guitar, acoustic guitar, bass and piano on the album, which also employed other top Brit and American musicians like Buddy Emmons on steel guitar, Jean Rousell on synthesizer, Pete Gavin on drums, bassist Joe Osborne, and a full chorale. Lee and Colton cowrote two songs, "Jack Daniels Old No. 7" and "Warmin' Up the Band," and Don and Colton cowrote six more. Don had but two songs of his own, both of which, "Helpless When You're Gone" and "Evelyn Swings," were clearly disguised references to his bitter aftertaste about Phil, both songs shifting some form of blame to a woman— in the former, one who, like a song, "fills you up and then it's gone / It reminds me of you," and in the latter, serrating lyrics about having "grown up closer than most," sharing beds and clothes and talking about everything, but that now "It's broken, I don't want to stay."

Other tracks were also on a knifepoint, about getting free of the yoke of L.A., most obviously in the almost gospel fervor of "Brand New Rock & Roll Band" and the closing track, "Southern California," his goodbye to Hollywood, sung as if he were Billie Holiday, warning from deep in his tortured and abused gut that those who "want to be a star" should "remain the way you are." On "Takin' Shots," he used war as a metaphor for the empty existence he faced as a fading star, surveying a row of "empty helmets and ammunition shells" and asking, "Ain't there anybody out there, takin' shots anymore? / Am I left here on my own?" But if he had doubts about where he was headed, there was always "Jack Daniels—Old No. 7," on which he admitted, "I just wander through a real bad dream / A-feelin' like I'm comin' apart at the seams." As overproduced and sometimes pretentious as it was, the album, released in late summer and mockingly called *Sunset Towers*, had a coherent concept and stinging personal confessions. Another genuine piece of bluesy, jazzy country rock, the cover art was a laughing, bearded, jeans-and-red-sneaker-wearing Don riding a bronco in a rock-strewn, post-apocalyptic L.A., a dilapidated building off in the background, as if this was Hollywood after the bomb dropped.

And, by pleasant surprise, it got him back onto the charts when, after the late summer release of the album, the single of "Warmin' Up the Band"—a joyful custard about dancing the moondog, shaking your fine tambourine, and cooing "mama you're alright . . . be-bop-a-lula tonight"—hit number 110 pop. Doing as good as he could get in this rocky period, he returned to L.A. but did little by way of music, normally spending his days tending to Karen, keeping a low profile. Then, early in 1975, his decision made, they packed up and literally said goodbye to Hollywood, Don putting his ranch north of Malibu up for sale. He bought a home in Nashville on secluded Hoods Hill Road, far from Music Row. He made Karen his manager, but for the most part he spent time loafing, reading, cooking epicurean meals, collecting fine art, and drinking wine at Les Amis du Vin tastings. If it seemed as if he had gone to Nashville to hide, Don differed. It was, he said, "the best thing I ever did."

○ ○

Phil also went back into the studio that year, and he too recorded his second album in England. With a lack of interest from record labels at home, he had made a modest deal with the British label Pye and went into a London studio with Terry Slater as coproducer and cowriter with him of seven of the eleven tracks, the crew kept to only four musicians, David "Foggy" Little and Joe

Moretti on guitar, Kenny Clayton on piano, Terry Campo on bass, and drummer Barry Morgan, who owned the studio. Two other songs were Albert Hammond's "We're Running Out" and country singer Thomas B. Knight's "Nothing's Too Good for My Baby" (not the Stevie Wonder song). Phil's one singly written song, "Goodbye-Line," was a goodbye to love that also had deeper meaning, such as with macho lines like "A man has got a right to be his own." The LP, *Phil's Diner*, quietly hit the market in December as did two Phil-Slater singles, "Old Kentucky River" and "New Old Song," the final cut, summing up his lifeblood as a refugee from Kentucky who hadn't forgotten his past, Not nearly as trenchant and self-dissecting as Don's album, his heavily echoed voice merging with backing singers sounded happier and less stressed, glad-handing "old friends" making it easier for him to have "been around so long.

He couldn't have been more adorable, the album cover having him pose hammily in front of a small-town eatery called Phil's Diner. Acting happy instead of tortured brought no surprise charting for the album. Yet it did keep him in the L.A. loop. There was a plan to unite him and John Sebastian as a supergroup with Lowell George, the mountainous frontman of the Southern boogie-funk supergroup Little Feat, but the plan fizzled out and Phil turned to his contractually obligated second album for Pye, *Mystic Line*, another coproduction with Slater in London, the session guys this time aided by Warren Zevon, who was a year away from his first major album and reputation as a certified musical genius. Zevon cowrote two songs with Phil, "Lion and the Lamb" and "January Butterfly," arranged all ten tracks, and made the long trip with Phil to play keyboards on the sessions. Phil cowrote three songs with Slater and five himself—one being a rockier redo of "When Will I Be Loved." Another, "Words in Your Eyes," was a lonely lament, his voice almost trembling, backed by an orchestral tide, that "the words in your eyes say you're gone."

Rather than preen, he rather meekly accepted having been stuck under the thumb of strong women. "Lion and the Lamb" relived being owned by a woman who "shot me down" and "laid me low," and that "You are the lion, I am the lamb." His

"Patiently" had him confessing, "It's always been the same old thing / You got me dangling on a string." The title tune "Mystic Line" pleaded to "mystics of the sky" to send down a woman whose string he could break from. The "When Will I Be Loved," redux, done in a sprightly reggae style, was an intriguing self-sample. As with Don's competing LP, it was worth attention, its cover an extreme close-up of an absinthian Phil, eyes staring daggers. But it didn't ignite and missed the charts, as did the single of "Words In Your Eyes."

Worse by leagues, only weeks later, on October 5, Everly family bonding took a further, tragic turn when Margaret called Don and Phil with jolting news. Their proud but long-pushed-aside father was in a hospital in Nashville fighting for his life.

○ ○

The seemingly impregnable Ike Everly had recently been diagnosed with pneumoconiosis, the proverbial Black Lung Disease, which he had actually been living with for decades as the result of all that thick coal dust he had inhaled while working the coal mines as a young man. He had been plagued by coughing fits ever since the boys were young, but on October 5, unable to breathe, he was taken to Parkview Hospital in Nashville where he was also diagnosed with pneumonia and put on a respirator. Margaret kept her sons apprised of his condition, but he deteriorated fast, slipped into a coma and on October 22, just days after his and Margaret's fortieth anniversary and a wraithlike rebroadcast of a 1971 segment by the Everly Brothers on the late-night *Midnight Special*, Isaac Milford Everly Jr. died at a too-hard-lived sixty-seven.

Don and Phil expected the worst, and felt guilty not having stayed closer to Ike, who through the years had become more and more a distant thread in his sons' complicated lives. As terse as he was, he had hidden his private resentment that they had sprinted so far beyond him that he was figuratively left in their dust. And while he appreciated the periodic tributes, they lost touch sometimes for months at a time, which the sons considered necessary given his lack of outward elation about and support of their careers. When Don broke up the act and Phil needed encouragement to go solo, he would recall later on, "my father told me I would never be able to match the Everly Brothers." Ike never stopped trying to prove himself as a music man. Only a year before, he and Margaret were among thousands who entered a national audition cattle call by the producers of the upcoming Burt Reynolds flick *W.W. and the Dixie Dance Kings,* which would be filmed in Nashville. Though they had never acted, they sent in pictures of themselves, hoping their country music past and identity as the parents of the Everly Brothers might win them a couple of small parts, which would be doing something their sons failed at. But that, too, didn't happen.

By the time Ike passed, Don had relocated to Nashville, but kept his distance. Phil came from L.A. for the funeral with his pregnant wife, Patti. The service was held at Tucker Funeral Home in Central City, Kentucky, and the burial at Rose Hill Cemetery, where Ike's simple stone would be the second, after the infant Mary Everly, to be sunk into the large plot he had paid for long ago to house the remains of the entire Everly family. All through the service, Don and Phil sat in silence, barely speaking to each other and the patriarch was then sent into his grave in the manicured section of the cemetery marked off by a large black stone with "EVERLY" carved into it. If he believed he had achieved a triumph in life, he never put it into words. It went down in the ground with him.

Out in Hollywood, nobody accused Phil of trying to hide, but when Pye's American label went under, he could find no label to sustain his solo career. He became a new dad again when Patti gave birth to their son, Chris, who, unlike Don and his children, Phil doted on along with his older son, Jason, who lived nearby with Jackie. Years later, Chris would recall him as "a full-blown dad the whole way. He taught me to ride a bike, drive a car and caught me when I came home at 3 in the morning." No showbiz dad, he left it up to his boys to determine if they wanted a musical career, and had to be persuaded to pick up his flattop and strum at any given time, getting more of a high out of throwing steaks on the grill by his backyard pool. Moreover, he would all but adopt Don's kids, each of whom would live in L.A. Opposites when they performed as an act, Don and Phil Everly were on different planets now, their three thousand miles apart seeming more like light years.

However, nothing the Everly Brothers could do to disappear from each other killed them off as has-been icons. Even now they could, as a team, make themselves and other people money. From 1974 to 1983, the recycled oldies, and even pedestrian songs and unreleased snippets, were pasted together on numerous albums, some leased to outside labels—*Don & Phil's Fabulous Fifties Treasury* (Janus), *The Everly Brothers' Greatest Hits* (Barnaby), *Wake Up Again* (GRT Records) in 1974; *Walk Right Back with the Everly Brothers (20 Golden Hits)* (Warner Bros.), *Everlys* (RCA) in 1975; *Greatest Hits Vol. 1* (Barnaby), *Greatest Hits Vol. 2* (Barnaby), *Greatest Hits Vol. 3* (Barnaby), *The New Album* (previously unreleased Warner Bros. songs) in 1977; *The Everly Brothers* (Teldec) in 1981. And of course they pulled in nice paydays from the cover songs, the bonanza being the March 1975 release of Linda Ronstadt's jumpy cover of "When Will I Be Loved," which went to number two.

Nor could they entirely put music out of their lives. On November 3, 1974, Don tentatively hit the stage, doing a casual two-night gig with country blues singer Linda Hargrove at the Lafayette Music Room in Memphis. And he found the studio again three years later, recording his third solo album, *Brother Jukebox*, for Hickory Records—with bygones being bygones, the label was owned by Acuff-Rose, and the album produced by none other than fifty-nine-year-old Wesley Rose at the Acuff-Rose studio. (Chet Atkins, having had surgery for colon cancer in 1973, had quit as RCA's country music president and cut back on his studio work save for cutting his own albums.) Don had written five of the LP's eleven tracks, the angle now being pure country, and the title tune by songsmith Paul Craft would become a number-one country hit by Mark Chestnutt in 1990. Don's own rendering of the song, with a jukebox being a proxy for "my only family left," was a howling Dixie ditty, a moonshine-soaked ball.

Another evergreen was written eons ago by Wesley's daddy, Fred Rose, "Deep Water," which had been sung by Bob Wills and His Texas Playboys, Ray Price, and Ferlin Husky.

The album was stacked with other old-time fare like Lefty Frizzell's "Yesterday Just Passed My Way Again" and S. D. Shafer's "That's the Way Love Goes" (which had been sung by Justin Tubb, the step-uncle of Don's daughter Venetia). The former brimmed with broken-hearted vibrato. And Don added a hearty redo of the Everly Brothers' 1960 "So Sad (To Watch Good Love Go Bad)," which had by then been covered often by country singers. The final three tracks, all by Don, comprised a hopeful trilogy of his new life's stages—"Oh, I'd Like to Go Away," "Oh, What a Feeling" and "Turn the Memories Loose Again," the last acknowledging that although life "can be a feather that's caught up in the wind" and success "a freedom or a chain," all he ever wanted was to sing, and that damn it, he still could. When the LP was released in March, the cover shot designed by Rod Dyer of a mop-haired Don, arms crossed, an Old Glory kerchief around his neck, three singles made the country chart, "Yesterday Just Passed My Way Again" (no. 50), "Since You Broke My Heart" (no. 84), and "Jukebox" (no. 96).

But Hickory Records was bleeding red ink and would go under, with the entire Acuff-Rose catalog to be taken over by Sony Music Publishing, which today owns the rights to almost all Everly Brothers songs. Left unmoored, it took him a year to perform again, when in 1977 he took to London for Britain's yearly country music festival. There, he told an AP reporter, "I'm loose now. It feels good. I'm not out to prove anything anymore. I'm not chasing anything." The reporter, though, seemed fixated on Don's larger waistline, which the once-svelte Everly said with a laugh was "the result of being laid back." The title of the story was "Don Everly Is Back, But He's Fat and Forty." And he was okay with that.

○ ○

Phil, too, had plenty of idle time, and he had no problem living with it. Down in his basement, he became obsessed with fiddling around trying to upgrade music technology to a new level of utility. His older son, Jason, who would also become involved in music, said that "he wanted to make a guitar—he always called it a *gee-tar*—with a speaker in it. It was heavy and it didn't really work and had tons of feedback. He had a record player with two needles so it would play real stereo. That's what he was trying to invent. [He'd say] 'What can we do? How can we make this better?'" Yet he couldn't upgrade his talent for screwing up marriages. His philandering caused the implosion of another when he and Patti amicably divorced in 1978, sharing custody of Chris. It left him downcast. "It's hard to get fluffed up about love anymore," he told an interviewer. "I've lived it. I try to avoid it. If I'm extremely fond of a woman, if I think I might really wind up walking down the aisle again, I go in another direction."

Music was always one such direction, his éclat helpfully built in. Seeking an outlet for another album, he secured a one-off deal with an old and diversified ally, Warner Bros. Records, shuttled to its Elektra/Asylum label owned by the pushy, twenty-something David Geffen. He was set up with producer Snuff Garrett, a very hip, Texas-raised good old boy who had produced massive hits for Bobby Vee, Del Shannon, and Gary Lewis and the Playboys for Liberty Records, then for Sonny and Cher and numerous others. Garrett furnished him with a cow-riter, former Ventures member John Durrill. They dashed off six numbers, with three more by Phil and the Everlys' road bass player from the 1950s, Joey Page; and under the new sway by Acuff-Rose, the songs with Durrill were published by the latter's Peso Music, owned by Steve Dorff, the others by Phil's newest publishing company, Bud's Red Hot Music.

The album, *Living Alone*, was his testament to, well, living alone. The title tune, the only song written entirely by Phil, confirmed that living alone sucked, but at least "you never have to say goodbye," something that had also happened when the Everly Brothers split. All the tracks sent the now-not-so-happy Everly down a self-pitying avenue, even a hoot like "Buy Me a Beer" a plea on a lonely Saturday night when "my baby's not here." In "I Was Too Late for the Party," he looked around and saw "my woman was gone," on "I Just Don't Feel Like Dancing" he laid blame on a straying woman, as he did on "You Broke It." Even a hopeful thought like "Love Will Pull Us Through" came with the hedge that "I'm still fool enough to think love's true." In "California Gold," love was a tableau of "midnight hookers and Midwest lookers" in "worn out bikinis" hanging with "sun-baked weenies." "Ich Bin Dein (I Am Yours)" proved that whatever language he used, "in my heart I knew I'd sail away." The last track, "The Fall of '59," was a play on words for the fall of impetuous dreams he'd had twenty years before, yesterday when he was young.

His sweet lilting vocals did make it affecting, nonetheless, and the "sun-baked weenies" line may have been the album's main highlight. But Garrett's plodding string, horn and synth arrangements designed to nibble into the dying disco miasma did nothing to make Phil into a lead vocalist instead of a mere harmony maker. The LP and two singles died quickly. Even so, the connection to Garrett paid dividends. When he produced the country-oriented soundtrack of Clint Eastwood's enormous hit *Every Which Way But Loose*, the one with the orangutan, he got Phil to write a song for it, which he did with Joey Paige, "Don't Say You Don't Love Me No More," and sung it with Clint's singer/actress girlfriend Sondra Locke on the soundtrack. And Clint also cast him and Mel Tillis in bit parts as honky-tonk singers at The Palomino, where Phil regularly played unadvertised gigs.

This then was the state of the Everly Brothers as the decade of their dissolution neared its end. At the least, they were there, in small but palatable doses. Phil, for example, singing harmony on J. D. Souther's "White Rhythm and Blues" in 1979. For the widowed Margaret Everly, whose emotions were always kept in check, seeing her sons keeping apart from each other, and from her, caused pain in her heart. Appearing years later on a BBC radio documentary about them, asked about her sons' sticky separation, she said, "It hurt. It hurt. I almost couldn't accept them going their separate ways," but added that "they needed some time to get away from each other to get to know who they were." The host asked if they had talked to her about it.

"No, they kept things from me," she said. "Phil wasn't always in the right place, and he would call me for reassurance. Don had a wife, but Phil was always more of a loner."

That might have been the answer to the jokey Smothers Brothers question that Don and Phil used to riff on when they sang together, about which of them "mom always liked best." But now it seemed neither one had much room for her in their disoriented lives. Margaret, like Ike, knew she was a casualty of their egos and petty grudges. And when the 1980s dawned, it must have seemed like a kind of cruel fate that there might not be room for *them* left in music as separate entities. Which was the reason why they wouldn't let themselves be shut out as an immutable team.

CHAPTER EIGHTEEN

Foreverly

To be sure, their classic songs and ambience were foreverly in terms of public consumption—an instructive moment being the *Midnight Special* episode of September 19, 1980, which ran current videos of The Rolling Stones' "She's So Cold," David Bowie's "Ashes to Ashes," and Paul Simon's "One Trick Pony," but also a grainy 1962 clip of the Everly Brothers singing "All I Have to Do Is Dream," which always seemed to fit any era. And rather than just fade away into memories, Don would make the brothers' first move of the decade, doing a gig on August 1 at The Venue Club in London at the urging of Albert Lee, who did a brief tour with him there. He also did a syndicated TV special called *Nashville Swings*. Phil also was visible, his first forays of the decade being to sing one of his solo songs and a medley of the oldies with host Dionne Warwick on *Solid Gold* and playing a gig in Vancouver in October 1981. Clearly, neither could stay out of the game, and despite all the disappointments, they had their place.

But their mulish insistence on staying relevant, if reduced, was also based on the fact that, other than making music, their lives were again lonely. The perfect union that Don believed he had with Karen fell apart at the seams like all the others. They both agreed they had lost their love for each other, but rather than dissolve in bitterness as he had when the end came with

Mary Ann and Venetia, he only praised her. And Karen was grateful for the sacrifices he had made for her, but they had grown apart, and the divorce amicably went through on March 8, 1983. (She would sadly lose her battle with multiple sclerosis in 2021.) As always, he had his next paramour lined up, a fledgling singer named Diane Craig, but that seemed tenuous at best.

Along the way, he admitted, "My personal life now is sort of strange. I really don't know what to say about it, hardly. I guess I'm with a girl called Victoria right now—but I'm still with Diane, too. I don't know how to describe this situation. You get your career straightened out, and all of a sudden your personal life goes."

He could say this because his career had indeed straightened out. Phil Donnelly, the Irish-born guitarist who had been a session player on Don's solo work, had moved to Nashville and put together a country rock band called The Dead Cowboys, with Tony Neman on drums and Rachael Peer on bass. Donnelly prevailed on Don to join them on gigs in town and in England. As this short stint occurred, there were months of feelers and negotiations between the Everlys' camps. This was mainly the doing of Albert Lee, the Brit R&B kingpin who also had woven himself into Don's life, visiting him frequently in Nashville. As Lee remembered, "I became Don's big buddy. We played local bars together, and he used to loan me his guitars. I was singing Phil's parts, so I actually was an Everly Brother for a little while."

Still, three more years went by, with feints and false starts. Then, in the early spring of 1983, Phil landed another fleeting deal, this time with Capitol Records, for which he recorded a song overseen by country producer Kyle Lenning and written by pop songwriters Kevin McKnelly and Don Stirling, "Who's Gonna Keep Me Warm." When released, it vaulted him back onto the country chart, getting to number thirty-seven, and into the Brit top fifty. That preceded an April release of his eponymous album *Phil Everly*, in collaboration with Terry Slater, recorded in England and Hollywood and produced by British bass man Stuart Colman, who played on most of the tracks, and featured backing and co-vocals by Christine McVie on "When I'm Dead and Gone." He dueted with Cliff Richard, backed by keyboard whiz Pete Wingfield, on "She Means Nothing to Me," which was written by guitarist John David. It ran up the British chart to number nine and was a favorite on *Top of the Pops*. (Two other tracks, "Who's Gonna Keep Me Warm" and its flip, "One Way Love [On a Two-Way Street]," were included on an expanded edition of the LP in 2011.)

It seemed like Phil just might have cracked the music code of the 1980s. And doing so well on English soil could have made Don feel like Phil was moving in on his territory. Not wanting to be upstaged, Don was suddenly receptive to Lee's oft-dropped opinion that this was the right time to reunite with Phil, if even just a one-night reunion concert. As the details were worked out for a two-nighter at Royal Albert Hall on September 23, though the brothers were still not directly speaking to each other, Don became more immersed. According to Lee: "He said: 'We're gonna do a record and we're gonna go on the road'—to my great surprise." Albert was contracted as musical director of the shows, which would be hyped to no end in the British press and recorded for a double album produced by Tony Clark to be released by the independent American label Passport Records.

A deal was also made with HBO, which, in the wake of MTV breaking open rock's video generation, had scored sky-high ratings for a similar taped broadcast of Simon and Garfunkel's reunion concert in Central Park in 1981—during which Art Garfunkel sang "Wake Up Little Susie," a cover of which by him and Simon would hit number twenty-seven, their last Top 40 hit—and also signed David Bowie for a 1984 concert show. The giant cable network, which paid the Everlys a $1 million fee, would videotape both of the Albert Hall shows and televise an edited version the following January. And so, with the negotiating over and the deals signed, Don and Phil, eyeing each other warily, started rehearsing with the all-Brit band of Lee and Martin Jenner on guitar, bassist Mark Griffiths, Wingfield on keys, and drummer Graham Jarvis.

"They'd have words, but most of the time everything was fun," Lee said. "They'd get a little bee in their bonnet every now and again about one subject or another, but it would blow over pretty quickly. I think they realized they weren't under the pressures that they were in the 60s."

To be sure, they were habitually programmed with each other, and the gears instinctively fell into place—being guaranteed an immediate hundred grand each and 50 percent of the album royalties didn't hurt—on the first night of the show. With all 5,232 seats filled, they were ready to fire on all cylinders, two guys in their forties, heavier in their almost kitschy black tuxes with white wing collar shirts and black bow ties, but firmly in their element. Unlike the disastrous previous attempt at a live album, they nailed this one. Albert Hall was a comfy locale for them, having played there before—with Ike as special guest—in 1971. Don was clear-eyed and sharp, Phil again biologically and professionally tuned in to his brother's every nuance. Entering from opposite ends of the stage to tumultuous applause, they threw an arm around each other's neck, easily smiling, Don's opening remarks being, "It's good to be back. I'm Don and I'm still the oldest, but Phil's catching up though," noting they had been on "vacation. . . . We enjoyed part of it and hated part of it." The opening song was a now-metaphoric "Crying in the Rain.

The setlists of the two shows would differ from those of the tightly edited, twenty-one-song double album and hour-long HBO show, the opening song on which was "Claudette," while the album began with "The Price of Love." The live shows stretched out a half-hour and half-dozen songs longer, with several medleys and some fans-only stuff like "Ebony Eyes," "Put My Little Shoes Away" and "Maybe Tomorrow." There were no pyrotechnics beyond overhead lights flashing, and the brothers stood rooted in front of the white-jacketed band, doing no more than twirling their guitars at times. But, under Lee's direction, the band didn't hold back; rather, they played louder and more rocking than the original recordings had been, with Lee hitting some terrific solos. As if catching the fever in the hall, the brothers sang with zeal. There were three encores, with "Let It Be Me" giving way to "Good Golly Miss Molly" and Jimmy Reed's "Baby What You Want Me to Do" before they could get off the stage.

The shows seemed to glide by, and the reviews uniformly agreed that, as an AllMusic retro review put it, the event wasn't a reunion but a "resurrection," in which the brothers "actually sound fresh and catchy to contemporary ears." It was as close as possible to finding their long-sought apotheosis, Don's summation after a rousing rendition of "Be-Bop-a-Lula": "You never grow old with rock and roll." Perfectly accurate on those two nights. One of the British critics, Penny Reel, even postulated that the "certain tension" between them "is the genius of their music. It's as if the lyrics . . . are directed as much to each other as any next party," even on "a night of reconciliation." Reel's closing line: "I miss Elvis and Buddy Holly, but at least I see the Everly Brothers."

○ ○

The Everly Brothers Reunion Concert, released in late September, charted at number 162 in America, 47 in England, and the HBO presentation has been sold, rented, bootlegged, and put online ever since. Some crabbier critics held back full praise, Robert Christgau for one mewling that "they sure didn't slough it off. But it's nostalgia anyway, adding nothing but a pushy drummer and a slight slackening of the voices to a superb body of work available in better record stores everywhere." Yet the reunion sprouted additional legs, mandating new tours and recordings, the first one, *EB 84*, done with a core led by Lee and Wingfield, and produced by Dave Edmunds, the baby-faced Welshman who as a performer had bridged new wave with covers of 1950s rock and rockabilly, and in 1980 produced the four-track tribute EP *Nick Lowe and Dave Edmunds Sing the Everly Brothers*.

Edmunds recalled that, after attending rehearsals for the re-union concert, he joined Don and Albert "putting away several pints of beer in a local pub." A few weeks later, the brothers had agreed to a two-record deal with Mercury Records and Don asked him to produce the Everly Brothers version 2.0. "Hardly able to contain myself, I gratefully accepted," said Edmunds, who was no small potatoes, having collaborated with both Paul McCartney and ELO frontman Jeff Lynne, both of whom he reached out to as album collaborators. As Everly buffs, they accepted. Paul told him, "Give me two weeks" to come up with a song, and kept to it, sending a demo of "On the Wings of a Nightingale." Edmunds had similar success with Lynne, who wrote "The Story of Me," and Dire Straits' leader Mark Knopfler, who wrote "Why Worry." But when Edmunds went to Nashville with songs for Don to approve, he said, "any song sounding remotely like the Everly Brothers, would be automatically discarded by them," no matter who wrote them.

Accordingly, the work, recorded in London's Maison Rouge Studio, could have been called "Don and Phil Don't Sing the Everlys," though for Edmunds getting them to sing at all was the problem, given that "they were strangely reluctant to actually do any work. Don would arrive at 3 p.m. and usually prefer to sit in the control room relaying humorous anecdotes from his legendary career, as though deferring the awful moment of commitment. Phil would arrive even later, and, both having made prior dinner arrangements, would leave the studio around seven. It was even more problematic coaxing Phil up to the microphone. At first, he suggested that Don should sing his part first, and that he would add his harmony later." And Don posed more problems:

> He sang completely differently on his own, constantly altering his phrasing, rarely singing anything the same way twice. It is inconceivable that Phil was not aware of this fact, but insisted that we do it his way. It was like trying to separate yin from yang. I found it to be a miserable experience, with Phil becoming frustrated and throwing the occasional primadonna fit. In virtually every record the Everly Brothers made, Don [sings] a solo passage, usually the middle eight bars, which I have always considered to be the epitome of soulful expression and perfect pitch. But when their vocals [were] finally completed, Don decided that he should re-record all his solo passages over again.

What made it worth the effort, he said, was when "Don and I spent several days working on it, and there were moments, listening to him, when I could feel the hair on the back of my neck stand on end. These were among the most satisfying moments I have ever spent in a recording studio." Once again, by rote, Don and Phil, he said, were so "locked in" to each other that Phil "constantly eyeballed Don to keep in sync with Don's phrasing. They just wouldn't let themselves be disjointed, and music veterans will tell you this codependency simply has not existed in anyone else's work; it was so absolute, so foolproof, that it was scary." Actually, it was scary in other ways. The British writer Ray Connolly, given access to the sessions, later published an indelible article in the *Daily Mail* that read:

> I got some idea of how far back the enmity went when a mutual friend who was working with them overheard a row between the brothers which carried on into the early hours in their motel room. Between the shouting and sobbing, over and over again she heard both referring to their father. "Daddy said this". . . and "Daddy said that" went the allegations and counter allegations. [Perhaps] there's some truth in the suggestion that Don always felt he was upstaged by Phil's sweet lilting tenor voice. "I've been a has-been since I was ten," he is alleged to have said. Each of the brothers may have felt, at times, in the other's shadow.

The finished album must have made Edmunds tingle, especially when McCartney came in and played guitar on his "Wings of a Nightingale," another of his melodic and harmless "silly love songs" that Edmunds punched up into a semi-chant of the title. He also contoured the brothers' impeccable harmonies to Bob Dylan's cooing semblance of country rock on the "Lay Lady Lay" cover, trading the original's haunting pedal steel for electric guitars, losing the simple yearning. Lynne's "Story of Me," with Lynne on bass and a streaming synth line, was a swaying lesson about discovering oneself. Frankie Miller's "Danger Danger" played to the 1980s trend of hard drum-machine beats and almost angry vocals, warning "the best little tease with the cheap thrill" of the dangerous game she was playing. Wingfield's "More Than I Can Handle" was the sequel, such love being "too much for me."

The only Everly-composed numbers were three by Don, "Following the Sun," "You Make It Seem So Easy," and "Asleep," with Edmunds pouring on the pedal steel on "Sun," jamming slide guitars into "Easy," and going soft rock on the somnolent "Asleep," with Don crooning, as if wishing for eternal peace, "It's like heaven when I sleep." All these were tangy curiosities, and the album clearly more independent minded, though among generally good reviews, there again were the professional crabs; to Christgau it was a "lacquered, interpretation-enhancing production, because mature interpretation will never be their forte . . . a certain emotional complexity eludes them." Whatever its faults, it worked as a comeback vehicle. The McCartney song, boosted by the first Everlys video (which for some reason made it about them finding a new car), hit number fifty on the pop chart, number forty-nine country, number nine of the Adult Contemporary, and number forty-one in England. A second single, Brit country writer Paul Kennedy's "The First In Line," the most overt country song, hit number forty-four country. The album itself reached number thirty-eight in America, thirty-six in England.

Not bad for a couple of near fifty-year-old farts, and it ushered in one more reunion-era work, *Born Yesterday*, which was recorded at the same studio with Lee, Wingfield, and company, and some supplemental recording at the Record Plant in L.A. This time, Mark Knopfler's "Why Worry" made it in, and the only Everly-composed song was Don's title tune, which would be the album's first single, a woeful remonstrance about learning his woman shitcanned him, such as by seeing her throw his clothes out on the street—perhaps not an imaginary scenario for him. Again, there were country flavors, but the most striking cut was another Dylan cover, the folkie "Abandoned Love," which went right along with "Born Yesterday," its condemnatory lyrics casting off the "ball and chain" yet realizing "I've been deceived by the clown inside of me." Edmunds bathed that one with steel-string and bagpipe bathos borrowed from Liam O'Flynn's

"Tin Whistle." "Why Worry," with its sad and languid intro by Lee modeled on "All I Have to Do Is Dream," was so good the Everlys would play it live with Chet Atkins on a local Nashville country music TV special in 1987.

Others included "Amanda Ruth" by Chip and Tony Kinman of the country band Rank and File, Brian Neary and Jim Photogio's "I Know Love" and "Don't Say Goodnight"; Nashville writer Jon Goin and Ozark Mountain Daredevil founder Larry Lee's "These Shoes"; Iain Sutherland's "Arms of Mary"; Billy Burnette and Larry Henley's "Thinkin' 'Bout You"; and Memphis blues rocker Larry Raspberry's "Always Drive a Cadillac," a bitching road song with Phil's throaty lead vocal sounding much like Bryan Adams or the early Springsteen. When *Born Yesterday* was released in November 1986, a review by Jay Cocks in *Time* opined that "The Everlys are back. They are back to stay." It peaked at number eighty-three on the pop album chart and number twenty-two on the country chart. The "Born Yesterday" single rose to number seventeen on the country chart, and they notched a final two-sided hit when the next single, "I Know Love"/"These Shoes" rolled respectively to numbers fifty-six and fifty-seven on the singles country chart.

With those relative successes, the manic two-year hitch with the Everlys was over for Edmunds, who had mixed memories about it.

"I never before encountered such a disparity of personalities and opposing values in two brothers," he said. "You get on well with one, at the cost of not getting on well with the other. I never met anyone who was close to both. While Don and I hit it off so well, I never managed to unravel Phil, and vice versa."

As it was, trying to unravel either of them seemed like a full-time job. But no one would need to do it in depth until these pages were written, for many years, perhaps because the Everly Brothers just never seemed to be finished with what they were doing out there on the horizon. And even after the reunion period, they still weren't.

CHAPTER NINETEEN

So It Was, So It Always Will Be

One measure of their yeah-we're-still-here presence was that they still argued. Man, did they argue. About *everything*. But they also managed to do selective road shows such as returning "home" to Shenandoah for a homecoming concert on July 5, 1986. And there was a last hurrah in the studio in 1989, recording an album called *Some Hearts*, again on Mercury. Recorded in four studios, three in L.A., one in Ft. Lauderdale, it was a team effort, with Albert Lee and Pete Wingfield making these trips with them, but none of the ten tracks were the products of both Everlys. Don wrote four—"Some Hearts," "Be My Love Again," "Can't Get Over It," "Three Bands of Steel"—Phil three, all cowritten with John Durrill, "Ride the Wind," "Angel of the Darkness," "Brown Eyes."

The title track was an eerie, part-Euro, part-Latin-sounding synth ballad alluding that "Love's sweet illusions sometimes can be the love you dreamed come true"—a hope dashed by "Be My Love Again" urging a fading lover to "Take away the silly games that's messing up our minds / Nobody's winning anyway." The non-Everly songs were country guitarists J. Fred Knoblock and Pat Alger's "Julianne," John Hiatt and Mike Porter's "Any Single Solitary Heart"—and the curve ball, Brian Wilson's "Don't Worry Baby," which saved the album from itself, easing the emotionally hollow 1980s acoustical blandness. Their cover of the latter—which like "Bye Bye Love" is a rock and roll Rosetta Stone—eschewed the frills for an early-1960s feel, complete with car obsession. Enhanced by Carl Wilson's backing harmonies, it proved that the Everly Brothers, when not trying too hard, were a hell of a cover band.

Mercury would release it as the only single from the LP, and though it or the album didn't chart, the song was also the A-side on a Capitol Records release called *The Everly Brothers with the Beach Boys—Don't Worry Baby*, the B-side coupling the original "Help Me Rhonda" and "Surfin' USA." But while the album was productive and fun, it would be their last album, its failure to chart a sign that they had probably gone one step over the line of fulfillingness.

Plainly, they needed to do no more now to prove they belonged. The reunion was the icing on a music revelation that would not stop reaching into people's lives, ever. Reproduction of music during their career had gone from vinyl to eight-track to cassette to CD to DVD to downloading MP3s off of computers, from record stores to digital streams. And in every format, there has been a release of Everly Brothers songs. Even as they bounced from label to label, studio to studio, the appetite for their songbook has kept recurring. Four oldies box sets came out between 1984 and 1988—*The Everly Brothers' 24 Original Classics* (Arista), *Home Again* (RCA), *All They Had to Do Was Dream* (Rhino), *Their 20 Greatest Hits* (Rhino), *The Everly Brothers* (Castle). Four more, including those gigantic anthologies and rarities, would come in the 1990s, four more in the 2000s, the door finally closing where it had first opened, with *Country: The Everly Brothers* in 2012.

They would also return to Royal Albert Hall six more times, in October 1987 and then in 1991, 1993, 1995, 1997, and finally on November 24, 2005—their final live gig. Some of their collaborators milked the Everly connection as well. Terry Slater, for example, began producing the quirky Norwegian synth pop band a-ha, who covered "Crying in the Rain" in 1990, which was a major hit everywhere except America. And then there were the honors. By design, *Born Yesterday* came out just weeks before the first Rock and Roll Hall of Fame inductions would be held, a creation drawn from the grandiosity of *Rolling Stone* publisher Jann Wenner and industry biggies like Atlantic Records boss Ahmet Ertegun. Notified that they would be in the initial class with Chuck Berry, Elvis Presley, Fats Domino, James Brown, Jerry Lee Lewis, Little Richard, Ray Charles, and Sam Cooke, they arrived in New York—separately, as usual—for the industry's rites of self-glorification and half-drunken glitz in the ballroom of the Waldorf-Astoria Hotel on January 23, 1986.

Don, who had to swallow his conviction that the industry was a giant scam run by liars, thieves, and swindlers, came to town with his sometimes girlfriend Dianne Craig, and Phil with his nineteen-year-old son, Jason. They sat tables apart, until brought to the wings as their induction speech was given by Neil Young, who spoke with great reverence of his own rituals trying in vain to sound like them, but "still couldn't get it." Unlike Neil, who wore a fringed coat and Civil War-general hat, after his speech the brothers came up to the microphone in their tuxes. Handled the statuettes, Phil's opening remark was perfect.

"Thank god," he said, "they gave us two. We don't have to fight over it."

Don cackled, and after Phil thanked the industry and said cryptically, "We made good choices when we were young," Don naturally was more existential, saying the honor was not personal but rather "a hat's off to rock and roll, which has changed all of our lives, the way we talk, the way we dress, the way we think. . . . [It's] been good to us, we hope it's been good to you." They then took their leave—this was before inductees would do a brief set after their thank-yous—and when the show closed as a jam session with the house band backing Chuck on "Reelin' and Rockin'," Billy Joel, Steve Winwood, John Fogerty, and Keith Richards joined in, but Don and Phil were nowhere to be found, leaving early to go their own separate ways again.

The same year, though, they did reunite, more fleetingly, at the behest of Paul Simon, to add a touch of resonance to the album that gambled his flagging solo career on opening mainstream doors to little-heard South African rhythms and idioms mainly submerged by apartheid. That, of course, was the *Graceland* album, his metaphoric homage to Elvis's beyond glitzy

Memphis mansion and death site, where empty decadence somehow lured tourists into near-religious visions of rebirth, including Simon after his career and marriage had floundered.

The title tune part-blessed and part-mocked this bizarre American liturgy, and Simon wanted to undergird the song with the harmony that blessed pop music and had a cellular hold on its adventurers. He brought the Everlys to an L.A. studio where Simon overdubbed the album he had primarily recorded in Johannesburg, violating the ban on travel to South Africa and irking anti-apartheid activists, though Simon was doing more for the cause by hiring Black musicians there at elevated pay rates.

The Everlys' part was small, blended with Simon's vocal on the choruses that ended with "Maybe I've a reason to believe / We all will be received In Graceland." Simon during the session was filmed in the control booth saying during early takes of the song there were "too many words for them" to keep the harmonies flowing. Yet the end result worked ideally, providing them with one more honorific, to be involved even if just a bit on one of history's most important albums. They also agreed when Johnny Cash asked them to do backing vocals on his 1987 rerecording of his 1968 "Ballad of a Teenage Queen" with his daughter Rosanne Cash in Nashville, a mild hit single from his *Water from the Wells of Home* album. They seemed to enjoy these sorts of laurels. But although Don had famously said you never grow old in rock and roll, he would find out otherwise. You do, and no one can stop it.

In the turgid world of music publishing, Don's songs were owned by Tropicbird Music, Phil's by Everly & Sons—though the masters of each were still owned by others who entered the picture long after the fact, Acuff-Rose having sold its catalog in 1984 to the Gaylord Entertainment Company, the Grand Ole Opry's parent company, for $15 million. (In 2002, it would be sold again to Sony/ATV.) And there were still nice paychecks for the taking. Although Don had sworn in the song he wrote about the town that he would never return to Las Vegas, he and Phil did a few more turns at The Orleans Hotel on the strip.

But he did hold to his odd aversion to his own kids, all of whom caught showbiz fever. His daughter Stacy branched out as an actress and sometimes singer, acting in low-budget 1980s flicks like *Vice Squad* and *Hollywood Vice Squad*. His other daughter, Erin, followed her own, manic path, hooking up with Axl Rose, the front man of the semi-crazed Guns N' Roses, who wrote "Sweet Child O' Mine" about her and put the shaggy-haired brunette into the video of it and another for "It's So Easy," with S&M jive like him putting a ball gag in her mouth—apparently the sort of thing they did at home. After marrying in 1990, she miscarried (a painful déjà vu for Don) and they divorced after ten months, launching lawsuits about who fucked up who the most. She married again, moved to Atlanta, divorced, and in 2010 was arrested for domestic violence, pulling a knife on her boyfriend, architect Matthew Klyn.

At the same time, her brother Edan also crept into performing as a glam rock singer and musician—his entry eased not by Don but Phil, who taught him to play steel-string guitar. When the Everly Brothers did a 1985 concert at the Pacific Amphitheatre, Edan sang backup. He then founded an eponymous band in 1992, the drummer being Frankie Avalon's son, and released a single called "Dead Flowers" and in the new century, two solo albums, *For the Insanity of It All* and *Songs from Bikini Atoll*, in 2011. Ironically, with his high-pitched voice he sounded more like Phil, who was contentedly watching his children grow up, his son Jason saying his old man was "gracious and ridiculously humble." Phil's younger son, Chris, went to school in L.A. with Tom Petty's daughter Adria, which brought the two rockers into a friendship. When the Everlys got a Hollywood Walk of Fame star in 1986, Petty made the presentation.

Jason got into the game playing his father in a musical review while attending Chapman College. Phil had told him, from experience, "I forbid you to actually make a career out of the business. If you make a lifetime commitment out of it, you're in trouble." Jason pushed on, doing some recording in Germany and the Philippines and as an actor, costarring in the 1997 Filipino romcom *Isang tanong, isang sagot*. When Phil had knee surgery and was confined to his home in Toluca Lake, Jason moved with him and the two made some home recordings, including a redo of Buddy Holly's "Rave On." After giving up on singing, Jason would settle into a different showbiz stake, as Phil's agent and overseer of his business, which primarily consisted of authorizing the use of their songs for use on movie soundtracks and accepting more awards.

The foreverly young brothers had become grandfathers but had long remained single, Don since 1982, Phil since 1977. Now, as if needing wives would seal their future, Don married a swarthy Nashville sister-act singer, Adela Garza, in 1997 when he was sixty and she was twenty-eight. When she moved into his home, her sister Adelaida moved in as well. The few times he was seen in newspaper pictures, such as one taken at the Kentucky Derby, dressed to the nines, she was anchored tight next to him. She also became his manager, running the Don Everly business profile under the name Adalida Music. However, this was no smooth ride. Adela would be in the papers numerous times, for the wrong reasons. In 2001, she was arrested for DUI and fined $500, pled guilty to implied consent on an unspecified charge, and apparently let go after an arrest for criminal trespass. As time wore on, the list of her arrests and court judgments would be arm's length, with uncomfortable propinquity to the aging Don.

Phil, meanwhile, who had insisted he had no interest in love anymore, married again in 1999, to another Patti, Patrice Arnold. The two had met at a New Year's Eve party Phil had hosted in 1994 and she had come with some of Jason's friends. She was forty-two, he sixty, and he told her, "I'm not looking for a girlfriend and I'm never getting married," but they became an item and married on August 22, 1999, in Las Vegas, when the brothers did a gig there. She quit her job as a police dispatcher, traveled with him, and hectored him to stop smoking, though he would be back on the Marlboros soon after, all but signing his own death warrant. He and Don would not be heard on a new recording for another decade—and if Don had any notion of doing so with Phil, he nixed it when in late 1994 a cover of "All I Have to Do Is Dream" that Phil recorded as a duet with Cliff Richard taking Don's part hit number fourteen in England. Don took this as a slap in the face. When the syndicated Nashville Network broadcast a documentary about the duo, *The Life and Times of the Everly Brothers*, in March 1996, Phil boycotted it rather than being interviewed with him.

They did consent to some more appearances, doing a brief return to the Ryman Auditorium on April 29, 1998, to help kick off a tribute musical about to tour called *Bye Bye Love*, before heading to Las Vegas and then to Australia and the Netherlands for more reunion gigs there. And while few may have noticed, they were on a double album from the Andrew Lloyd Webber rock opera *Whistle Down the Wind*, which had closed quickly in December 1996. On the album, with songs composed by Webber and Jim Steadman and sung by the likes of Tom Jones, Boy George, Bonnie Tyler, and Donny Osmond, they performed "Cold," a harmonica-enhanced stomp. It would be the final Everly Brothers single and unwittingly would provide in one line the context of where they were as the new millennium arrived—"It's cold and getting colder."

But it *still* wasn't over. In 2001, they were inducted into the Country Music Hall of Fame. Then they found themselves again being invited into the cosmos of Simon and Garfunkel, agreeing to appear on the latter's own reunion tour of 2003, "Old Friends," starting with an October 3 show at the Pepsi Center in Denver. As the staging had it, in mid-show Paul and Art reminisced about their youthful elan for the Everlys before introducing them. The Everly Brothers who proceeded to the stage were in their sixties, bore little trace to the "Asiatic"-looking eels of eons ago. They were big around the middle. Don's once hawk-like face was plump, sweaty curls framing it. Phil's once puckish grin now was jowly, his devilish eyes sunken. They took their usual positions, Don to the right, Phil left, as they did four-part harmony with Paul and Art on "Bye Bye Love," which would be taken from one of the shows and included on Simon and Garfunkel's *Old Friends: Live on Stage* album. Don and Phil would then have the stage alone for a few minutes and perform several of the oldies (two of which, "Wake Up Little Susie" and "All I Have to Do Is Dream," would also be on the *Old Friends* DVD). Recalling the historic intersection of perfect harmonies, Simon laughed.

> It was hilarious that the four of us were doing this tour, given our collective histories of squabbling. They hadn't seen each other in about three years. They met in the parking lot before the first gig. They unpacked their guitars—those famous black guitars—and they opened their mouths and started to sing. And after all those years, it was still the sound I fell in love with as a kid. It was still perfect.

They did twenty-four shows through July 31, winging through America, including a sellout crowd at Madison Square Garden and another in Nashville on June 22, then Canada, England, Amsterdam, Germany, and Copenhagen, ending in Oslo on June 24, 2004. It was long and grinding, and when it was over, they filed it away as their last tour, swore on it. And why not? They were both secure millionaires, if less so because of their divorces, having milked the industry that had ripped off many of their 1950s contemporaries to the tune of around $20 million each. Except for family matters—such as Phil adding his voice to his younger son Chris's fleeting attempt at a singing career as well, covering the Delmore Brothers' 1949 tune "Blues Stay Away from Me"—recording was also over with. Swore on that, too.

They could not swear their feuds were over. Phil kept his main residence in L.A., but he too came "home" to Tennessee when he bought a rather historically tainted home near Columbia, in Maury County, one built in 1846 for the infamously racist general Nathan Bedford Forrest, whose ghost Phil would swear he had night visions of haunting the place. He also bought a woody country inn on the outskirts of Lake Malone state park in Dunbar, Kentucky. Not to be outdone, Don in

May of 1997 bought a different property on which to open a fifty-five-room resort inn by Lake Malone and, by happenstance, Lake Adela, in his hometown of Brownie, which had since been incorporated into Central City. He spoke cheerily about making the place a music beehive, drawing revelers with Everly Brothers memorabilia festooned around the lobby and bringing in local acts to perform at a summer music festival. The plan was, he said, "something I can do with music and grow old gracefully." Rock and roll, he added sentimentally, "has kept me in my adolescence."

But none of this would happen. Mired in debt and diffidence, Don would have to sell the unprofitable Everly's Lake Malone Inn in 2004. Furthermore, this chapter wouldn't end without more woe. During the hotel's descent, he had fired the manager, Ann Morgan, who filed a lawsuit against Don and Adela, and subsequently, Adelaida Garza, who replaced her as manager, for allegedly accusing her of embezzling "vast sums of money," as well as a three-wheeler and pontoon boat. The damages from the settlement of the suit forced the sale of the place, which suffered the ultimate indignity when, before it could be resold, burned to the ground in July 2005.

○ ○

Because the scenery of these peaceful mountains and lakes was spectacular, it was where the Everlys united to do interviews such as one on Labor Day 1999 with Bob Greene in *Look* magazine, whom they invited to tag along on a trip into the woods by Lake Malone. As Greene recalled, "Don and Phil drove separate cars. I rode with Don up Route 431 in Muhlenberg County. He said: 'The town where I was born doesn't exist anymore. It was called Brownie—just a few miles from here. It was a coal mining camp. When the coal was all gone, they tore the town down.' Later that day I sat in that bare-bones cafeteria with Phil, and he told me: 'There's an acceptance of us here. They know who we are. They know our kin.'" It was during this trip that Don, in a reflective mood, made a confession that, to Greene, was the product of "never quite fit[ting] in with the gleaming and glitzy rock idols who were their fan-magazine-cover contemporaries [and] because, as boys, they had so little in common with the others. 'I had this haunted feeling all my life,' Don said to me, 'of being odd man out.'"

Phil eventually sold his hotel, too, and though he would remain a West Coast guy, he kept the old Confederate general's "haunted" house in Columbia, and bought another getaway place, a summer beach house in Alabama. The last thing on his mind, or Don's, was making music. "Studying the charts is no kind of occupation," Phil said. "What kind of occupation is that? You get scared and a scared person can't sing."

Scared as they may have been in their old age to keep trying to fit in, their voices were as entrenched as ever. In 2003 came one more compilation, *Stories We Could Tell — The RCA Years* and a year later *Country Classics* (BMG). In 2005 there were three: *Too Good to Be True* (previously unreleased takes from the late 1950s, on the Varese Sarabande label) and two Bear Family surface scratchers, *Studio Outtakes* and *The Price of Fame*; and the voluminous box set *Chained to a Melody* a year later. Their limited time with Mercury got them into Hip-O-Select's thirty-four track *On the Wings of a Nightingale: The Complete Mercury Studio Recordings (1984–88)*, which included their previously unreleased Andrew Lloyd Webber and Jim Steadman song "A Kiss Is a Terrible Thing to Waste" from the *Whistle Down the Wind* album. And it was also in 2005 that they gave their last public performance, at the Regent Theatre in Ipswich. The next time an act would perform under the "Everly" name anywhere in the world would be when a new English band emerged, The Everly Pregnant Brothers.

In December 2009, a year when both Everlys had reached their seventh decade, sixty-four-year-old John Fogerty played New York's Beacon Theatre, singing "When Will I Be Loved" with sixty-year-old Bruce Springsteen. And a year later, Phil and Don made technically their final recording as backup voices on a recording virtually no one heard, Edan Everly's "Old Hollywood," which was ground that Don Everly had covered thirty-five years before on *Sunset Towers*, only proving that where rock and roll goes, the Everly Brothers got there first.

○ ○

For Phil, it was by then a struggle to sing at all. His lungs had paid the inevitable price for chronic chain smoking. By the time he was seen in public as an invitee when Buddy Holly was given a star on the Hollywood Walk of Fame in 2011, he had been diagnosed with obstructive pulmonary disease—essentially the same condition that had killed Ike Everly. Coughing up blood and black resin, he had acceded to Patti's stringent demand for him to quit smoking, and he meant it this time, but it was much too late. By 2013, he needed to wear an oxygen mask to simply be able to breathe and a wheelchair to get around. Knowing he would not live much longer, when Duane Eddy came by the house and they went over ideas for songs, one of the lyrics Phil wrote would break Patti's heart. As she recalls, "He wrote, 'You'll love again after I'm gone,' which I won't."

She assured him of that while she went through living hell. "In the middle of the night," she said, "you look over to see if [he's] still breathing. Pretty soon, all you're waiting for is death." She kept on him during the day to swallow twenty medications, and every day was a blessing. "He still has that smile. He was at peace. He'd done all he ever wanted to do. He had us all with him. He was ready to go."

Dipping in and out of consciousness, he went into Providence Saint Joseph Medical Center in Burbank around Christmas time. Patti, Chris, and Jason kept a vigil by his bed, and opened Christmas presents. As Jason said, "he was a fighter." But on January 3, sixteen days before his seventy-fifth birthday, he could not be woken, his breathing irregular, and doctors told them he would not survive the day. Late that afternoon, he stopped breathing. The inevitable had come. They kissed him and hugged each other, in tears.

○ ○

Across the country, seventy-six-year-old Don Everly had been kept informed by Patti and Jason about Phil's deteriorating condition. When she called to tell him his little brother was gone, it felt like a kick to the stomach. He would say he had thought a lot about Phil as he neared death. His first statement to the press reached for a higher ground, saying that he had been told just as he was listening to the radio and an Everly Brothers song came on, which he called a "spiritual message" from the beyond, aimed right at his soul. It was of course the sort of thing any brother would say, but Don's friends said he was shaken up, unable to process that his kid brother had gone first.

Because Phil had been a good-time kind of guy, the burial and funeral on January 18 was more like a hoedown. The memorial service at the Merle Travis Music Center in Powderly near Central City, where the Everly Brothers had performed often at benefits for the city, around two hundred people filed in, many carrying objects of memorabilia, singing along with Kentucky singer-songwriter Marty Brown. Margaret Everly, now ninety-three, sat with dozens of Everly family relatives, some of whom gave folksy speeches about Phil, including one by Billy Harlan, who had played in rudimentary bands with the Everlys as teenagers before he became a session player, and their cousin David Everly. But Don, just as when he was too anguished to attend Buddy Holly's funeral, apparently did not attend. There would be no burial service, as Phil had chosen to be cremated and his ashes sprinkled into the Green River, where John Prine's ashes would be deposited six years later in keeping with the lyrics of his song "Paradise": "When I die let my ashes float down the Green River."

At Rose Hill Cemetery a few miles away, a small, flat stone would be implanted for Phil in the plot that Ike had conscripted for the family, a few feet from Ike's stone and that of Mary Everly, which had become covered by overgrown grass, all but forgotten by the Everlys. In the coming years, a small country music museum would open in an abandoned storefront down the road from the cemetery, a stop-off for tourists who came to take pictures of Phil's gravesite. In the end, Bob Greene's elegy for the Everlys years before in *Look* was epitaphic. In it, Greene wrote that Phil was "soft-spoken and seemingly quite shy; there was an underlay of pain that somehow felt omnipresent" but "he didn't feel compelled to dwell upon."

Don would carry on alone, and further address his brother's death in media interviews, saying that although they'd had "a very difficult life together" because of their "vastly different views on politics and life, I always thought of him every day, even when we were not speaking to each other. I think about him every day, you know. I wake up, and this thought comes to me. I have a bit of his ashes here at my house. And I go by, and pick the ashes up, and I sort of say good morning to him. That's a funny way to do it, but that's what I do."

○ ○

Not only was Phil gone, but so were many who had aided them, like Archie Bleyer, Wesley Rose, and Chet Atkins. Don went on living the simple life in Nashville. Seen rarely, he became grayer and needed glasses but seemed less seething and more appreciative of huzzahs that still were an undercurrent of his life. On October 25, nine months after Phil's death, the Rock and Roll Hall of Fame held its annual Music Masters series in Cleveland honoring the Everly Brothers. That night, various pairings performed their songs, including Graham Nash and Vince Gill, Emmylou Harris and Alison Krauss, Bonnie "Prince" Billy and Dawn McCarthy, Ledisi and Keb' Mo', J. D. Souther and Krauss, and Waddy Wachtel and Nash. Albert Lee led the band. And Don, who came to the State Theater with Phil's widow, wasn't scheduled to perform but near the end of the show, standing with the cast on stage, he broke into "Bye Bye Love" with Nash, echoed by all the others.

Two years later, a presidential election year, he was making public pitches for Hillary Clinton, explaining that he had held off on political endorsement in the past to keep peace with Phil but felt "liberated" being able to do so now. Of course, he was still locked in with Phil on the plethora of repackaged compilations and box sets. As he reached his eightieth year, he was close friends with the liberal writer and radio monologist Garrison Keillor, the British art and architecture writer Lucinda Lambton, and painter Peter Blake and his wife Chrissy. A *Guardian* writer described him as "a glutton for life and a connoisseur. He had always seen the latest film; he read widely; he was interested in modern art and, on a modest scale, collected it. An avid explorer of restaurants, he loved to talk of food and to cook it." But he was also a riddle—"moody and irresponsible" and "ruthless, rude and self-centered" but also "warm, generous, very charming and excitable." But Chrissy Blake saw him in a simpler light, as a deep thinker with "lots of the qualities of a child"—a characterization that seemed to be sadly apt when his life became all but ruled by Adela, whose bouts with the law were by now a regular occurrence in Nashville and its surrounding areas, and apparently a clear danger to Don Everly.

Davidson County Municipal Court records show that she was arrested on July 11, 2017, whereupon her scowling mugshot was put up on Jackson, Tennessee's WBBJ Channel 7 website, which reported that Adela was "in custody after [holding] a relative against her will in a vehicle on Interstate 40 Wednesday morning before leading Tennessee Highway Patrol troopers on a chase. Court documents say Everly was speeding, driving off the road, and hit a THP trooper's vehicle [and] just before 8 a.m. [she] allegedly turned into the front passenger side door of the trooper's vehicle, causing the window to shatter and leaving 'significant damage' to the vehicle [and] nearly hit three other vehicles. [She] is charged with reckless driving, felony evading arrest, kidnapping, aggravated assault on an officer, four counts of reckless endangerment with a deadly weapon, and leaving the scene of a crash resulting in property damage."

While the "relative" in the car was her sister and roommate, Adelaida, after she was also booked for "criminal contempt—violation of Order of Protection"—it came out that the order had been filed by Don in March 2016, three years after Adela had been arrested for assaulting him and Adelaida. And, as it happened, Adela and Adelaida both had arrest records dating back at least to 2004, when a small item in the "crime reports" section of the September 28 edition of the western Kentucky *News-Democrat & Leader* reported under the headline "Woman Attempts to Pull Gun on Police," that Adela had led Nashville cops on a very similar chase in a black Lexus SUV. When pulled over on West Ninth Street and given a sobriety test, Adela—who was not identified as the wife of Don Everly—had "attempted to draw a concealed handgun from underneath her clothing but was physically controlled and disarmed [and] taken into custody and transported to the Logan County Detention Center." She was booked for "DUI first offense (aggravating circumstances), carrying a concealed deadly weapon, possession of controlled substance first degree (oxycontin), and resisting arrest."

Yet not only was Don kept in the background, the Nashville papers seemed to either ignore or embargo this quite juicy story, and the charges were quietly resolved, seemingly setting the pattern for downplaying future violations of protection orders—despite the fact that there was a pretty fair amount of hidden melodrama going on between the three house-sharing residents. Rumors, never confirmed, had it that Adela had learned of a possible affair between Don and Adelaida, who herself had brushes with the law, being busted in 2019 for DWI, criminal trespass, evading arrest, and her own kidnapping charge that was neither explained nor apparently seriously prosecuted beyond nominal fines of $500 for both sisters on the DUI charges. All this cringeworthy chaos seemed to paint a picture of Horror on Hood's Hill, However, while Don was reported to have filed yet another protection order not long after, the dam didn't ever break open. If anything was known about it at all, Adela's wild ride on I-40 was brushed aside and the "Three's Company" storyline of the Everlys home life simply went on as if on a need-to-know basis.

For Don, this actually was some sort of normalcy. Neither he nor Adela seemed much bothered by the messy but forgotten details and neither spoke in public of the craziness; and the press may have done him a solid keeping it mum. Photographs would appear of the happy threesome at public events. One of those was an eightieth birthday celebration for Don at a Nashville restaurant attended by Michelle Phillips, with one report noting, "There was a lot of laughing at the table." Adela and Adelaida accompanied him to his last performance, when Paul Simon's 2018 farewell concert made an emotional stop in Nashville's Bridgestone Arena on June 20 and Paul invited Don to come and sing "Bye Bye Love" one last time.

His last public sighting came at the Nashville-based Musicians Hall of Fame in July 2019, when he received the Iconic Riff Award for his guitar intro on "Wake Up Little Susie," which he proved he could still play by heart. By then he needed a cane to come to the stage. But he was the essence of senior cool, wearing specs and a pink pashmina around his neck, salt-and-pepper hair neatly styled. And while some of those who knew of his disharmonious marriage wondered how he had gotten himself into it—a reminder being Adela's arrest again for domestic assault in 2020, with the case again filed away without major penalty—it seemed that he needed any remnant of love, or at least steady companionship. He may have bent willingly or unwillingly to Adela, but something about her, her spunk or high intelligence, even her rebel nature, kept him in love, and his mind remained sharp. What's more, though his time was growing short, he would not let go without fighting for one last battle he just had to win.

○ ○

Back in June 1980, miffed that he'd given Phil cowriting credit on sixteen songs he wrote alone, Don had gotten Phil to sign papers that Don was the sole composer, including of their biggest seller, "Cathy's Clown." Phil signed five notarized documents titled "Release and Assignment" upholding Don's sole authorship on the songs. And although Phil had a three-year legal window to contest it but did not, after Phil died Don went to District Court for the Middle District of Tennessee on November 8, 2017, to lock in a declaratory judgment. This was not solely based on ego. Given that Everly Brothers songwriting royalties were worth a bundle, and "Cathy's Clown" the showstopper, ownership of just those songs was worth millions. And he prevailed, when in a two-day bench trial that took until April 2021 to adjudicate, the judge ruled in his favor.

But Patti, Christopher, and Jason appealed to the Sixth Circuit court, contending that Phil had "inalienable" termination rights and Don had harassed him to sign the agreement. They obtained a deposition from Joey Paige that one call from Don to Phil on the matter became "violent verbally," and that Phil gave in to "keep the peace," with Jason testifying that Phil told him he said to Don, "Screw you. Send me the goddamn paperwork and I'll sign it." The court agreed on November 6, 2018, that the case should go back to the District Court. By now, it all boiled down to "Cathy's Clown," and the case would drag on for another five years.

In the interim, steps had been taken to make sure the brothers were united in perpetuity. In July 2020, the clans of Don and Phil united to help finance a park named in their honor in Knoxville, one of the financial contributors being Don's long-estranged daughter Venetia Ember Everly, whose mother, Mary Sue Ingraham, had died in Nashville in 2008. Another dedication came on June 15, when ground was broken for the installation of bronze statues of the Everlys and John Prine in Festival Square in Central City.

Don didn't have that much time to spare, but he did live to see the District Court on May 4, 2021, reaffirm its ruling that he wrote the song. He had three months to savor it. Then, on August 21, in the thick of a hot, humid Nashville summer, Don Everly died in his sleep, his ticker giving out in his eighty-fourth year of trying to ease his troubled soul. A statement from Adela that morning was posted on the internet. "Don lived by what he felt in his heart," it said. "Don expressed his appreciation for the ability to live his dreams. Living in love with his soulmate and wife, Adela, and sharing the music that made him an Everly Brother. Don always expressed how grateful he was for his fans."

As rounds of tributes poured in—Jerry Lee Lewis, for now the last living original rocker, who would die a year later, said, "There's a lot I can say about Don, what he and Phil meant to me both as people and as musicians, but I am going to reflect today. God bless Don Everly and long live rock and roll music"—Adela arranged a funeral service. It happened two days later at Phillips-Robinson Funeral Home that was kept so private that virtually no one knew who was there. Unlike the service for Phil that drew hundreds and became a tribute concert and reunion for family members, Don seemingly just disappeared into the mist. As with Phil, he was cremated and his ashes sprinkled into Green River—but, unlike Phil, there would be a mystifying postscript: there would be no stone put in the family plot at Rose Hill Cemetery, the absence of a marker beside those of his father, brother, and his first daughter befuddling the steady flow of tourists to the plot. In fact, on the findagrave.com website, Don Everly's burial ground is incorrectly given as Rose Hill, perhaps by assumption. Whether or not his avoidance of just such a burial was something he had commanded of Adela, or whether it was her decision based on his estrangement from the family, it was the perfect end note for a man who went through life sure he was the "odd man out."

Margaret Everly had her own lawsuit against Don that she wanted to settle before she passed on, having to do with ownership of the house Don and Phil had bought for her and Ike in 1958. They had originally put the title in Ike and Margaret's names while making all the payments and taking questionable tax deductions on the property. In 1966, the IRS came after them about the deductions and they had their parents cede 80 percent of the value of the title over to them to justify deductions. But after Ike's death, Margaret sued her sons, claiming they had promised but failed to transfer the title back to her. Phil did so with his 40 percent, but Don held onto his. Margaret's court claim asked for a ruling that he had abused his "confidential relationship" with her. Yet, in one of the longest running cases imaginable, possibly because Don's lawyer kept filing additional documents and requests to delay it, three decades later the suit languished in the courts.

Margaret, who had been too ill to attend her elder son's funeral, died only four months later on December 17 at a robust 102. And she too would not be buried in Ike's rather lonely family plot. Instead, she was interred in the Embry family plot in Nashville's Woodlawn Memorial Park and Mausoleum, the same cemetery where Boudleaux and Felice Bryant, Marty Robbins, Eddy Arnold, Porter Wagoner, Red Foley, and Tammy Wynette are buried. Margaret's death meant her home was left effectively in Don's estate, over which Adela Everly controlled every detail. Don had made Adela its administrator, in partnership with his estranged children. Apparently, all agreed that the house would be torn down and the property put up for sale. What's more, the deaths of Don and Phil did not mean the end of what became known as the "Cathy's Clown" suit. In 2023, more appeals led the families back again to the District Court's full three-judge panel—the case now identified as *Garza v Everly*, with Adelaida Garza oddly listed on the plaintiff's side as the "Representative for the Estate of Isaac Don Everly" against the defendants Patti, Jason, and the now disabled Chris Everly. Finally decided on February 10, 2023, Don again won—or rather, Adela did, cementing her ownership of the publishing and permission rights of Don's songs. That catalog was and never won't be a bonanza. Many of the songs were still being used in cable TV movies like the *Sopranos* prequel *Many Saints of Newark* and two episodes of *Dexter: New Blood*. There was also another compilation package, developed by both families, *Hey Doll Baby*, released in 2022 by Warner Music Group and produced by Adria Petty in conjunction with both families, featuring stunningly clean remasters of many of the old evergreens.

This was yet further proof of the grip they have on the ever-enduring rock generation—how else to explain the 2023 cover of "Bye Bye Love" as a duet by eighty-one-year-old Ann-Margret and seventy-seven-year-old Pete Townshend? Art Garfunkel's epitaph of the Everlys, that "Every syllable can shine" is still felt on a microcellular level about them, with a special shine in Nashville. When the young and bold Everly Brothers told the Grand Ole Opry to go to hell in 1960, they knew change was in the air. And today, despite all the pushback from the jerkoffs at the State House and resilient racists in country music, the sound moves more and more to the beats of a new culture.

They still wear big cowboy hats and shiny spangles there, but they sing songs like Kacey Musgraves's 2014 LGBT anthem of inclusion, "Follow Your Arrow," which won Song of the Year at the Country Music Association awards. There are even openly gay bars like TRAX, The Lipstick Lounge, and Pecker's, where one popular act is known as the "gay masked cowboy," Orville Peck. An early favorite to win the mayor's race in 2024 was a liberal female candidate who had once played in a touring band. As for Don and Phil—given names that can only apply to two specific people with the same surname—they can't be found on street signs in town. There is that memorial park down in Knoxville, with tributes from Dylan, Carole King, Paul McCartney, and others carved into the cement stones built into the ground. But the Everly Brothers are more spectral than in common rites like these, having engendered a new style of music without doing what Jerry Lee Lewis and the other frothing rockers did, which Jerry Lee once said involved "draggin' the audience to hell with me."

The appeal of the Everlys wasn't measured in great balls of fire but in soothing sighs of resignation and pain that coaxed and caressed, in complete harmony even when each one was repelled by the other, and by a world they rarely seemed at ease in. But even the most tortured one knew in his gut what really mattered. "When we get together, we sing," once said Don Everly. "When Phil and I hit that one spot—I call it the Everly Brothers spot—it's not me or it's not him. It's the two of us together." If only Brother Don and Brother Phil could have let it matter enough—to them. Because to everyone else, the wind they rode on was never too high or lonesome. It only embraces, and makes us young and fearless again for around two and a half minutes, which as Don and Phil knew is a hell of a lot better than nothing.